F190

D0905847

Imagining the Middle East

Imagining the Middle East

Thierry Hentsch

translated by Fred A. Reed

BLACK
ROSE
BOOKS

Montréal/New York

Copyright © 1992 BLACK ROSE BOOKS LTD.

No part of this book may be reproduced or transmitted in any form, by any means, electronic or mechanical, including photocopying and recording, or by any information storage or retrieval system, without written permission from the publisher, except for brief passages quoted by a reviewer in a newspaper or magazine.

This book has been published with the help of a grant from the Social Science Federation of Canada, using funds provided by the Social Sciences and Humanities Research Council of Canada.

BLACK ROSE BOOKS No. V179
Hardcover ISBN: 1-895431-13-1
Paperback ISBN: 1-895431-12-3
Library of Congress No. 91-72982

Canadian Cataloguing in Publication Data

Hentsch, Theirry, 1944 –
Imagining the Middle East

ISBN: 1-895431-13-1 (bound) ISBN: 1-895431-12-3 (pbk.)

1. Europe — Relations — Arab countries. 2. Arab countries — Relations — Europe. 3. United States — Relations — Arab countries. 4. Arab countries — Relations — United States 5. Persian Gulf War, 1991. I. Title.

DS44.H46 1991   303.48′240174927   C91-090492-8

Cover Design: Werner Arnold

Mailing Address

BLACK ROSE BOOKS
C.P. 1258
Succ. Place du Parc
Montréal, Québec
H2W 2R3 Canada

BLACK ROSE BOOKS
340 Nagel Drive
Cheektowaga , New York
14225, USA

A publication of the Institute of Policy Alternatives of Montréal (IPAM)

Printed in Canada

Table of Contents

Translator's Preface

Translators are often beset by the hoary cliché of contradiction between textual faithfulness and aesthetic infidelity, and vice versa. But Thierry Hentsch's *Imagining the Middle East* presented me, as a translator, with a singular opportunity, and with a challenge: that of steering between the Scylla and Charybdis of Yes and No, between slavish verbality and unjustifiable liberty, into the zone which George Steiner has described as "an exchange of parity within a field of magnetic force and tension, a dynamic, intense equilibrium in a very complex system."

Hentsch's text — ostensibly erudite, yet thoroughly subversive of erudition-as-system — commands that the effort be made, thus my attempt to recreate the peculiar elegance and complexity of its probing manner, while simultaneously reinvesting it with some of the vigour of polemical English. Ever attentive to the injunctions of the author, I have sought to give free reign to the text as subject.

Ultimately, translating *Imagining the Middle East* would have been impossible without the close cooperation of the author. In the process my own grasp of the historical, cultural and mythical dimensions of the frontier between the West and the Islamic Orient has been strengthened and clarified by Hentsch's relentless, often ironic scrutiny and analysis.

Though the book's sources are primarily French, many are readily available to the English-speaking reader. Where footnotes do not refer to an English edition, I have assumed responsibility both for the translation and for all possible errors. Finally, I would like to express my thanks to the staff of McGill University's Institute of Islamic Studies Library for their assistance; and my gratitude to my daughter, Eléni Reed, who reconstituted the book's references with verve and painstaking accuracy.

Fred A. Reed
Montréal, Québec
September, 1992

Foreword

This book is not about the Orient. It is about us.

The Orient is elusive; omnipresent yet evanescent. As close at hand as books or paintings; on our television screens, in the street; so near yet so remote.

At once a locus of cliché, synonym for the exotic, catalyst of contradiction and excess; wise and irrational, ascetic and voluptuous, cruel and refined…The Orient is immemorial, the primeval dawn and night of history…The Orient is immense; an immense repository of our own imagined world.

The Orient is in our minds.

Outside our Western minds, the Orient has no more substance than does the West itself. The West is an idea which inhabits us, as surely as does its opposite. But we feel no defining impulse; after all, are we not ourselves the West?

But are we, really? Are we indeed the obverse of the Orient? The Other's other? The positive pole, the affirmation? For there are times when we become the diametrical opposite: the negative image of the positive. In those few brief instants the ancient symbols spring to life: the Orient suddenly becomes luminosity, universal soul, enchanted magnet drawing us inward to the space within, distance separating us from our unwieldy modernity. But come the smallest incident, the first spattering of blood and the light flickers, then fails. The Orient recedes into the dark night of our fears to vanish, forgotten, before reappearing as dream. Or as a quavering, ever-receding mirage; an apparition.

The Orient is elusive; this book makes no effort to ensnare it. Nor does it propose a definition of ourselves. No; we are its principal focal point; we and the Other; we as we see ourselves through the Other. Not as the Other sees us, but as we reveal ourselves through our way of seeing. This book proposes to bring our largely instinctive expression of self to the surface of our consciousness. Is this not the task of history? From our vantage-point atop the historical pinnacle we must stoop to reexamine the substrata of our daily existence, to excavate the layers of sediment. Part myth they may well be, but this in no way affects their crystal-hard reality. Myth, like stone, may be eroded over time, but attempting to "destroy" it (as some suggest) serves no purpose. Instead, I propose we redouble our efforts to reread myth, the better to understand how it functions over time — and how it functions even today.

Taken both as excavation in the geological sense, and as political act, the search for understanding through our view of the Other takes us to the wellsprings, to the very source of that which eludes our understanding: the necessity of reflecting upon ourselves and upon our political attitudes toward the Other. The simple solution would be to define our attitudes in terms which most Western media would have us accept as our own, an acceptance which comes all the more easily as it rests upon the same sustaining substratum with which we claim such easy familiarity.

But how great is our familiarity? Do we ask ourselves persistently enough why, to our Western eyes, "Arab" terrorism and "Islamic" fanaticism seem perfectly normal propositions? Indignation at these grotesque simplifications is simply not enough. We must go to the roots. But does the explanation lie with the Muslims or with ourselves? In their history or in ours? The answer is far from simple; this book makes no pretence of presenting it in finished, capsule form. Its overriding aim is to state a presupposition, a capital presupposition: any study of the Other is futile unless we first observe ourselves face to face with it, and in particular, unless we attempt to understand how, and why, we have studied and represented this self-same Other down to the present day.

This book probes the depths of the Orient as fashioned by the power of our imagination. It makes no pretence of definition, of passing judgement, on the reality or unreality, or even on the pertinence — or lack of same — of the Orient as concept. The clear necessity of these reservations is, I believe, clearly demonstrated in the pages that follow.

The Orient may well be a construct of our imagination, but it is still immense. Within it is embedded a kaleidoscopic profusion of images constantly forming and re-forming into distantly familiar shapes, the same material displayed in a thousand and one ways. As concept, the Orient is kaleidoscopic both in terms of its limits, and in terms of its inexhaustible possibilities. Its component parts are few, but they can be fashioned into an infinity of permutations to express our multifold phantasms.

I make no pretence of exhausting these permutations. My intention is to draw from them their formative elements; elements which are essential, but by no means immanent. Quite the contrary: these elements have appeared, each one superimposing itself atop the one below, over the course of centuries. Our kaleidoscope does not assume its ultimate shape, its principal components are not fully incorporated, until the 19th century. This book is an attempt to retrace the pivotal stages of a long process of construction.

First, the question of space. What are the geographical contours of our imagined Orient? Paradoxically, as concept, the Orient of the imagination constitutes the antithesis of the West, and as such has no precise boundaries. It can expand to subsume the rest of the world: whatever the West considers neither as its own nor as its direct emanation. But if the Orient has come to represent, in our eyes, the supreme degree of otherness, it is because this otherness (excepting the concept of the state of nature) has almost always been projected onto Asia and its great civilizations. In purely practical terms, however, Asia is too vast, its 'Orients' far too numerous. They have not all held the same significance for Europe. Thus we have limited ourselves to the Orient nearest us, that Orient with which we have been in intimate contact down through the centuries, which shares with us in the history of the Mediterranean. This is why I have called it the Mediterranean Orient, a far less ethnocentric term than Near or Middle-East. By it I mean the Arab world plus Turkey and Iran, a region which also embraces North Africa (itself indissociable from the history of the Arab and Ottoman empires). No possible geographical outline can meet criteria whose rigor is absolute. But we may at least rest assured (or dismayed, depending on our point of view): we shall not be adventuring into the imaginary West of India, China or Japan. To the East, the boundary seems clear.

It seems hardly less clear to the West. Does the Mediterranean itself not stand as a clear-cut boundary? Still, we accept this notion too willingly, too uncritically, almost as though it represented immutable historic knowledge, as though Europe itself had always been unequivocally "Western." But the matter is by no means so simple. Seen from London or Paris, do the Balkans belong to the West or the Orient? Everything depends upon the moment, upon the issues, even upon the individuals involved. Whatever our ultimate criteria, the geopolitical boundary (that discrete yet intimate interplay of colours on a map) can never be drawn with perfect clarity, for it remains an imaginary line. Where exactly has our imagination located it? The Aegean, or the Adriatic? Or does the frontier itself ebb and flow with the advances and retreats of history? Which brings us suddenly to the heart of the matter. The frontier is not merely place; it is moment. When does our collective imagination draw the imaginary boundary line between the West and the Orient? This is the first question we must ask ourselves.

Naturally enough, it is also the subject of the first chapter. As we shall see, the question cannot be separated from the West's own self-awareness. To trace it back to the battle of Marathon would be anachronistic. Should we then seek the first stirrings of European (Western) self-awareness in medieval Germano-Latin Christianity? Is first contact with Islam the revelatory moment? What is the significance — and the consequence — of Catholicism's anathema upon the religion of Mohammad? Or, to rephrase the question: to what extent is the medieval Mediterranean a locus of opposition or of symbiosis? These are the questions implicit in Chapter II, which concludes that the most significant cleavages are not always those we assume. These considerations lead us to a close study of the critical period of the "long 16th century" (late 15th to the early 17th). During these decades, the Mediterranean becomes at once the theatre of sharp military conflict (particularly between Turks and Spaniards) and of an immense flanking movement which signals the beginning of the great explorations.

In Chapter III we shall see how this decisive historical moment shaped the European view of the Ottoman Empire. Could this be the moment when the concept of Orient as a political formulation of identity and otherness first takes shape before us? The answer is far more complex than would appear at first glance. Contrariwise, from the mid-18th century onward, and even more clearly during the Enlightenment, as Chapter IV will demonstrate, the Orient emerges as the representation of an all-embracing otherness. At the same time, several key concepts (such as despotism) emerge, to describe it in political terms.

But it is only with the spirit of the 19th century, subject of Chapter V, that our collectively imagined Orient is made to gather into itself all that which we are not, to become the antithesis *par excellence* of modernity. At the same time, European philosophy incorporates the high ancient civilizations of Western Asia into its universal history, into an ethnocentric vision of the world and of its evolutionary course which dominates Western thought down to this day. This dominating vision is our legacy. But on the periphery, the legacy is inexorably being eroded by the decline of Europe and by the relative decline of the entire West. The pangs of remorse which are our inheritance from the colonial era have cast a pall over this vision. Today, among people of good will, the result has been a turn toward reconciliation with the Other, a desire for reparation. Chapter VI seeks to provide a context for both the limitations and the pitfalls of this desire. What use can be made of our manner of seeing the Other; on what conditions can we contemplate a dialogue?

This brief outline should provide a first insight into the spirit which underlies this book and which gives it, I believe, its interest and its originality. But in a field already so well explored, nothing could be less obvious.

Works on the Western view of the Orient are abundant, and I have made abundant use of them. I am particularly indebted to Maxime Rodinson's *Europe and the Mystique of Islam*[1] and to Hichem Djaït's *Europe and Islam*,[2] the only works which, to my knowledge, present a succinct historical overview of the question from the Middle Ages down to the present. Without them, the task of finding my way would have been far more laborious. Their bibliographies were particularly useful to me in my own choice of references. However, both take a descriptive, rather than an analytical, approach to the Western view of Islam. The stages through which this view has passed are duly noted, but not incorporated into a broader context which seeks to identify their significance. So while they helped stimulate my appetite, they ultimately left my hunger unsatisfied. It is this hunger which has driven me back to the sources.

Other, more detailed, works limited to a particular moment, or to a particular aspect of our view toward the Other proved invaluable: for example, Norman Daniel's classic *Islam and the West*,[3] for the religious dimension.

Nearer in time, we clearly must acknowledge Edward Saïd's biting analysis of *Orientalism*,[4] a book to which we will frequently return. Saïd's book has become the corridor through which all examination and discussion of Orientalism must pass. It is so richly documented, its analyses so accurate, the overweening ethnocentrism of the learned and not-so-learned orientalists is so often deflated, that a reader might well conclude, on finishing the book, that nothing more remains to be written on the subject. This too: Orientalism as a learned discipline emerges so bruised from the encounter that a sense of repugnance seems to pervade the entire exercise. Undoubtedly it was necessary to hammer the message home over and over again — or, more precisely, to hold up before us the unrelenting, wearisome succession of orientalist clichés themselves. The work has now been done; it would be useless to attempt to repeat it. Particularly since Saïd's attack focuses on only one limited aspect of a wider problem. The Orientalism which he brings under such detailed scrutiny remains confined primarily to the colonial era, whose spectre Saïd, a touch abusively, projects back in time beyond the 19th century. The European view of the Mediterranean Orient becomes, in his hands, little more than the forerunner of the imperialist enterprise, seen even then as the full expression of Western contempt and rapacity.

But Orientalism — on condition that we set its origins before the 18th century — cannot be reduced to a predatory extinct in academic clothing. And since it only represents one aspect of the Western view of the Orient (as Saïd himself notes), care must be taken not to exaggerate its impact. "Scholarly studies," warns Rodinson, "exert a great deal less influence on the ideas current in a given society than the latter exert on intellectual milieux."[5] Observations by "scholars...eager to arrive at general conclusions"[6] often find no basis in their own research, and are little more than a reflection of the temper of our times.

This book makes no pretence of denouncing either Orientalism or the ethnocentrism which pervades it. Critical evaluation of our vision remains necessary; in fact, it has become indispensable to all even remotely lucid work about the Other. But criticism can rapidly reach the limits of the very ethnocentrism it condemns if it merely censures the worst excesses, and withdraws into smug satisfaction. Nothing could be simpler than to string together insulting or grotesque quotations from Western literature on the Orient. But to what end? We would only be belabouring the obvious, without advancing our knowledge of the phenomenon by more than a fraction; as if awareness of our biases was enough to surmount them. Ethnocentrism is not a flaw to be simply set aside, nor is it a sin to be expunged through repentance. *It is the precondition of our vision of the Other.* Far from offering us absolution, this precondition compels us constantly to return to our point of departure, if only to grasp the internal and external imperatives which shape our curiosity about the Other.

Desire for self-knowledge is the innermost motivation of this book. The Orient, finally, becomes a vector. I may well be reproached for this ultimate use of the Other and criticized for my own latent ethnocentrism. Deservedly so. But with this proviso: my approach is conscious of its ethnocentrism, focusing as it does on the forces which make such an approach necessary. This perspective is of primary concern to us as Westerners — though I ardently hope it will also stimulate interest among non-Westerners. But it advocates neither self-withdrawal, nor exclusion. Instead, it is an attempt to create the conditions under which we can make intellectual use of the Other and of its experience. I have adopted the Western point of view simply because I can adopt no other without false pretences. Readers who may not yet agree will, I hope, understand by the end of the book.

Now that all the necessary precautions have been taken, I can sum up my approach more concretely. This book details the principal stages in European political thought around which our collective imagination of the Mediterranean Orient has slowly coalesced. It seeks to place each of these historical moments in the general context from which it arose. This work of collective imagination is bound up with the temper of the times; it cannot be reduced to an assortment of illusions, or of falsehoods, though it reveals much more about the onlooker than about the looked-upon. Bluntly, it is our history's vision of the Arabs, of the Turks, or of Islam. It is also how we viewed — and still view today — these peoples, their cultures and their institutions: in short, what we take to be their "mentality." All this has profoundly impregnated our own mentalities, with inevitable political consequences.

More than in any other region of the globe, the political incoherence of the Western powers in the Middle East clearly shows that policy is shaped not only by material or strategic imperatives, but also by passions of which the leaders and the peoples of the West are largely oblivious. If we wish to understand ourselves in our complex and conflict-ridden relations with the region alongside which Western Europe emerged, we must seek out these roots. And in a more general way, our research leads us to consider the study of other cultures, and our professed desire for dialogue with them.

All of which leads to the question of sources. Where are we to seek, where to choose those expressions which best represent each moment of our collective imagining of the Mediterranean Orient? Even when limited to a fraction of the field, the source material is inexhaustible. Inexhaustible in terms of sheer bulk, but repetitive in substance. Read two or three accounts of 17th century travellers and you have read dozens. Representations have crystallized into models. If you seek the archetypal form of "oriental despotism" you need only read Montesquieu. If you wish to understand the position of the Orient in our historical vision, you need only read Hegel. If you wish to experience the sense of heartbreak you will turn to Massignon. A particular set of problems articulated around several key authors corresponds with each historical period, with each "founding moment." The pool is both broad and deep. I will surely be reprimanded for omitting Tasso, Cervantes, Lane, Weber and many more. Perhaps the gallo-centrism of my selections will be criticized. I happily confess: I have not read everything, and I have read primarily in my own language. Are my choices significant enough; can my analyses be properly verified? This is the crux of the matter. From the sociopolitical viewpoint — mine in this book — they are indeed significant. My intention is not to shed a uniform light on every facet of our representation of the Orient. It should come as no surprise that literary and artistic exoticism occupy relatively little space in comparison with their importance in the poetry, in the novel, in stories and in the plastic arts of the West.

To characterize is not to exclude. Each historical moment carries with it infinitely more than itself; it conveys what has gone before, proclaims what is to come. I shall have ample occasion to repeat, but let me state it once and for all: the great historical "epochs" overlap, change is virtually never sudden (above all in collective mentalities); sharp breaks coexist alongside continuity. The spirit of the Renaissance is already present in the Middle Ages, and that of the Middle Ages persists into the Renaissance. The 19th century did not signal the total collapse of the Enlightenment, and our 20th century remains very much of the 19th in many ways.

But methods, in their multiplicity of aspects, can rarely be drawn up before the fact. Method emerges alongside discourse. Should this book provide food for thought on how we expand our knowledge of the Other, it should also constitute an underlying process of enquiry into method. But the reader should not be put off by what may appear as the siren-call of seriousness. Ultimately, my wishes are few and modest: that the reading of this adventure arouses as much interest among readers as I experienced in the writing — and, above all, that this interest not be confined to specialists. This book has not been written for them specifically, but — dare I hope? — they may certainly profit from it.

I do not consider myself a specialist in the Orient. My field is international relations, and it is in this capacity that I have taught and written on the Near East in the international system, and on the Arab-Israeli conflict.[7] The idea of investigating our own imagined Orient slowly took shape over the course of discussions with an Iranian friend, Mojtaba Sadria. The discussion continues; and this book is the product of that friendship.[8]

NOTES

1. Rodinson, Maxime, *Europe and the Mystique of Islam,* translated by Roger Veinus. Seattle, University of Washington Press, 1987.
2. Djait, Hichem, *Europe and Islam,* translated by Peter Heinegg. Berkeley, University of California Press, 1985.
3. Daniel, Norman, *Islam and the West: The Making of an Image,* Edinburg University Press, 1966. See also Daniel's *The Arabs and Medieval Europe,* London, Longman, 1975.
4. Saïd, Edward, *Orientalism,* New York, Pantheon Books, 1978. See also Saïd's *Covering Islam,* New York, Pantheon Books. 1982.
5. Rodinson, Op.Cit., p.129.
6. Ibid., p.89
7. The first two chapters of this book were published with different titles in *Études Internationales* (Sept. 1985 and Sept. 1986). I thank the publishers for authorizing their re-use in this book.
8. The friendship of Nicole Morf made the reading of this book's manuscript possible. Thanks as well to Marie De Broin for her painstaking efforts in preparing the French-language version of the typescript, and to the Université du Québec à Montréal for its financial support.

I

The Mythical Frontier

Shaped by the secular forces of opposition and proximity, the pairing of East and West, Orient and Occident, has every appearance of a constant in Mediterranean history. It has been a curious liaison: two fundamental essences cohabit, influence one another, intermingle in peace and war yet never lastingly become one. As essences they are complementary, yet as distinct as oil and vinegar: the blend is often savory, but the fine line separating the two seems always to reappear. The line seems always to have existed; as though, from Antiquity onward, the Orient and the West have been locked in ceaseless and unrelenting combat, with the Mediterranean as its epicentre, its shifting field, its zone of demarcation.

But can we really trace the line back to Antiquity? To the east of precisely which West do the great civilizations of Egypt and Sumer lie? Through what historical transformation does the Mediterranean become both median and interior? Three millennia later, in spite of first Phoenician then Greek colonization along the Mediterranean littoral, Alexander sought to make Mesopotamia the centre of his empire. It was not until Rome, not until the Punic wars, that the Mediterranean was truly to embrace its etymology, to become "the sea amidst the lands." How sweepingly these words reach back into a past for which they were not created! Geopolitical toponymy is an anachronism which — beyond the convenience of habit — carries within it a second significance, the key to the power and the immutability of the images which have been brought into being by the dominant version of history forged in the West.

Even so the Mediterranean remains a critical zone, the ineluctable physical and historical point of departure for the study of relations between the Orient and the West, with Antiquity as its all-but-obligatory genesis. But it is a beginning which must be described with care. From the inception of the East-West nexus, and throughout the history of the Mediterranean world, fiction and reality have woven a tight-knit, complex fabric. The further we move back in time, the fewer our direct sources, the more difficult it becomes to separate the two. The space occupied by myth so expands that the mythical dimensions of the most distant past take on a life of their own, replacing a reality beyond our grasp. No demonstration that the Trojan war did or did not occur can alter the evocative power of the

Homeric legends to fire our imaginations even to this day. This is the point at which myth assumes its full explicatory function. The interpretation may be just or false — no matter. Myth's power of representation has imprinted it upon collective memory, has brought a real weight to bear upon the future. And at deeper levels still, myth shapes our behaviour and thus becomes a part of reality.

My prime concern is a particular facet of the reality: the manner in which the founding myth of the rivalry between the Orient and the West has been articulated. And the form in which it makes itself manifest today. How has it influenced the contemporary West's view of the Orient, and of the Mediterranean Orient in particular? For the Mediterranean world represents the supreme meeting place where contact between the West and the Third World, as we term them today, has been the most enduring and the most intense. It is the crucible in which the images that to this day shape the one's perception of the other were forged. In an era of world economic crisis, which is simultaneously a crisis of Western civilization, these images are particularly pertinent. To this day the Occident looks anxiously toward an Orient — its eternal antithesis — which continues to escape its grasp. And in the West emerge sporadic fears that, ultimately, its prosperity and security may depend upon this selfsame Orient.

Appropriating the past

No matter how far back we trace the opposition between Orient and Occident, the two extremities are not of the same age. We, as Westerners, must make our pilgrimage to the sources, the first great civilizations of western Asia and of Egypt.

Before Homer (8th century B.C.) and even down to the classical age of Athens (5th century B.C.), the modern West draws its principal cultural references from the Fertile Crescent, stretching from the Tigris to the Nile. With good reason: the Chaldean civilization of Mesopotamia, stretching back to the fourth millennium, calculated the movements of the stars, the lunar and solar cycles, divided the year into 360 days, and invented a numerical system based on the "positions in relation to the ecliptic"[1] (which remains ours to this day, but which Rome was incapable of mastering). The Egyptians created architectural monuments whose innermost workings continue to escape us. With the Code of Hammurabi (18th-19th century B.C.), Babylon founded a system of law "before either Rome or China," writes René Grousset, who underlines the "recognized precedence of the civilizations of the eastern Mediterranean and the Near Orient."

From these civilizations emerged "the great poetry of the Semites, who were possessed from their very origins by the breath of the sacred." The

Gilgamesh Epic, "possibly the oldest epic poem of the human race,"[2] is the precursor of Job, and of Prometheus.

> It is the eternal glory of the Semitic genius to have, from the very first, posed with such acuity, such intensity, such violence, the problem of evil and of human destiny, which is to say, the metaphysical issue in its entirety...Already 'the third millenary' the Pascalian shiver of man in the face of destiny, in the face of 'the eternal silence of these infinite spaces', the whole of metaphysical anguish.[3]

The sweep is broad, even breath-taking. In one fell swoop the West takes on unexpected historical depth. From Gilgamesh and Job to Prometheus and Pascal, the trail has been blazed. The Semitic genius and the religious intensity of a Pascal resonate across the millennia, laying down the trajectory along which the Orient proceeds, through Judaism and Greece, directly to us. The expression of the universality of the human condition, of the metaphysical anguish which the West considers as one of the great philosophical conquests of its own modernity, here become the bridge which links us to the Origins. Our sense of exaltation arises not so much from Semitic genius as from the lineage that joins us with it: as we discover its true grandeur we share in its "eternal glory."

By asserting the anteriority of this genius, we acquire a near-existential certitude: civilization must have a beginning, or at least a particular point of origin at which and of which we may partake. It is no coincidence that George Deniker, Grousset's disciple and successor, describes China, whose claim to antiquity is significant but whose past is less-well-known, as "rising before us, at the extremity of the Eurasian land mass, like a huge, isolated bloc," or: "China's particular version of humanism developed in a vacuum."[4] How quickly we relegate one quarter of humanity to a gigantic parenthesis by locating its culture, no matter how remarkable we judge it to be, beyond the universal stream which rises in western Asia to irrigate Europe. Could this marginality have something to do with the fact that China was never extensively colonized by the West? Whatever the case, direct cultural lineage between China and the West would be much more difficult to establish than with the ancient "Near East."

India is a different matter. Long colonized, it has provided Europe with several fundamental elements of its culture, drawn particularly from the extended Indo-European linguistic family. In spite of the relative isolation of the Indian sub-continent, it can still be linked to the Mediterranean world with relative ease via Iran and the Indo-Afghan passes of the northwest. "For it is through these very passes that the history of India is joined with universal history."[5] The link becomes all the more crucial in that Iran is now called upon to play a key role in the mythology of our origins.

Iran, in fact, should be properly seen as a parcel of Europe in Asia. Moving eastward from Mesopotamia to the Iranian plateau, Grousset notes, not without an almost audible sigh of relief:

> In several stages, in the invigorating air of the high plateau, we have moved from Asia back to Europe. Like the trees and the plants, the men are from our common home. Of what significance the Arab or Turkoman invasions which, from one era to another, swarmed up from Irak or from Transoxania? Of what significance are the often times secular occupations which may have been the result?...For the Caspian plateau, by its altitude, reminds us of our own European climate, and the Indo-European type (in the strictly European sense of the term) has been marvellously preserved here, finally imposing itself on the non-natives minorities.[6]

Providentially the geographer extends a hand to the historian, helping it leap over the centuries and eluding the prickly question of Islam. How important is history, how significant the successive layers of sediment it deposits, as we search for immanence and transcendence beneath the fine dust of time!

> Perhaps the geographical explanation could be carried even farther. Might there not exist a secret harmony between Iranian thought and the environment in which it was shaped?...For Iran is one of those lofty regions of the earth where, from the dawn of time spiritualism has soared skyward in vertical flight.[7]

From the dawn of time, indeed, for "in reality, the mother of our civilizations did not arise at Ur, but on the slope of the Iranian plateau, at Susa..."[8] This affirmation of antiquity is fraught with consequence for us, if we admit that "Iran, in terms of its thought, remained essentially Indo-European. From its earliest origins, Iranian thought has infinitely more in common with the loftiest of Indian speculation or the most spiritualized thinking of Greece than with the primitive conceptualizing of Babylon."[9] Implicitly, the Semitic genius is relegated to a secondary position, while an earlier pre-dawn gleams, pregnant with the glimmer of Greek light.

We should react cautiously to the division of ancient western Asia between Semites and Indo-Europeans. How can Iran of the fourth millennium be "Indo-European" if not by virtue of a symbolic mythology? What then is Europe? This fantasy-driven anachronism is all the more astonishing when, in an earlier work devoted to the question of the Orient, Grousset establishes the cleavage between Asia and Europe at the Persian Wars (5th century B.C.),[10] or barely two centuries after Zoroaster, symbol of the spiritualism which so characterizes the Iranian essence. Had the "land of the Aryans" become "orientalized" in the meantime? But Grousset, and many like him, believe Xerxes stands for the ancient commonplace of "Oriental despotism." Why, after two millennia of Indo-European Iranity, in fewer than two centuries had the Medes come to symbolize Asia as against Europe? The answer is quite simple: the appearance of classical Greece, and the rise of Athens.

Before Greece, we have no alternative but to seek the European heritage farther afield, in the depths of Iranian antiquity. But in the dazzling light of Hellenic civilization, this necessity evaporates. Iran may now shed its European character and sink back into Asia; the distinction between the Orient and the West may begin. *Must* begin, for from this moment on, the appropriation of Greece by Europe not only fulfilled the need for historical depth with which the West sought to invest its culture, but at the same time allowed it to establish, against Asia, the anteriority of its identity and, paradoxically, the universal character of its modernity.

With Greece, we cross the symbolic threshold separating the West from the Orient. But Grousset has shown us how to imagine a Europe which for millennia lay at the heart of the Iranian plateau. The tendency for any dominant civilization to reduce humanity to its own dimensions may be an irresistible one, and Grousset a rather emphatic expression of this reductionism. But since the publication of *La face de l'Asie* (1955) Western sensibilities have changed, superficially at least, upon contact with the political and ideological renaissance of peoples engaged in the process of decolonization. The difference in language is greater than in underlying attitude. In the West, "third worldism" tends to be an expression of guilt among intellectuals confronted with the stigmata of colonialism (a guilt which has long since ebbed) or acts out the urge to seek, in the awakening of the Third World, a sense of hope absent from our societies. (Today this hope has been all but betrayed.) In short, the Western view of history has not been radically changed. The need to legitimize our "universalizing function" (to borrow Denis de Rougemont's phrase) has remained so tenacious that we find ourselves incapable of not tracing our identity as far back as possible along the course of our history. "Homer had already described Zeus as *Europos,* an adjective meaning 'who sees into the distance'," cautions Rougemont, who appears to have borrowed his own eyes from those of the god of Olympus, the better to scan the twenty-eight centuries of consciousness which he ascribes to Europe.[11]

In the quest for these far-distant foundations, Greece, now assigned the place of the earlier civilizations of West Asia and Egypt, has clearly been given a central role.

The Hellenic connection

The idea of Europe begins with a myth. A Greek myth woven, in all probability, on a Semitic loom. In it the goddess Europa, one of the numerous brood of sisters called the *Oceanides* (another of whom is Asia), is seduced and abducted from her Asiatic homeland by a fair-haired bull incarnated by Zeus. Astride the animal she flies off to Crete where she is impregnated by her divine abductor. It is told that on the night before her abduction she dreams of "two lands locked in conflict for her favor, the land of Asia and the land which faces it."[12] Even though, as Herodotus notes, Europa "never set foot in this land which the Greeks now (5th century B.C.) call Europe,"[13] it is easy to imagine the fertile symbolism of this fabled abduction. In fact, it is hard to imagine qualities more satisfying to the ideology of origins and identity which is the West's constant source of nourishment. From Asia, birthplace of the first great civilizations, Europa, alone among her sisters, is chosen, torn from her native soil to receive the Jovian seed which both transforms her descendents and predetermines them to domination. The Europa myth, created to establish the authenticity of both Greece's Asiatic lineage and her specificity, was taken up by the heirs of the Hellenic legacy. "A part of the globe will be given her name,"[14] Horace was later to note. Europe's appropriation of the myth casts light, in turn, upon its place of origin: Greece, having founded Europe, must belong to it, which moves Rougemont to remark that Mycenae represents "the birth of Hellenic Europe."[15] The bond which must exist between Asia and Greece, then between Greece and Europe, originates in myth. In the first instance, the link is little more than a simple transition, while between Greece and Europe, the bond is a lasting one, deeply rooted in their common origin. From its very beginnings, Europe is latent in Hellenic civilization which, in the face of Asia, is so immediately "European" that Elie Faure is able to assert:

> There is a much stronger relation between the art of the caverns in France and Greek art, taken as a whole, though one or two hundred centuries separate them, than between this selfsame Greek art and the art of Asia which barely precedes it, follows it immediately, or coexists with it.[16]

Seen from this perspective, the Persian wars seem, quite logically, to be the first conflict between Orient and Occident. But well before them came the Trojan wars. Aegean Troy, however, was no less "Greek" than was Argos or Mycenae. For those who listened to the Homeric epics (which were particularly popular in the 7th century B.C.), the Trojans were not foreigners but adversaries sharing the same culture, to whom Homer accorded the support of a powerful cohort of Olympian deities, and whose heros are no lesser men (aside from their ill fortune) than their Achaean besiegers. In short, mythical Troy is too much a part of the Hellenic heritage to be cast in opposition to Greece.

The Persians — who stand completely apart from the Greeks in both language and political organization — are an entirely different matter. The Persian invasions directly threatened both the independence of the Greek city-states and their prospects for expansion as naval powers against the immense, hierarchically structured empire of Darius and Xerxes. But the response of the city-states to the incursions of the great king was far from uniform; some, in fact, sought his arbitration in their internal quarrels. The Persians were "Barbarians" of course, that is to say non-Greeks, foreigners, people of another nation, another culture. But they belonged to the familiar, the civilized world. The Hellenes may have been loath to submit to imperial authority, they may have held fast to their identity, but they held no disdain for Persian civilization. In *The Persians*, Aeschylus both magnifies the invader (how better for the victor to magnify himself?) and upholds Athenian democracy against Persian monarchy. The victory of Salamis, like that of Marathon before it, was due in large measure to the consciousness of the Greek soldiers and sailors that they were fighting for their own liberty, their own land, in their own waters. "They are neither slaves, nor subjects of any man," says Corypheus, remarking on their valour.

Little more was needed to transform the Persian wars into the first salvo, and symbol, of a millennia-long struggle between Europe and Asia — and to read, in the military successes of the Greeks, the "victory of Western intelligence and liberty over the materialism and the despotism of the Orient."[17]

In an epigram to *Les Orientales*, his poem celebrating the victory at Navarino (where a Franco-Russian squadron defeated the combined Egyptian-Ottoman fleet in 1827), Victor Hugo harks back to the lamentations of the Persians, according to Aeschylus: "Alas, alas, our ships alas, have been destroyed." Suddenly the Greek war of independence resonates with the Persian wars. The reference could hardly be more natural: the history of Greece is part and parcel of the European cultural patrimony. By delivering the land of Homer and Phidias, Europe was restoring its own past. "At the time of the great Greek civilization," wrote André Siegfried in 1943, "the world's centre of gravity was located in the eastern Mediterranean, with a certain limited contact with Asia. Already the West was distinguishing itself from the East, and Greek culture, *as we still understand it today*, was Western."[18] "In opposition to the Persians," he goes on, "...incontestably, the Greeks of antiquity were already, genuinely, Westerners. Marathon should, for us, be a shrine."

Grousset is just as categorical. In a book devoted to "the evolution of the frontiers — spiritual and political — between Europe and Asia," he unhesitatingly draws the boundary along the eastern shore of the Mediterranean.

> The European spirit became conscious of itself for the first time in Greece, in the fifth century before Christ. It set itself in opposition to the Asiatics during the days of Marathon and Salamis, which, in establishing the liberty of Hellas, ensured for eight centuries the independence of the Greek spirit, that is to say, the appearance of the European spirit. Since that time, the notion of Europe has expanded, become more substantial, without its foundations ever being too radically modified.[19]

So it was that from the 5th century B.C. onward, the European spirit ranged freely, from East to West, across a Mediterranean which it had made its own. For, says Siegfried, quoting E. M. Forster, "It is in the Mediterranean that humanity finds its norm." The Mediterranean may well be a "hyphen" between Occident and Orient, "yet it remains part of the West."[20] Fustel de Coulange's warning to the Philhellenes of the last century appears to have gone unheeded, or else quickly forgotten. "That which we have inherited from them, that which they have bequeathed to us," he writes, "leads us to believe that they resembled us; ...but almost always, we are the ones who see ourselves in them. And this is the source of frequent errors."[21] But to speak of errors is to risk posing the wrong questions, as though only historical veracity were at stake. The question is not whether or not modern Europe was right in appropriating ancient Greece, or whether the lineage it pretends to establish does or does not exist — but at what level. No one can deny its existence. It has given nourishment to European thought for far too long to have had no effect on our conception of the world. But we must realize that it is our's, and our's alone.

Why should the ancient Greeks have considered themselves Europeans? During the century of Pericles, the "European spirit" means nothing whatsoever. We may speak of the Greek spirit, of the social and political organization of the city-state — or more properly, city-states. And we shall see that no two are organized in the same way: here, an oligarchy, there a duarchy, there a tyranny. Athenian democracy is often projected, abusively at that, upon all of Greece. The Greek "model" stands in only marginal relation to our Western democratic ideals (no matter how thwarted in reality). Our values are not at all the same — far from it. But the lustre of the 5th century draws us toward it, dazzled by its brilliance. Imagined affinities spring to life — it is all too normal for modern Europe, at grave risk of anachronism, to attempt to contemplate itself flatteringly in the prestigious Athenian mirror. But the differences remain enormous. From the penumbra of the familiar classical heritage emerges a world which is, in many ways, profoundly foreign to us. A close reading of the Hellenists themselves reveal as much.

André Aymard, in his startled reaction to what he terms the two paradoxes of Hellenic antiquity — slavery and undeveloped use of machines — is a striking example. For many years efforts have been made to explain, or even justify, the first by the second. But for Aymard, the reverse holds true: the practice of slavery — the solution of facility — impeded the development of the machine, in Greece as elsewhere in antiquity.

> With infinite patience, the most ancient East accumulated empirical observations, and yet utilized them only to create astrology and magic; the quality of the materials at hand warranted better than those false sciences. The Greeks were possessed with a true scientific spirit, and it was entirely in their hands to find practical application for the principals which their reasoning had discovered...All was in place for progressive, yet radical transformation of everyday existence. But this transformation never occurred.[22]

Aymard's thesis is a controversial one: slavery is undoubtedly not the only, nor perhaps even the principal cause of this missed opportunity. It is not my place to resolve the issue. What fascinates me here is the Hellenist's disillusionment at one of history's missed opportunities — a disillusionment which reveals a spiritual difference at least as considerable as the Western intellectual's empathy for Greece. This particular intellectual bemoans the Greeks' clear disdain for applied science; he deplores the gratuity of knowledge, so profoundly contrary to the spirit of modern science. Above all, he condemns the silence of the philosophers in regard to slavery; he cannot understand. Is he not right in concluding that, in this particular case, the Renaissance has "disavowed the very Antiquity which it claimed as its own."[23]

The affinities we feel today with ancient Greece cannot permit us to measure the distance which once may have separated Greece from Persia. The best method of evaluating this necessarily subjective distance remains an examination of how the Greeks defined themselves in relation to the rest of the known world, and particularly in relation to Asia and to Europe.

We should recall, at the outset, that Europe did not yet exist as a historical concept. Mythological references to the goddess Europa aside, the concept was to remain a purely geographical one for the Greeks. Herodotus (5th c. B.C.) describes it as "a Nordic region ill-distinguished from Scythia, which is the Russian plain,"[24] and of which Greece is apparently not a part. Nor is Greece seen in opposition to Asia. Denis de Rougemont, that great European in heart and spirit, finds the "first known parallel (or contrast) between Asia and Europe"[25] in a passage attributed to Hippocrates (one generation after Herodotus). Europe, he writes, has a harsher climate which is less favourable for agriculture; therefore — in a first attempt at a theory of climate — its inhabitants are "more courageous," "disposed to action," but also "wilder, less sociable, more impetuous in nature"; while those of Asia are "pusillanimous, lacking in courage, less warlike" (primarily because they are "dominated by Kings"), while being "gentler, more perspicacious in spirit."

But what position are we to attribute to the Greeks? Hippocrates gives us no clues, but we do find an answer in Aristotle's *Politics* (Book VII, Chapter 6):

> The nations inhabiting the cold places and those of Europe are full of spirit but somewhat deficient in intelligence and skill, so that they continue comparatively free, but lacking in political organization and capacity to rule their neighbours. The peoples of Asia on the other hand are intelligent and skilful in temperament, but lack spirit, so that they are in continuous subjection and slavery. But the Greek race participates in both characters, just as it occupies the middle position geographically, for it is both spirited and intelligent; hence it continues to be free and to have very good political institutions, and to be capable of ruling all mankind if it attains constitutional unity. (Translation by H. Rackham)

For Aristotle, Greece is no more a part of Europe than of Asia: it lies at the crossroads of two worlds, and stands as their best possible synthesis. The resulting superiority awaits the unification of the Greeks under the authority of a single government. With the Macedonians, Philip and Alexander, pupil of Aristotle, this unifying, conquering power was to emerge. But their government was to be monarchical, the contrary of the principles of independence and liberty which were emblematic of the political organization of the Greek city-states. Still, even if we concede that Alexander's first victories in Asia Minor were a sort of "Panhellenic retribution" for earlier defeats suffered at the hands of Darius and Xerxes, we cannot escape the fact that Alexander ultimately adopted and made his own the system — and the ambitions — of the kings of Persia. With Alexander, asserts Grousset, "the boundaries of Europe, suddenly extended to cover what had been Near Asia, reaching to beyond Samarkand and Lahore, to the threshold of Central Asia."[26] But, he admits, Alexander and his successors are guilty of "sins against the Greek spirit." "The unexpected consequence" of their hegemony was to be "the penetration of the Hellenistic world by the spirit of the Orient."[27] Alexander had carried Europe too far, diluting it in the vastness of Asia.

European myth here slides into excess. While the existence of the Hellenistic world tends to demonstrate that the differences which separated Greeks from Barbarians were far from insurmountable, the myth would have us see this symbiosis as the corruption by the Orient of the European spirit. There could be no other way to perpetuate the East-West rivalry born with the Persian wars. Any lessening of tension could only be the product of a decline by one or the other of the two antithetical poles. And if Hellenistic Greece was no longer precisely Greece, if Athens was no longer the focus of a world whose centre of gravity had shifted eastward, the West could no longer have a champion. Providentially, to the west of Greece, a new power was arising to take up the combat which Europe, after the Alexandrian adventure, had almost abandoned.

The yearning for Roman unity

Though Rome draws from the Orient the key elements of its culture and mythology — the *Aeneid* bearing symbolic witness (in it Virgil confirms his Trojan origins) — with its rise, the Mediterranean politico-military centre of gravity shifts toward the West. For several ensuing centuries, the centre was to hover close to the geographical mid point. The shift was providential. It opened the gates of history to the northeast Mediterranean, writes André Aymard, "abandoned until then to peoples isolated from one another, and living in backwardness,"[28] and corrected the Alexandrian aberration in which Europe narrowly avoided being drained away into the boundless expanse of the Orient.

Curiously, with Rome the question of European lineage seems no longer to preoccupy Western historians. Rome, after all, *is* Europe. The colour that slowly creeps along the Mediterranean littoral needs no explanation: it is, first and foremost, our colour. From Augustus, if not before, and for more than four centuries thereafter, the sea merits its name, and appears to fulfill its destiny as a crucible of unification. All this bears no relation, in our Western mindset, with the merging of West and East:

"under Roman domination," writes Siegfried, "the Mediterranean became the centre of the Western world."[29] As for the Orient, it was now where it should be: outside, beyond the eastern and southern shores of *Mare nostrum*. Even today, the image of Mediterranean unity haunts us still. Fractured again and again, its legacy has been a disfiguring of the unitary political landscape for which Rome has left us to yearn.

The Romans, unlike anyone before, or since, created viable organic relations among the Mediterranean peoples through an imperial economy designed to serve, and to service, the metropolitan centre. Under Rome the differences which distinguished the two principal basins of the Mediterranean (with the exception of Carthage) were gradually eroded. But differences in level of development (as we would say today) remained, never to be entirely effaced. Despite "the prodigiously exceptional nature of Roman universalism,"[30] the eastern extremity of the Mediterranean (particularly after the destruction of Carthage) maintained cultural and economic ascendency over the western throughout antiquity. With the administrative division of the Empire, with Italy in decline, stripped of much of its power and its markets even within the Roman world, this ascendency was bound to increase.

Paradoxically, a clear demarcation between the West and the Orient, reaching its culmination in the splitting of the Empire into two distinct political entities with the death of Theodosius (395), is formally consummated under the insignia of Roman unity. But even prior to separation came administrative division corresponding to a parcelling out of powers and responsibilities between the Augustuses and the Caesars. Imperial Rome's Orient was little more than one of the four administrative divisions of the Empire. But already, by the time of emperors Valerian and Diocletian (late 3rd century), the eastern portion was considered the most interesting: thus they kept it for themselves, leaving the Gallians or the Maximians the task of ruling Italy. And when, in the following century, Constantine the Great was to reestablish the administrative unity of his Empire beginning from its Western domains, he chose Byzantium — soon to become Constantinople — as its nerve centre. Some historians consider his reign to mark the true founding of the Eastern Roman Empire.[31] And in point of fact, from that time onward, Italy entered into inexorable decline.

Decline, and the shift from the West to the Orient of the economic, cultural and political centre of the Roman world, echo the marginalization of Athens during the Hellenistic period. The slide toward the Orient weakened the solidity of the Roman virtues, just as it had debased the purity of Greek classicism. Edward Gibbon's description of the reign of Constantine has become one of the classic evocations of the decline of the Roman Empire:

The manly pride of the Romans, content with substantial power, had left to the vanity of the East the forms and ceremonies of ostentatious greatness. But when they lost even the semblance of those virtues which were derived from their ancient freedom, the simplicity of Roman manners was insensibly corrupted by the stately affectation of the courts of Asia.[32]

Thus, the eastward passage accentuated and accelerated the decadence which had infected the Empire's institutions and political life. But precisely what were these vanishing Roman virtues, aside from the formal frugality of power which prevented neither political assassinations nor civil wars, neither demagogy nor a host of other crimes and infringements of the legalism of senatorial oligarchy? They were, of course, realism, pragmatism, the gift of military organization and administration of the conquered; on the intellectual plane, the moral and legal accomplishments of the elites which evidenced, contrary to the Greeks, little taste for scientific and intellectual speculation. Good soldiers, excellent legal minds, efficient builders of roads and bridges, tireless organizers imbued with a universalist vision: these are the virtues the modern West loves to recognize in the Romans. But what are we to make of Rome's "scientific inertia," the "despotism" of the Neros and the Caligulas, of the elaborate ceremonies and superstitions (infinitely more important in Rome than in the Greek city-states), the cruelty of the circus (in stark contrast with the Greek games)?[33] In fact, these ingredients of Roman decadence, particularly in the political sphere, are at work deep inside Rome well before its shift to the Orient. If the decline of the Empire was accelerated by its decadence, how are we to interpret the fact that its eastern section resisted invasion so immeasurably better and longer than the Western rump? The question impels Gibbon to temper his judgement. Constantine cannot be Asia alone:

...and although the laws were violated by power, or perverted by subtlety, the sage principles of the Roman jurisprudence preserved a sense of order and equity unknown to the despotic governments of the East.[34]

If classical Rome under Constantine can still mount a resistance against the deleterious influence of the Orient, a mere two centuries later the Byzantines merit hardly more than Gibbon's scornful dismissal for having dishonoured by their vices the names of Rome and Greece.[35] However, the reign of Justinian is not without its grandeur. Gibbon is obliged to agree, attributing Justinian's ephemeral military successes to "the Roman virtues" of a peerless military leader. General Belisarius was the exception which confirmed the rule.[36] But though Justinian may have restored the universal sweep of the Empire, may indeed have brought together in his celebrated compilations the sum total of the Roman legal heritage, he remains an unworthy heir.

Was the empire of Constantine, in fact, more "corrupt" than that of Antony or Severius? Was it more equitable or at least better organized than its contemporaries, the Sassanids or later, that of Justinian? These are embarrassing questions which elicit largely subjective answers. The notion of Oriental "contagion" dates neither from Gibbon, nor even from the late Empire. Under the Republic itself, Cato the Censor warned the Senate against conquests to the East, against the corrupting influence of Greece on the Roman *virtus*. If our aim is to decry the influence of the Orient, we must go back several centuries before Constantine. But for us who, as Westerners, claim the double heritage of Greece and Rome, it would be unthinkable to call Hellenism into question. In reality, contempt for Byzantine "decadence" coupled with the incoherence of its justification seems to rouse in European historians like Gibbon a keen disappointment at both the loss of Mediterranean unity and the eastward advance of Roman civilization. This double phenomenon impugns, too, the notion of continuity from Greco-Latin antiquity onward, for this continuity can be tolerable only if we form a part of it. In order that "true" continuity be the lot of the West, it is necessary that the obvious and immediate successor of the *imperium romanum* founder on contact with the Orient. No sooner has the golden age of Roman unity and universality been extinguished than the dichotomy of Orient and Occident raises its head once more. Certainly, neither the West nor Europe existed as historical concept in the 6th century. But the conditions which were to allow the concept to emerge were slowly being put in place: under the guise of barbarianism, the "true" heirs of Greece and Rome were preparing to assert themselves.

The war of the Roman succession

Beneath the fissured surface of the Roman Empire, and despite the political erosion of its Western reaches, one significant element of unity and continuity subsisted throughout the Mediterranean world: the Christian faith. Having become the State religion even before the final partition of the Empire, Christianity was firmly rooted and maintained an enduring structure virtually everywhere. While to the East religion constituted an instrument of primary importance in the hands of the Emperor, to the West the Church managed to survive and to consolidate itself in spite of, and even through the great invasions — particularly when invaders like the Goths and later, the Franks, were to embrace a Catholicism still associated with the symbolic prestige of Rome. Though the Barbarians took over and in many ways perpetuated Roman institution and custom, the Church was probably the Empire's most lasting structural and ideological legacy. After the political break-up of the Western Mediterranean, the Roman Catholic hierarchy enjoyed an independence which the Byzantine clergy never did, becoming the sole central authority of the Western world. It is hardly surprising that Papal Rome hastened to assert itself as the spiritual capital of all Christendom, and as the true guardian of the grandeur and of the mission of the Roman Empire. In so doing, Rome could not but collide with the "Caesaropapist"[37] ambitions of Byzantium itself which, even after the failure of the glorious campaigns of Justinian, never relinquished its design to restore the unity of the Mediterranean and the universality of the Empire under its own hegemony. The first conflict between the Orient and the West takes shape within the very bosom of Christianity; and at its core lies the issue of succession. The outcome of the conflict still resonates in contemporary European historiography.

Who, West or East, can lay the most legitimate claim to the heritage of Rome? The dispute between Rome and Byzantium extends, in fact, down to the present. While the Western Empire was "succumbing to the barbarians," writes Hélène Ahrweiler, "the Eastern Empire became the bastion of Christendom and the refuge of Greco-Roman culture."[38] It was a precarious refuge indeed, when we think back to the severity of Gibbon's judgement. But it will not do to simply lash out at the East's ineptitude at preserving the Roman virtues. It must also be demonstrated that the West did not simply let them languish, that the Germanic barbarians were not simply safeguarding them for a better day. Thus, to the West, the consequences of the great invasions would be downplayed. "From whatever standpoint we regard it," notes Henri Pirenne, "the period inaugurated by the establishment of the barbarians within the Empire…introduced no absolute historical innovations."[39]

Pirenne does well to call into question the suddenness and the sharpness of the upheavals caused by the great invasions. To admit the fact would force historians to revise their views. Such an exercise is rarely sterile in a field where the great verities, because of their plural and contradictory nature, can often be turned on their heads. But Pirenne's reversal (largely accepted today, in any event) concerns me less than his stubborn determination to demonstrate it.

It is as though continuity between Rome and the Merovingians must be established at all costs, in order to present the advent of the Carolingians as a historical "cataclysm."[40] We can sense a paradox at work. Does the ultimate break with Roman antiquity come with the Carolingian Empire and the consecration of Charlemagne in Rome — events which, for Gibbon, signified the "restoration of the Roman Empire," "the link which brings together ancient and modern, civil and ecclesiastical history"?[14] A break had indeed occurred, to the extent that this new Western Empire, despite its short life-span, may be seen as the first manifestation of Europe as historical consciousness. Not so much in opposition to the Saracen incursions, as Rougemont[42] would have it, but in opposition to the *Imperium Romanum* of Constantinople. The "imperial tenure" which Charlemagne, with the support of the Pope, took upon himself constituted, according to Arhweiler, "the first major schism in Christendom."[43] Even though the Emperor of the new Rome was ultimately to grant, in exchange for strategic concessions, the title of *basileus* to him who sought consecration in ancient Rome, he never considered Charlemagne as anything more than a barbarian adventurer. The cultural chasm separating the two Empires was as wide as it was deep.

For the majority of historians, the central question appears to be, in one form or another, that of Mediterranean unity. Whether the loss of unity is the result of the slow drift of the Roman Empire, of social, economic and political forces which finally led to the final split in Christendom, or whether the sundering of the Mediterranean world is the by-product of a brutal outside event is at the core of the theses Pirenne defends so spiritedly. The question is to know, at the risk of overshadowing the significance and the extent of the great schism of Christianity, who, the Nordic or the Southern invaders, were the original destroyers of the indivisible legacy left by Rome to the whole of the Inland Sea. So it was that the end of the Empire inevitably raised the question of succession (which the modern West, until today, has generally settled to its advantage); but the end of Empire also cries out for answers to the causes of the destruction of more than half the Mediterranean perimeter. And if Pirenne staunchly holds for Merovingian continuity as against the Carolingian rupture, it is because the groundwork must be laid for the decisive appearance of Islam, and the Arab expansion.

The mythical rupture

The Arabs must thus bear responsibility for the decisive split which rent the Mediterranean in the 8th century. Not only did their irresistible expansion reduce "the territory of Christianity to Europe alone" (an affirmation that can only be hazarded if Byzantium is not considered part of Europe), "it was presently the cause of the great schism which finally divided the West from the East."[44] True, its impact on the internal development of the Frankish kingdom was a radical one. By cutting the sea in half, and by launching raids against its southern coasts, the Saracens succeeded in "bottling up" Carolingian Europe, interdicting maritime commerce and driving it ever further northward. The decline of trade, which in turn reduced the flow of revenue into the royal treasuries, forced the Carolingians to use land as remuneration, and gave the economy a much more land-based form than before.[45] This accounts for the rather surprising title of Pirenne's book, *Mohammed and Charlemagne*. For without the one, the other is "inconceivable."[46]

The growth and dynamic expansion of Islam indeed form a chain of events of enormous significance, events whose consequences are still being felt thirteen centuries later (in comparison with a weary Christianity, to limit ourselves to the strictly religious dimension, Islam remains extraordinarily vital even today). Pirenne's thesis is a forceful one. And it has the added merit of drawing an accurate picture of interdependences: Europe could have hardly arisen in isolation from external upheavals and impingements. From this perspective, the relative isolation in which the Arab invasions contrived to place Charlemagne's Empire may even be seen as a withdrawal, an essential precondition to the rebirth of the European Middle Ages three centuries later. But this is far from being Pirenne's viewpoint. Rather than a stimulating force, Islam, for him, represents an untoward event, rather like a break in the unitary destinies of the Mediterranean.[47] It is the sea which Pirenne describes as "essentially European" at a historical juncture (6th century) when he can rejoice in its being "reopened to Western navigation."[48]

But the return of *Mare Nostrum* to its "essence" is not whole, nor will it ever be. In the 7th century, something irremediable has occurred.

> With Islam a new world was established on those Mediterranean shores which had formerly known the syncretism of the Roman civilization. A complete break was made, which was to continue even to our own day. Henceforth, two different and hostile civilizations existed on the shores of Mare Nostrum. And although in our own days the European has subjected the Asiatic, he has not assimilated him.[49]

Neither colonization nor the crushing material superiority of the West — one has to admire the clairvoyance — can brush aside what Arab expansion achieved twelve centuries earlier. Pirenne's sense of regret is profound. The Europeans remain inconsolable at the loss of Mediterranean unity which they had claimed as their own. It matters little who — the German barbarians or the Muslim invaders — bears greater responsibility for the "loss." The real and the symbolic are too closely knit to be easily distinguished. Here, a tangible event assumes all the appearances of a founding myth: centuries removed, Pirenne experiences the Mediterranean rupture with an intensity which reveals its impact, and its significance, in the imagining vision of the West. With greater intensity, surely, than experienced by Charlemagne and his contemporaries.

For them, the Saracens were little more than one group of enemies among many, and far from the most worrisome. Charlemagne's determination and consistency are much more pronounced in his struggles against the Saxons and the neighbouring Lombards than against the Umayyad Emirate of Cordoba. His limited expeditions south of the Pyrenees were subsequently magnified by legend, as was the importance of the battle won by his grandfather, Charles Martel, near Poitiers (a skirmish among many, which by no means signalled the end of the Arab expeditions north of the Pyrenees). When he affirms that "Charlemagne was almost constantly at war in the region of the Pyrenees,"[50] Pirenne, with a complacency alarming in a great historian, falls victim to the mythology which the *Chanson de Roland* would help root in the collective imagination of Christian Europe three centuries later. But the *Chanson* is a much more faithful reflection of the spirit of the Spanish *Reconquista* (which began in 1031) and of the First Crusade (1096-1099), than of the Carolingian era.

In a general sense, the Western perception of Islam and the Arabs remained imprecise. "There was no need to know any more about them," writes Maxime Rodinson.[51] Notwithstanding the devastation caused by the Saracen raiders in the West, the Byzantines — not the Franks — faced the greatest shock at the hands of the Arab armies. Constantinople was twice besieged within the space of forty years (674-678, and 717-718). But these threats, dire as they were, touched off not a flicker of solidarity among the Christians of the West, where consciences were hardly ruffled by the idea that the resistance of Byzantium "saved Europe and in saving Europe, it saved Christianity," as Pirenne[52] boldly asserts, twelve centuries later. The absence of a Christian collective consciousness is hardly ringing support for the thesis of anti-Islamic Mediterranean unity. It is difficult to understand how the division of Christendom could be attributed to the sudden appearance of Islam. As much, if not more than the Arabs, the Byzantines sought to monopolize trade in the eastern Mediterranean, which in turn contributed, following the second siege of Constantinople (718) to "cutting off the Frankish kingdom from its economic ties with the Levant."[53]

In sum, the Arab expansion of the 7th century does not seem to have been the Christian West's main concern. If, like Rougemont, we are to push the sense of belonging to a European entity so far back in time, if we are to date Europe's entry into history as consciousness of itself from that remote point, then Western consciousness should take shape against Byzantium rather than against Baghdad, Damascus or even Cordoba, which the Occident discovered three centuries later. If we must absolutely speak the dichotomy of East and West, this dichotomy — political, economic and cultural more than religious — cuts right through Christendom itself. Dichotomy of the West and the Orient cast in the form of Christianity versus Islam does not yet exist.

Beyond doubt, a new and vigorous force had arisen in the eastern Mediterranean, defying the established Empires of Persia and Byzantium. From the three-way meeting of Greek, Persian and Arab cultures, a brilliant civilization rapidly sprang into being, one from which Europe was later to borrow much more than it preferred to admit. To depict the emergence of this new civilization as a "cataclysm" which threw "an insuperable barrier" across the Mediterranean "at the very moment when Europe was on the way to becoming Byzantinized"[54] is an exercise in reverse extrapolation of how the West was to perceive the Orient and Islam much later. It echoes the same anachronism which arose from the Persian wars. And underlying both anachronisms is nostalgia for ancient Greece and for Roman unity. For the unity of Rome perpetuates to this day the brilliance of Greece despite the rupture caused by Islam, which amputated from that splendid continuity a significant part of the Mediterranean world.

From that moment hence, the Other must bear responsibility for our loss of unity. In our imagined collective vision, from the instant that the West and the Orient met in combat at Salamis, only to collide again at Poitiers and at Roncevaux, the resemblances, the economic and cultural symbioses which continued to exist in the Mediterranean, the great currents which swept ceaselessly from one end to the other, seem unimportant. Despite it all, the mythical frontier which separates the West from the Orient along variable meridians and longitudes exists as part of the fabric of history, reappearing century after century, down to our day. The mythical dimension of relations between western and eastern Mediterranean is so solidly grounded in the evolution of the Western view of the world since the Middle Ages that it still dominates the European history of these very relations. It is hardly surprising that we tend to ground them in an epoch where the East-West dichotomy as we understand it simply made no sense.

Very little sense, indeed. But the depth of the dichotomy is greater today, as confrontation and attempts at dialogue between Islam and Western intellectuals, and between the producers and consumers of black gold, are plagued with misunderstanding, ambiguity, and repressed fear. The distortions and secular images clearly call for a reevaluation of relations between East and West in the Mediterranean. But the process of reevaluation must be informed by an awareness of the mythical dimension which pervades the Western view of the Orient, and, to begin with, the ancient Orient. Nothing could better illustrate the urgency of reevaluation than to see Edward Saïd, merciless critic of the Western vision of the Orient, himself caught up in the snare of myth.

Asia suffers, yet in its suffering it threatens Europe: the eternal, bristling frontier endures between East and West, almost unchanged since classical antiquity.[55]

But the "eternal frontier" is eternal only in myth. If Saïd had not allowed himself to be carried away by the very orientalist tradition he attacks, he would have observed that the break between East and West does not date from antiquity, or if so, only *a posteriori*. The cracks, as we understand them today, only appear many centuries later.

NOTES

1. Wolff, Philippe, *The Awakening of Europe*. Translated by Anne Carter. Harmondsworth, Penguin Books, 1968. (Pelican History of European Thought, Vol. 1), p.119.
2. Grousset, René et Denicker, George, *La Face de l'Asie*, Paris, Payot, 1955, p.11,7.
3. Ibid., p.13-15.
4. Ibid., p.233.
5. Ibid., p.134.
6. Ibid., p.70.
7. Ibid., p.70-71.
8. Ibid., p.67.
9. Ibid., p.69.
10. Grousset, René, *L'Empire du Levant*, Histoire de la question d'Orient, Paris, Payot, 1949 (3e ed.) p.22.
11. De Rougemont, Denis, *Vingt-huit siècles d'Europe, la conscience européenne à travers les textes d'Hésiode à nos jours*. Paris, Payot, 1961. p.8.
12. Ibid., p.13
13. Ibid., p.12
14. Ibid., p.20
15. Ibid., p.18
16. Faure, Elie, *Histoire de l'art antique*. Paris, Le Livre de poche, 1964, p.71.
17. Badi, Amir Mehdi, *Les Grecs et les Barbares, L'autre face de l'histoire*. Lausanne, Payot, 1963, Vol, 1, p.12.
18. Siegfried, André, *The Mediterranean*. Translated by Doris Hemming. London, Jonathon Cape, 1948, p.32, 211.
19. Groussant, *L'empire du Levant*, op. cit., p.7.
20. Siegfried, op. cit., p. 26,27,32.
21. Quoted by Badi, op. cit., p.15.
22. Aymard, André, Postface à l'*Histoire général du travail*, Vol. 1, Préhistoire et Antiquité, sous la direction de L.-H. Parias. Paris, Nouvelle Librarie de France, 1962, p. 371-372.
23. Ibid., p.377.
24. De Rougemont, op. cit., p. 38.
25. Ibid., p.36.
26. Grousset, *L'empire du Levant*, op. cit., p.23-24.
27. Ibid., p.7,34
28. Aymard, André et Auboyer, Jeannine, *Rome et son empire*. Paris, P.U.F., 1954, p.81.

29. Siegfried, op. cit., p.211.
30. *Rome et la conquête du monde méditerranéen*, Vol. 2., Genèse d'un empire, sous la direction de C. Nicolet. Paris. P.U.F. (Nouvelle Clio), 1978, p.173.
31. Ahrweiler, Hélène, *L'idéologie politique de l'empire byzantin*. Paris, P.U.F. 1975, p.13.
32. Gibbon, Edward, *The Decline and Fall of the Roman Empire*, The Modern Library, Vol. I, p.521.
33. Aymard, André et Auboyer, Jeannine, Rome et son empire, op. cit., p. 184, 224, 393.
34. Gibbon, op. cit., Vol. I. p.560.
35. Gibbon, op. cit., Vol. II. p. 520.
36. Gibbon, Ibid., Vol. II, p.241.
37. Perroy, Edouard, *Le Moyen Age*. Paris, P.U.F., 1955, p.34.
38. Ahrweiler, op. cit., p. 18,39.
39. Pirenne, Henri, *Mohammed and Charlemagne*. Translated by Bernard Miall. London, George Allen and Unwin Ltd., 1939, p.140.
40. Ibid., p.107.
41. Gibbon, op. cit.
42. De Rougemont, op. cit., p.47.
43. Ahrweiler, op. cit., p.40.
44. Pirenne, Henri, op. cit., p.214.
45. Ibid., p.202-210. It must still be demonstrated that it was really the Arab-imposed lack of Carolingian sea access which determined this new political and economic orientation. Pirenne concedes that Charlemagne could have profited from the protection demanded of him by Venice of becoming a maritime power. "But it did not avail itself of the opportunity." (p. 177)
46. Ibid., p.234.
47. Ibid., p.149. "The Arab conquest which brought confusion upon both Europe and Asia was without precedent."
48. Pirenne, Henri. *Economic and Social History of Medieval Europe*. New York, Harcourt, Brace and Co. 1937, p.30.
49. Pirenne, *Mohammed and Charlemagne*, p.152.
50. Ibid., p.159.
51. Rodinson, Maxime, *Europe and the Mystique of Islam*, op. cit., p.5. Hichem Djait, in *Europe and Islam*, says virtually the same thing, p.10.
52. Pirenne, Henri. *Mohammed and Charlemagne, op. cit., p. 175.*
53. McNeill, W.H., *The Rise of the West*. New York, Mentor Books, 1963, p.488, note 38, which is based on Archibald Lewis' *Naval Power and Trade in the Mediterranean, 500-1100*. Lewis adds that Franco-Byzantine rivalry in Italy was of no encouragement to Constantinople to end its restrictive practices. McNeill notes: "This is Pirenne's famous thesis turned upside down." The same refutation is made by Perroy, op. cit., p.96-97.
54. Pirenne, Henri, *Mohammed and Charlemagne*, op. cit., p.164.
55. Saïd, Edward, *Orientalism*, op. cit., p.250.

II

Symbiosis and Conflict

In the preceding chapter we examined how the West has endeavoured to ground its history and its specificity as a civilization in Greek antiquity. There, went the common belief, lay the source of all that differentiated West from East. How much better to appropriate a Mediterranean which Rome had successfully made "our own." But, seen from this perspective, the rapid expansion of Islam under the Arabs challenged Western dominion over the Mediterranean basin, and caused what seemed to be a radical, irreparable rift. Under the impetus of Islam, the imagined East/West fault line shifted from the eastern reaches of the Mediterranean hinterland to the very heart of the inner sea. Arab expansion thus came to be burdened with responsibility for the destruction of Mediterranean unity. Though denying neither the scale of the expansion nor the magnitude of its aftershocks, I concluded that such an extreme ethnocentric interpretation of history (which remains to this day the dominant interpretation in the West) was made possible by a series of anachronisms firmly rooted in our collective consciousness, and that the rift between the Orient and the West, in the sociocultural sense which we understand it today, came about much later.[1]

But if not with the Arab upsurge, when did it come about? The hypothesis which first springs to mind would have the rift appearing in the age of the Crusades, from the 11th to the 13th centuries. Indeed, this is the era when European Christendom (perhaps more accurately described as Germano-Latin to distinguish it from the Greco-Byzantine variant) truly enters into contact with Islam, and begins to become concerned by "Mohammedanism." Much can be gained by examining the circumstances and the amplitude of a first encounter which remains, to this day, engraved in the collective consciousness of the West.

We can trace back to this encounter the images from which European Christendom shaped its rival. They are the same images which continue, indirectly, to permeate the everyday Western view of the Mediterranean Orient which has become, over time, modern Europe's "Other" *par excellence*. But here, too, myth and reality are closely intertwined. Though Western Christians of the 11th and 12th centuries were undeniably sensitive to the opposition between Islam and Christendom, we today stand at risk of misleading ourselves over the original significance and extent of this opposition.

In this chapter, I propose to take up the question of significance and extent. Can the encounter between Germano-Latin Christendom and the world of Arab Islam be reduced to the clash of two armed, implacably opposed religions? Did it alone give rise to a medieval West fully conscious of its own specificity when confronted by the discovery of what, even then, seemed a radical alterity? Was the Mediterranean then broken asunder, or did it remain a zone of cultural symbiosis, and if so, to what degree?

To answer the question with some certainty, we must have at our disposal the most authoritative sources. These sources are abundant and oft consulted, but, for the most part, they reflect the outlook and attitudes of elites, and only imperfectly mirror popular feelings. Our reconstructed image of Islam remains essentially the creation of a relatively narrow literate stratum of Western Christendom — the rest would be risky conjecture. But the discrepancy can be overcome if we remind ourselves that these very images, the products of an elite, have also shaped collective mentalities down through the centuries. Their study is far from futile: these are the images which call our very beliefs into question and, even today, give shape to our relations with the Arab world — which is precisely what interests me. I make no pretence of writing history; my reading springs from a synthesis of existing work.

For centuries the Crusades have been the subject of a literature as inexhaustible as it is varied. Several definitive books published in recent decades have placed events in a more balanced perspective though, outside the limited circle of specialists in the period, few conclusions have been drawn. The mythology which quickly sprang from the largely fantastic epics woven around the theme of expeditions to distant lands still permeates our commonly-held image of these events, and colours our view of the Mediterranean Orient. Still, though the first true encounter between Western Christendom and Islam (as a society) was couched in terms of war and religion, there was infinitely more to the encounter. The true depth of Germano-Latin Christianity's opposition to Islam (as a religion) can only be grasped in the light of the full range of Mediterranean relations, including both Byzantium and the Christians of the East. Furthermore, it must take into account the prevailing situation within Western Christendom itself.

How then do the West's terms of encounter with Islam make themselves manifest? This is the question which must be taken up before examining the many facets of a historical meeting.

Terms of encounter

The birth and rapid expansion of Islam in the 7th and 8th centuries of the Christian era were earth shaking events that touched off long-lasting shifts in the political and religious geography of the Mediterranean, over-turned the existing order and determined the future of the societies established along its eastern shores. Muslims and Christians entered into contact on two levels: as communities and individuals in the lands conquered by the Arabs, and as states and empires. At each level, the terms of encounter were strikingly different.

For the Christians of the Orient, the Arab invasion represented considerably less than the historical calamity we are so readily inclined to imagine. Already partially Arabized by the gradual migrations which drew the nomads of Arabia toward the more fertile zones of Syria and Mesopotamia, the populations which were living in proximity to the peninsula welcomed the troops of Abu Bakr and Omar as much with relief as with dismay. The Arab armies brought an end to the administrative intimidation and religious intolerance of a remote and unloved Byzantine power. The majority of these populations, like those of Persia and North Africa later on, rapidly converted of their own volition, half out of conviction, half out of economic and political opportunism. But, side by side with the Muslim majority, there remained sizeable Christian and Jewish communities whose members enjoyed "protected minority" (*dhimmi*) status which allowed them to live under the protective wing of Islam while conserving their religious beliefs, coupled with payment of a special tax and observance of a certain number of restrictions of varying severity, depending on time and place (for example: riding a horse and carrying a sword might be forbidden, marriage to Muslim women prohibited, special dress required).[2]

Though hardly idyllic, the situation of the Christian communities of the Orient appears nonetheless to have been bearable. The ever-so-slightly condescending tolerance which Islam and its leaders demonstrated toward them derived from the fact that Mohammad did not establish his new religion in opposition to the two monotheistic creeds which preceded it. He situated it, instead, in the Abrahamic continuity which links them. From Abraham to Jesus, the Qur'an "contains" all previous revelation which it reveals in turn and in its own way to the Arabs, thus bringing to an end the Judeo-Christian duopoly:

> And they say: None entereth Paradise unless he be a Jew or a Christian. These are their own desires.

For:

> Those who believe and do good works: such are rightful owners of the Garden. They will abide therein.

And:

> Abraham was not a Jew, nor yet a Christian; but he was an
> upright man who had surrendered (to Allah), and he was not
> of the idolaters.[3]

The reference to Abraham, ancestor of monotheism, places the
Qur'anic discourse outside of time, transforms it into a message at once
universal and specifically Arab in its origins. Though the Word transmitted
by Mohammad follows after Jesus, it belongs to all eternity. At the same
time, it "defends the rights of his people before God"[4] by opening the doors
of a more authentic, purer monotheism. Islam, and even more so Islam
triumphant, needed feel no envy toward a Christian religion which sacral-
ized suffering, humiliation and defeat (the crucifixion of Christ). More, it
rejected the divinity of Jesus, and even the possibility that this remarkable
man might have died on the cross[5] — an interpretation which abolished the
intractable confusion caused by the concept of the Trinity, long a source of
conflict between the Christian churches.

Those new subjects of the caliphate who conserved their beliefs were
not necessarily expressing bitter resistance to the new dominant religion,
nor were they excluded from the *cursus honorum*. Christian communities
subservient to Muslim law found themselves released, in a manner of
speaking, from the dogmatic exigencies of Byzantine "Caesaro-papism"
and were, paradoxically, able to practice their respective rites in an atmosphere of greater tolerance under the new regime. Christian intellectuals
held high-ranking positions in the hierarchy of the caliphate, and viewed
the faith of the conquerors with relative serenity. One such man was John
of Damascus, the son of a highly-respected court official, who became such
a trusted advisor to the caliph that he was suspected by Byzantium of
having "Mohammedan leanings."[6] The moderation of his writings on
Islam (compared with what Western Catholic literature on the same theme
were to become) convey a certain sense of superiority: in his view, the
doctrine of Mohammad, whose longevity the Damascene could not have
anticipated, was founded on instruction the prophet was alleged to have
received from a Christian monk of the Arian (thus heretical) persuasion.
Though not entirely free of pettiness, the theological controversy launched
by John of Damascus belonged to the tradition of "Byzantine" disputations
and was tempered, above all, by its author's day-to-day contact with the
Muslims.[7] Just as later in Spain, systematic, fierce antagonism between
Christians and Muslims did not exist in the lands of Islam. Cohabitation
was not only possible; it was often felicitous.

State-to-State relations were often quite different, varying from one
part of the Mediterranean to another. Both Christian and Muslim States

attempted to channel the religious ardour of their subjects against the adversary. Even then, as the spirit of conquest faded in the Islamic lands, the distinction in Islamic law between *dar al harb* (house of war) and *dar al Islam* (house of submission) lost its force. With the disintegration of the Arab empire and the rise of "internal" rivalries, alliances with Christian potentates became part of Muslim politics. Nor did religious divergences constitute the fundamental principal of international relations on the Byzantine side. When the *basileus* took up the sword against Islam it was to preserve his empire's territorial base rather than to save his soul. Relations between emperor and caliph shifted constantly between war and peace, between hostility and civility, in response to prevailing political and economic conditions. The Byzantines and the Arabs were familiar with one another, and held each other in esteem.

The situation was diametrically different in the Christian kingdoms of the West. Prior to the late 9th century, these realms had been virtually unaware of the Islamic world, which in turn was unaware of them, despite some four centuries of confrontation and conflict between the Saracens and the Italian city-states of the Mediterranean. This reciprocal ignorance stemmed from the totally different levels of cultural, economic and political development of the two societies. The poorly educated clerics and the roughhewn military chieftains who ruled over fiefdoms which had barely begun to recover from the multiple invasions which wracked Europe from the 4th to the 10th centuries, found themselves face to face with a full-formed and flourishing civilization, even though its political unity had collapsed. Only abuse of language can explain why the notion of Middle Ages (understood as the West's long transition from the end of the Roman empire to the first signs of the Renaissance) still subsumes, for many historians, the whole of the Mediterranean world. This notion, already unconvincing in terms of the immense Western European historical reality it purports to designate, enfolding as it does the idea of decline and retreat, is totally inadequate to describe the upsurge of Islam and of Arab civilization.

Hardly one century after its initial expansion, Islamic civilization had already achieved a degree of refinement and flowering totally beyond the ability of the Carolingean empire to comprehend. Islam had produced a scientific outpouring which Europe would only truly begin to grasp and to equal from the 13th century onward. By the end of the first millennium, the curious and inventive spirit of the Muslim elites, their taste for rational explanation and for the experimental method, the sum of their knowledge in fact, stood in sharpest contrast to the mystical revival of Western Christianity, to the ignorance of its knighthood, whose chiefs often boasted of their illiteracy. Measured against that which the West, partially under Arab influence, was later to enshrine as the cardinal criteria of "civilization," the

Christian kingdoms were mired in "barbarism." It is hardly surprising that the world of Islam could barely deign to learn more about these "backward" lands which, in their turn, were closed to developments beyond the Pyrennées. The situation was exacerbated by the fact that, following its political disintegration, the Arab empire had ceased to expand its zone of domination. By the beginning of the 11th century, Arab classicism and the Christian Middle Ages touched without coming to know one other.

But the political deterioration of the Muslim world was to allow the Christian warlords of the West to go over to the offensive in Spain, in Sicily, even in Syria, while the intensification of transmediterranean trade was to bring Italian traders into ever-increasing touch with the port cities of the Levant. Thus contact developed between Western Christendom and Islam. Through commerce, war and politics, and despite the ire and the interdictions of the Church of Rome, the least refined societies were gradually to absorb from much more advanced societies — not always overtly and often unwittingly — a significant part of their arts and sciences.[8]

Such was, in the early 11th century, the general context of the encounter: on one side, emerging kingdoms and Christian princes distinguished above all by their military power, and on the other, a brilliant civilization, powerful in its knowledge and economic development, but weakened by its internal divisions. There were two zones of prime contact: southern Italy and Spain. But a third, declining power also existed: Byzantium, which sought to impose its authority in the eastern Mediterranean as the necessary mercantile intermediary in the face of increasingly vigorous competition from the Italian city-states.

Clearly, the encounter between the Orient and the West must be expressed in more complex terms than first meet the eye. It cannot be reduced to antagonism between Islam and Christianity, nor to the Islam-Christendom binomial, which in turn gives rise to an intriguing terminological problem. Western science uses one word to designate, in the case of the Oriental Other, two distinct realities between which it draws a careful distinction: Islam as religion (which would correspond to "Christianity") and Islam as historical and social reality (which would correspond to "Christendom"). In Arabic, however, the expression *dar al Islam* designates the geopolitical territory of Islam, while *umma* stands for the community of the faithful.[9] For the West, ignoring time and space, Islam-as-religion enfolds Islam-as-society, with the second being no more than the consequence, the reflection of the first. "Understanding Islam in history is not identical to understanding Islam," notes a perceptive religious historian.[10] The formula should be adopted, and reversed: the desire to "understand Islam" has often contributed to obliterating the socio-historical dimensions of the *dar al Islam*.[11]

While it may or may not be true, as Djait insists, that "it was Europe that invented the cultural notion of Islam as a totality,"[12] there can be no doubt that this totalizing vision meshes perfectly with the modern Western intellectual tradition, and particularly with the immutable Orient-Occident dichotomy. Why should we be surprised that, today, it has become so difficult for us to grasp the complexity and the diversity of the relations which were formed in (or have simply continued from) the Mediterranean in the 11th and 12th centuries?

But this diversity of relations — and of perceptions — has been all but obliterated by the simplistic imagery which agglutinated around the Crusades.

The Orient of the Crusaders

The Orient of the Crusaders began with a fiction before becoming reality in the Crusades themselves.

The fiction was that of the Holy Land to be delivered, compounded with an ill-defined yearning for a hidden Eden. "Paradise is situated in the regions to the East," wrote Isidore of Seville (530-636) in his celebrated *Etymologies*, anchoring a tradition which was to continue unchanged throughout almost the entire Christian Middle Ages. Astride the path towards Paradise lay Jerusalem; Jerusalem the mythical, city of the Passion, Orient of Western fervour, and orientation point for the physical structures of churches, large and small. Among the little people, "the voyage, whose conditions they scarcely understood, was intimately connected with biblical reminiscences until the very last stage, by which time it had become all but impossible to distinguish between the earthly Jerusalem and its celestial counterpart."[13] The Holy City represented a symbolic place, and the Crusades, an adventure within Western Christendom, not only in the religious, but in the social and political sense.

Though the problems of the Byzantine Empire had some bearing on the origins of the first "overseas" expedition, the campaign had no connection with the situation prevailing in Palestine, and even less with the state of Christian-Muslim relations in the Mediterranean. As we have seen, Christians in the Muslim States lived well on the whole, and sought nothing from their Western coreligionists.[14] Moreover, the very two societies into which, for the first time, Muslim subjects were being integrated (reconquered central Spain and Sicily under the Normans) "were not to participate in the Crusade"[15] — a significant abstention. There remained the question of pilgrimage: the brigandage and ransom-taking to which Western pilgrims en route toward the Holy Land were exposed are well documented.[16] The land route via Asia Minor had become "all but impossible" because of the Turkoman invasion, but the sea routes remained open.[17] But at the same time, Christian merchant vessels had begun to ply the eastern Mediterranean, drawn by expanding trade between Fatimid Egypt and the Italian cities.[18] The explanation for the Crusades must be sought in Europe itself, and more specifically, in northwestern Europe: precisely the region which enjoyed the least direct contact with the Mediterranean and with Islam.[19]

Warlike energies had begun to overflow in the northwestern corner of Europe, energies which Pope Urban II, himself a native of northern France, sought to muster in the service of his European policy. There can be no doubt that the Pope's plan to enlist Western knighthood for the "deliverance of the Holy Sepulchre" was, in part, a response to a petition from the Byzantine emperor Alexis Comnenos who, 24 years after the crushing defeat of the Byzantines by the Seljuk Turks at Manzikert (1071), dreamed of recovering the lost lands of Asia Minor. But Urban's solemn appeal to the Council of Clermont in 1095 stemmed above all from a desire to strengthen the Papacy in its struggle against the Holy Romano-Germanic Empire. By recruiting Western rulers and knights of Europe to an expedition against the Turks, Urban consolidated his prestige and power, and confirmed the Papacy as a force for unity overarching the divisions and internal struggles in which these princes and warlords were depleting their resources and their forces.

The Crusades absorbed political unrest which might well have been ruinous for Christian Europe: an excess of knights in search of a fiefdom and the wars of feudal expansion which followed, such as those waged by the Normans in Italy, Sicily and England, or by the French in Spain, or by the Germans in the northeast corner of the continent.[20] Urban successfully redirected these forces outward by setting them a faraway goal, Palestine; a symbol, the Cross; and the image of a common enemy, the Infidel, profaner of the Holy Places.

> Oh, what a disgrace, if a race so despised, base, and the instrument of demons, should overcome a people endowed with faith in the all-powerful God, and resplendent with the name of Christ![21]

The Pope's fanatical exhortations had more to do with fabrication of an image than with the expression of widespread feelings of hostility. It drew on the South's painful memories of marauding Saracens, and linked these memories to the religious fervour of the peoples of the North (who knew nothing of the Saracens), to create an anti-Christian enemy of purely mythical generality. This generic adversary had one sole function: to bring about unity by channelling energies into a venture which would quickly become a "colonial expedition."[22]

The incontestable popular appeal of the sermon at Clermont was stark evidence of the zeal, at once religious and warlike, which had permeated the whole body of Western Christendom. But the Pope's discourse posited an imagined "liberation" (the people of Jerusalem saw no need to be liberated) and an arbitrary foe: the "Turk" (Seljuk, as it happened), a new arrival in Anatolia who had no connection (except by religion) with the Saracen raids on the southern and western shores of the Mediterranean. The misunderstanding was total, embracing both adversary and cause, as well as the very people whose rescue was vital, be they the Christians of Palestine — for whom "the Crusades were first a source of suffering, and then a great disillusion"[23] — or the Byzantines.

The Byzantines experienced the first shock: the Poor People's Crusade — an unforeseen consequence of the sermon at Clermont — which, led by Peter the Hermit, had set out without waiting for the seigniorial armies. This throng of pilgrims, visionaries and paupers easily infiltrated by common bandits, lived off the land, wreaking havoc in the countries through which it passed. When finally, preceded by its dismal reputation, the rabble arrived before Constantinople it resembled nothing so much as a horde of undisciplined marauders whom the terrified Byzantines promptly transported across the Bosphorus — and to slaughter at the hands of the Turks.[24]

This first, ill-fated contact between Crusaders and Byzantines was almost symbolic. Not that the real armies which, several months later, converged on Constantinople either looked or behaved like their luckless predecessors. No, the mail-clad knights were impeccably disciplined; their power inspired another kind of fear, of the political variety. In reality, the emperor Alexis Comnenos had not wished them to come; mistrust, even hostility marked his first encounter with the Crusader chiefs. But had the Frankish knights not come at his bidding? Not really. This was the first misunderstanding. We do not know the details of the pact between the Pope and the emperor, but all the evidence suggests that the latter wished to recruit mercenaries in the West, or at least, troops which would be under his orders.[25]

Alexis, after all, had little or no control over a foreign expeditionary corps driven by a will independent of his own and prepared for, at most, an alliance with him. The emperor was seeking a military tool to further his political aims. Byzantium had not foregone diplomatic means for attaining its ends (the recapture of part of Asia Minor), and had made the use of military force conditional upon the results of the talks then in progress. For Constantinople warfare held little glory; it was never anything more than a stopgap measure, the last political resort, even when the enemy was Muslim. Intrigue, corruption, and the political exploitation of the adversary's weaknesses were much preferred methods.[26] It comes as no surprise that the knightly cavalry, driven by faith and the thirst for combat, for whom warlike virtues were supreme, and exercised in the name of Christ, filled the emperor with apprehension. He distrusted these lords in quest of new kingdoms to conquer, new fiefdoms to carve out of lands the Byzantines considered their own, though occupied by the Turks.

Byzantine sovereignty over the future conquests of the Crusaders could only be established by inducing them to swear an oath of allegiance; the Crusader chieftains finally agreed, but not without ulterior motives. It was only the first in a long succession which was to last the length of the Crusades, with Greek and Latins occasionally confronting one another as declared enemies. Who can be unaware that the Fourth Crusade took the form of a Venetian-Norman alliance against Constantinople, which fell in 1204 and became, for a half-century, a "Latin Empire" before being retaken by Michael Paleologos in 1261. The First Crusade was not quite as extreme, but the sight of a great Western army drawn up beneath the walls of the capital could not have been particularly comforting. The emperor would have had no choice but to assist the Crusaders' campaign against the Turks, if only to help them move on. But the assistance went no further than the capture of Niceae. The Crusaders soon felt "betrayed" by the suzerain under whose authority they had pretended to place themselves.

Above and beyond political divergences, the failed encounter between Western Christians and those of the Orient laid bare the cultural chasm dividing the two worlds. The two worlds enjoyed incomparably different levels of civilization (or decadence, depending on the viewpoint), shared neither the same view of politics or warfare, and experienced their common religion in sharply opposing ways. While amongst the Westerners, the ideal of the pious Christian warrior provided mutual sustenance, "it was too blatantly paradoxal for the logical Greek mind to accept."[27] Byzantine Christianity was less ardent and less fanatical than the Western faith; it seemed more humane, more humanitarian, closer to the attitudes of its Muslim neighbours. So it was that the Christians of the Orient and the Muslims agreed not to practice forced conversion. The Muslims themselves were, in that long-ago era, far removed from the fanaticism which the West has so often ascribed to Islam, irrespective of time or place. So far removed, in fact, that they could ill understand how the Crusades could possibly have been motivated by religious considerations (in which respect they were only half wrong...).[28] The Christian populations which the Crusades "delivered from the Muslim yoke" quickly came to look back fondly upon their subjection to Islam when confronted by the new occupying forces so estranged from their culture.[29]

Succinctly put, both the Byzantine Christians and those of Asia Minor and Syria had far greater cultural affinities with the Muslim world than with their Western coreligionists. "A Byzantine felt more at home in Cairo or Baghdad than he would feel in Paris, Goslar or even Rome."[30] Greeks and Muslims concurred, according to virtually every surviving account, in denouncing "the Westerners' savagery."[31] The bloody massacre which followed the taking of Jerusalem contributed powerfully to propagate this image, and had a direct effect on the manner in which the Muslims looked upon and waged war against the "Infidels."

Conversely, the Crusaders — or a significant number of them — used their accounts to fashion an "extremely deprecatory" vision of their Greek coreligionists. Far more negative, in fact, than their accounts of the "Saracens." Should we be surprised?

The Crusaders seemed more often disappointed with their allies than with their enemies; as masters of the art of warfare, they could appreciate the adversary's true worth. "Who can be wise enough, and learned enough to make bold to describe the sagacity, the warlike gifts and the valiance of the Turks," wrote an anonymous warrior and chronicler of the first crusade.[32] The attitude was reciprocated by the other camp. Ibn Jobair and Usama, despite their declared hostility to the occupiers of Palestine, could still pay homage to the "justice of the Franks."[33] War, contrary to what we might imagine, was not total: certainly there were outbursts of armed hostility, but just as certainly, peaceful interludes, as shown in this account by Beha-eddin of the atmosphere which prevailed during the siege of Acre by Saladin (Salah al-Din) during the Third Crusade.

> As each side was continually attacking the other, the Christians and the Moslems ended by drawing closer, getting to know each other and talking together. When they were tired, they laid down their arms and mingled together; they sang, danced and gave themselves up to every enjoyment; in a word, the two sides became friendly until, a moment later, the war started again.[34]

These moments of fraternization among the troops were a perfect reflection of the relationship which grew up between the two leaders: Richard Coeur de Lion and Saladin (through the intermediary of Malik-Adil, Saladin's brother, and heir) carried on a courtly dialogue, exchanged gifts, and finally signed a treaty (October 9, 1192) by which Saladin promised to respect the rights of all pilgrims to travel to Jerusalem. Richard offered his sister to Malik-Adil in marriage; had the sister not refused, the marriage would have been concluded.[35]

Paradoxically, war, in the general sense, was as much a vehicle, a bridge, an agent of human intercourse as it was a confrontation. The war-induced encounter with hard reality was a source of differentiation and nuance; appreciation of this reality at ground level was indispensable to the effective (though not necessarily non-bloody) conduct of politics. The first Crusaders may well have been zealous, hot-blooded men, but their combative ardour gradually waned as their customs fell under the influence of the more refined civilization with which they rubbed shoulders. This was particularly true of those who decided to settle in Palestine: Foucher de Chartres declaring, "We who have been Occidentals have become Orientals." Or Usama cautioning, not without irony, "the Templars, who were friends of mine"[36] to "instruct" the newly arrived Franks in sensitivity to Muslim manners and customs. As Edouard Perroy notes, the Crusades were a permanent institution, through which a regular process of coming and going between Europe and Asia came into being.[37]

The Crusades, as an institution, supplemented the Mediterranean's existing networks — primarily trading networks — and contact zones (Sicily, Spain) between Latins and Muslims. Some authorities contend that the Crusades even stimulated commerce between the Italian city-states and the Levant. Without going quite so far, it was noteworthy enough that despite the Western invasions,[38] trade continued to thrive: a clear indication that contemporaries — travellers, at least — had no sense of living in a bipolar world. They moved and functioned in a variegated Mediterranean, rich in possibilities, contacts and multiple opportunities, where religious differences did not play a preponderant role, and — crucially — raised no insurmountable West-East or North-South barriers. The "silent complicity of the traders" writes Lopez, gave rise to a "reciprocal esteem" which even war seems not to have shaken.[39] But, above all, as Claude Cahen notes:

> Neither the Christian nor the Muslim side (nor anywhere else) looked upon the war as political or religious in the same totalitarian sense as today. Trade and the circulation of goods were almost sacred customs.[40]

The Crusades generated more than economic activity; they spawned political contacts — and curiosity. These political contacts reached their diplomatic and peaceful apogee in 1229 with the Sixth "Crusade," whose leader Frederick II obtained Jerusalem, Bethlehem and Nazareth from the Sultan of Egypt, El-Kamil, through negotiation, without a blow being struck. Granted, it was an ephemeral acquisition, but the method was significant. The Church, however, was obliged to condemn the example: for Rome, coexistence with Islam was unthinkable, ungodly. The Pope struggled, without success, to destroy the agreement, signed in Palestine. The short-lived success of imperial diplomacy did not, however, end the Catholic Church's ideological domination over a large section of Western Christendom. For the common people with no direct experience of Islam (primarily in the northwest), the word of the Church carried substantially greater weight and, had a more immediate impact than did the cosmopolitan views of an enlightened elite.

Maxime Rodinson is correct to warn against too broad an interpretation of the contacts established at the time of the Crusades. Among the common folk, interest in both the living Orient and the political Orient, its history and its divisions, remained virtually nil. What the Crusades and their mythology were to create was "a huge market for a comprehensive, integral, entertaining and satisfying image of the enemy's ideology."[41] This thirst for simplification did not however, even on the popular level, result in a uniformly negative image of the Other. Rodinson reminds us that Saladin, a full century after his achievements, continued to "inspire overwhelming admiration among Westerners." But the admiration stopped short of the Muslim faith of the hero upon whom it was lavished: "Surely such a perfect knight could not be excluded from the Christian experience. Therefore, his mother was said to be a Christian countess of Ponthieu who had been shipwrecked in Egypt by a storm; and it was recounted that Saladin himself had been converted on his death-bed."[42] Once again we have the classic desire to appropriate: for those who never forsook the dream of reconquering Jerusalem, it was a simple matter of "seizing upon its most celebrated conqueror."

But the "christianization" of the Arab (or Turkish, or "Saracen") hero was by no means a condition *sine qua non* of his use. The generosity of the Arabs could be expressed above and beyond all religious considerations, as Sigrid Hunke so enthusiastically notes:

> In the personage of the "noble pagan" who forgoes his victory, throws down his sword and extends his hand to his courageous adversary without regard for national or religious barriers, the pious Wofram von Eschenbach raised up an undying and moving monument to the generosity of the Arabs: it is the 'pagan' Feirefiz who teaches the hero Parsifal how to attain the summit of true knighthood...[43]

Feirefiz, Parsifal's half-brother, may have been only half Oriental (by his mother), if I understand his genealogy. But it is of little importance, since the fraternal duo of gallants partake of both the Orient and the West. The glorification of Christian chivalry did not necessarily imply hostility to the Arabs or denigration of their culture, even at the popular level. What we have encountered is a will to appropriation, the relatively rough-hewn culture's natural approach to a more refined one. Régine Pernoud may well be right in concluding, from her study of texts on the Crusades, that the Christian Middle Ages, like Islamic civilization, "were innocent of race prejudices."[44]

Instead, analysis of the Crusades suggests that prejudices were at work on altogether different terrain: that of religion.

The image of heresy

The pejorative image of the Other does exist: it is shaped like a heresy. In the 11th and 12th centuries a "plebeian image"[45] of Islam as religion took form in Western Christendom. This image was to sink deep roots in the collective unconscious,[46] and then in the collective subconscious, roots so deep that the image remains insidiously active, always ready to spring back to life in Western public opinion. When I read "Arabs get out!" scrawled in crude black letters on the walls of certain French universities, I am reading the present: the sense of disquiet and resentment toward North African workers and students in France. There is also the recent past: the dismay and the rancour of those who could never accept the war of national liberation or the "loss" of Algeria. Not to mention the barely conscious expression of that omnipresent undercurrent of mediocrity and insecurity: the need for reassurance of the value of one's own identity through exclusion of the Other, a mechanism which Sartre has stripped bare in his portrait of the anti-semite (applied here, *mutatis mutandis*, to the anti-Arab).[47] But the raw materials which go to make up the average European's near instinctive devaluation of Arabs or Muslims come from far away indeed, originating in the venomous discourse of the Catholic Church on "Mohammedan" heresy and imposture which began in the 11th century — a discourse which has continued, in a variety of barely concealed forms, interspersed with occasional bouts of open virulence, until our century. Only recently, in fact, has it been abandoned and condemned by the highest echelons of the Catholic hierarchy in its recent efforts to drape the Christian message with the cloak of universality.

Why Catholicism's unremitting ideological hostility toward Islam? Why at this particular point in history?

That the systematic vilification of Islam coincided, however approximately, with the rise of the Crusader spirit (as distinct from the real contacts created by the Crusades themselves) is far from startling. It constituted the key element of Catholic power's drive to unite a European Christendom no longer threatened by pagan incursion (Norman, Magyar and Slavic invaders had been converted and integrated into Christianity) against a common foe (be it purely mythical in its generality) whose ideology Europe was only beginning to grasp. Not only did the Church of Rome appreciate more fully the power of Islam's religious contagion — and particularly its progress in North Africa — but it had come to better understand the fundamentals of Islam through the intermediary of the Christians of the Orient, and, above all, of Spain. Could not this understanding have stimulated rapprochement given that Islam, far from setting itself in opposition to Christianity, claimed continuity with it? But continuity also meant modification, refinement: Islam, over and above its Arab specificity, also claimed universality and asserted itself as a final and perfect revelation which "corrects," where necessary, the messages which preceded it. But what corrections they were: Christ was no longer God become man, but simply a man; a great prophet, certainly, but second in the hierarchy of prophecy after Mohammad, the ultimate and irrefutable messenger.

Consider for a moment the repercussions of such a doctrine within a Church already hard pressed to establish the notion of the Trinity as the cornerstone of its entire edifice, particularly in the "deepest, darkest" West, the northwest, where geographical and cultural distance further deepened the doctrinal chasm. We have seen how, for the Christians of the Orient and even of Spain, everyday contact with Arab civilization had a tempering effect on the theological quarrel with Islam. But nothing of the sort took place in the West. The Western Church had no reason to display moderation toward what it viewed as a dangerous and invasive heresy, whose rigor and propagative power seemed unaffected by the collapse of the political and military power of the caliphate. Heresy it was indeed: the Christian message was diluted, betrayed and challenged; and the heresy became all the more pernicious, perfidious in its attempts to legitimize itself by reference to Holy Writ. Its author could only be an impostor, a magician, a malefactor, an agent of subversion in the service of Satan. No words were strong enough to discredit this lewd (polygamous) mystifier who enticed zealous followers with lascivious images of a promised paradise. Is there any point in dwelling further on these gross caricatures? They are well known, frequently recurring in Western Christian literature, even among authors considered as enlightened.

In his definitive *Islam and the West*, Norman Daniel provides a systematic, in-depth analysis.[48] Daniel's close examination of the Christian literature of the Middle Ages reveals that the circulation of slanderous images of Islam was far more the work of malice than of ignorance. From the early 12th century onward, works containing "certain accurate observations"[49] on Mohammad and Islam began to appear in the West, primarily in Spain. Alongside the fabrications and the calumnies appeared a more honest, more straightforward approach, symbolized in France by the patronage of Pierre the Venerable (1092-1156), abbot of Cluny. Pierre's efforts were far from disinterested: his aim was to grasp, through a more cool-headed, sober understanding of the Qur'an, what and who the Church must combat: the Other must be studied the better to be refuted. The same attitude was to persist with little modification right down to our day: information on Islam available to most contemporary Catholics serves, in the final analysis, to "encompass" it within the Christian faith, an ultimate attempt at neutralization under the guise of benevolence and sympathy.

Returning to the 12th and 13th centuries, we may safety affirm that the image of Islam disseminated *ad usum populi* remained grossly pejorative, unenriched by whatever progress the scholars and clerics of the age had achieved. Even in the best of circumstances, their attitude remained ambiguous and often contradictory. But no matter how obscurantist the ecclesiastical authorities toward Islam-as-religion, the Western elites, though religious themselves, could neither close their eyes to, nor staunch their curiosity toward, the sheer volume and depth of the Arabo-Islamic thought whose inexhaustible riches they had only begun to discover.

Attitudes toward Arab science

In Arab or Muslim science,[50] the learned elites of the West realized that they were dealing with a culture considerably more advanced and refined than theirs, and with a body of knowledge upon which, however poorly understood, they were not loath to draw, whatever the attitude of the Church might be. In fact, the status and authority of these new European scientific elites came as a direct result of their contact with Arabo-Muslim thought. Adelard of Bath (1070-1150) admitted that "to gain approval for his own ideas, he often attributed them to the Arabs; so pervasive was the 'fashion for Muslim science'"[51] in Christendom. Nonetheless, science in general, and Arab science in particular, were looked on with suspicion and worse yet, condemned by the Church. Secular medicine was highly suspect. As late as the Lateran Council of 1215, Pope Innocent III proclaimed:

> Upon pain of excommunication, it is forbidden for a physician to care for an ill person unless such person has made his confession, for his sickness is an emanation of sin...[52]

The transgression was all the more serious if the physician was not a Christian, but a Jew, or a "Saracen." But Arab medicine, founded in clinical observation and the experimental method, was so much more advanced that it could not fail to fascinate those Europeans who were not inclined to permit Church doctrine to govern the art of healing. The same held true for the natural sciences and astronomy: the mysticism of the Christian Middle Ages, in the 11th century at least, could hardly have encouraged the study of natural phenomena when it was not actively condemning such study. But it never succeeded in blocking the penetration of a spirit of scientific curiosity which had awakened many Christians beyond the Pyrenees. In the 10th century, the figure of Gerbert d'Aurillac (938-1003) symbolized the contradictory situation in which learned men of the Church, stimulated by the scientific discoveries of the Arabs, were to find themselves. The future (authoritarian) Pope, who was to reign as Sylvester II, was an astronomy enthusiast who had received his education in Cordova. Both the breadth and the Arab origins of his knowledge roused the suspicion of his contemporaries, who openly accused him of sorcery. The accusations were not enough to stop him from ascending the papal throne, but they were testimony to how far Gerbert stood "ahead of his time,"[53] an eloquent illustration of the then-ambivalent status of science. Or perhaps the ambivalence is ours, in our 20th century obsession with compartmentalizing knowledge, in almost instinctively setting the rational scientific method against the religious method, as belonging to another order. The fact remains that by the 10th century, the general status of knowledge (compared to what it had been even five centuries before in the Roman and post-Roman world) had deteriorated; what had remained of this corpus of knowledge and what re-emerged from the bedrock of Arab and ancient science cannot be easily classified.

Though an upsurge of mysticism took place at the end of the first millennium, neither Saint Augustine (354-430) nor Boetius (480-525) were ever entirely forgotten. It was widely known that the two great thinkers of medieval Christianity had attempted, in their writings, to place reason and knowledge at the service of faith. "Understand in order to believe" and "believe in order to understand," argued the author of *The City of God*. Boetius harked back to Plato and Aristotle in developing a Christian morality grounded in reason.[54] Though invasions and the resulting general insecurity they created in the 9th and 10th century tended to favour millenarian anxiety and divine entreaties over theological reflection ("A society cannot with impunity exist in a state of perpetual terror," writes Marc Bloch[55]), the corpus of theology did not vanish. Nor was it able to impose rigid limitations upon thought. When "the efforts of the learned to provide the Christian mysteries with the prop of logical speculation" resumed at the end of the century, "Catholicism was still very far from having completely defined its dogmatic system, so that the strictest orthodoxy was then much more flexible than was to be the case later on, after scholastic philosophy and the Counter Reformation had in turn exercised their full influence."[56] Added to this was the fact that "Catholicism had incompletely penetrated among the common people."[57]

All of this would indicate that, despite the Church's apprehensions and prohibitions (which only partially mirrored the spirit of the age), the 11th and 12th centuries cannot be considered obscurantist with regard to science. On the contrary; they were an age of intellectual awakening; the rediscovery of Greco-Roman thought drew sustenance from the proximity of the Arabs. Montgomery Watt is correct in insisting that "the (Arab) contributions were not perceived by Europeans as something foreign, a threat to their identity."[58] Neither in status nor in breadth was knowledge equal in Europe and the Arab world. But in their curiosity, Christian emulators partook of the spirit of their Muslim masters, who were indeed the true "educators" of the West.[59]

How then could medieval Christian Europe, and more precisely an intellectual elite coinciding almost exactly with the scholars of the Church, and profoundly imbued with the Catholic faith, reconcile its admiration for Arab philosophy with its impassioned, even grotesque condemnation of "Mahometanism"? Maxime Rodinson offers this explanation:

> One could escape these apparent contradictions about the Muslim world by assuming that their philosophers opposed the official religion of their own countries. Although both simplistic and too general, this opinion can be substantiated from accurate accounts. From the Western perspective, the Muslim philosophers seemed to accept certain religious dogmas and doctrines that could benefit the ignorant and barbaric among their people. By exaggerating the gap between reason and faith in Islam, some in the West went even further, claiming that the philosophers secretly ridiculed the Qur'an and were persecuted by the authorities.[60]

Could Rodinson be yielding here to a kind of anachronism, as opposed to the "mystique of Islam" into which he is attempting to initiate us? As he reminds us, in the 12th century "philosopher" and "Muslim" were, for certain European men of learning, virtually synonymous. For example, Pierre Abelard (1079-1142), "exasperated by his problems with the theologians of his own country,"[61] is said to have dreamed of taking up residence in a Muslim land. But it is unlikely that these learned souls would have grasped the subtleties which Rodinson (drawing on Daniel) now attributes to them. There can be little doubt that the Christian interpreters of Arab thought ill-judged the influence of certain writings in the land of Islam. A case in point was the celebrated Averroës (Aven Roshd), whose considerable influence in the Arab West was "hardly perceptible" in the Orient. Europeans exaggerated the importance of the Andalusian philosopher's polemic with the philosopher and theologian Ghazali, himself described as "proof and guarantor of Islam" and one of the "best organized minds in the Islamic world."[62] Similarly, because of Ghazali's efforts to set limits to philosophy, the Latin scholastics simply overlooked the fact that he was, first and foremost, a theologian. This may have been the consequence of access to truncated sources, as Henri Corbin[63] explains. More likely, it was the product of prejudice: it was hard to believe that a philosopher of Ghazali's stature could have placed all of his science at the service of a far-reaching illumination of Islam *because it is a "heresy,"* and not because of a "conflict between faith and reason," a thoroughly modern concept. The heirs of Saint Augustine and Boetius, beyond the confessional prejudices and the anathemas, shared a desire to reconcile faith and reason, the better to fight dogmatism and obscurantism within the Church, as did the Muslim philosophers in their own world. In this respect, "intellectuals" from both shores of the Mediterranean were more alike than unlike. They shared the same sources and the same concerns. Had this not been the case, their mutual borrowings would have remained incomprehensible: a further indication that the Western Christian's hate-filled contempt and suspicion of the Muslim centered, not on culture or thought, but on religious deviation.

A Mediterranean world

From the late 11th century to the 13th, feudal Europe broke out of its isolation and turned increasingly toward the Mediterranean which, despite its political fragmentation, had preserved its character as a cultural melting pot. But did Europe, in that era, truly exist as anything more than a geographical designation? There is little reason to believe that it did. What did exist was a Germano-Latin (as distinct from Greek) variant of Christendom whose southernmost fringes had never lost contact with the Mediterranean. Contact grew more vigorous in the 11th century, and intensified over subsequent centuries with the ebb and flow of warfare, politics, trade, art and science, and *in spite of* religious hostility. Not all of Western Europe played an equal role in this Mediterranean awakening, but the spirit of renewal was unmistakable — and drew sustenance from a cultural space which, contrary to prevailing opinion today, was undivided; a space whose cultural fault-lines did not necessarily follow religious boundaries.

Two 13th century historical figures, one from the political realm, the other from the intellectual, illustrate, beyond division and confrontation, a uniquely Mediterranean symbiosis. They are Frederick II of Hohenstaufen, king of Sicily in 1197 and Emperor of the Holy Romano-Germanic Empire from 1212 until 1250, and Thomas Aquinas, or Saint Thomas, who lived from 1225 to 1274. These two exceptional men probably less reflected the prevailing mind-set of their time than they contributed, powerfully, to shaping it.

Whether Frederick II treated the Muslims in a spirit of true tolerance or out of political calculation (from which cruelty was never entirely absent) is a secondary consideration. No need to overstate the man's character to appreciate the historical significance of his policies, which were but a continuation of those of his predecessors.[64] When they arrived in Sicily the Normans, rapidly concluding that they had much to gain, adopted the majority of the institutional, scientific and artistic accomplishments of Muslim society as their own. The cohabitation of Islam and Christianity was part of the Arab heritage (though not always free of conflict), and involved too distinct a positive component to be sacrificed to the triumph of the Cross. From the 11th to the 13th century, due in part to the contribution of Muslim civilization, Sicily experienced a flowering and a prosperity which stood in marked contrast with the other countries of Europe. There were only a few other exceptions, each significant: Spain, southern France, and Italy.

As a Germanic emperor Frederick II barely resembled his predecessors (German affairs bored him and he dealt with them perfunctorily). But as king of Sicily he found himself perfectly at home: out of place north of the Alps but in harmony with the Mediterranean world from Palermo to Jaffa — where, as we remember, he negotiated a *modus vivendi* for the Holy Land with Sultan Al-Kamil. This Islamo-Christian treaty, signed in 1229, symbolized less that "the Orient and the West had reached out to one another"[65] than it illustrated, in a manner of speaking, the Mediterranean's recognition of itself. For Frederick II, the world of Arab art, architecture, science and philosophy was his world: a world less foreign to him than Germany.

But could the man himself have been too "Arabized," too much the exception to be significant? Probably less so than we would imagine today, influenced as we are by what has become the traditional polarized vision of the Mediterranean world. Arab culture imbued not only Frederick II, but all of Sicily, the south of Italy and "reconquered" Spain where Alfonso the Wise, king of Castile from 1252 to 1284 cultivated the arts and sciences with the active support of artists and men of learning of the three religions (Muslim, Jewish and Christian). In reality, the entire southern fringe of Europe drew sustenance from Arabo-Islamic civilization, whose ideas pervaded the learned guild structures of the day and extended their influence as far afield as England and Germany. Michael Scot (astrologer at the court of Frederick II), Robert Grossetête, Roger Bacon (despite the intensity of his Christian proselytising), Siger de Brabant, Albert the Great and his celebrated disciple Thomas Aquinas: all had encountered Aristotle, but the encounter was by way of Averroës and Avicenna, without whom debate on the thought of the great Greek master would neither have taken the same direction nor had the same significance.

A community of concern existed on both sides of the Mediterranean. When Acquinas attempted, in his own way, to reconcile faith and reason he was much nearer intellectually to his Muslim predecessors and fellow-students of Aristotle, such as al-Kindi, al-Farabi, Avicenna and, of course, Averroës, than to the dignitaries of his Church. Aquinas's opposition to Averroës, or more precisely, his quarrel with a Latin interpretation of the Muslim philosopher which claimed that faith and reason exist in two hermetically sealed worlds, removes nothing from his direct and indirect debt to the Andalusian philosopher. Through Acquinas, who embodied an innovatory, even audacious instant in Christian philosophy, Arab thought in its "age of enlightenment" illuminated Western Christendom. One of the central aspects of this innovative spirit was Aquinas's synthesis of the Orient, or rather *Orients* (the biblical, the Greek and the Islamic) and nascent Western thought: an exceptional, yet typically Mediterranean achievement. Michel-Marie Dufeil has demonstrated that Acquinas is "oriental to his every pore and mystical cultural reflex," but also, he adds, "a man of intellectual reason and an academic rationalist."[66] But need there be a contradiction between the two? Does "Oriental" mean the same thing today as it did seven centuries ago? If there existed, in the 13th century, an intellectual opposition between the Orient and the West, the same dichotomy also cut right through the Muslim world: "Oriental" philosophy was that which, at the eastern extremity of the Arab zone, drew a portion of its source material from the "wise men of ancient Persia" (the "oriental theosophy" of Sohrawardi, and before him, Avicenna).[67] At the opposite extreme, Averroës represented the "West" of Muslim philosophy, which caused Henri Corbin to remark:

> ...The names of Avicenna and of Averroës could well be taken as symbols of the respective spiritual destinies which awaited the Orient and the West.[68]

The West (our West) was to be fertilized by the trend of Arab thought which was geographically closest to it, and which was also the most "Mediterranean" of the two, through the work of a thinker — Thomas Aquinas — who was also a Mediterranean, in spite of his long visits to Paris.

> As much as he (Thomas) scorns, shuns and attacks the barbarian West of which he is not a part, so also he is the universitarian in its first flowering, which presaged and procreated the rational cultural modernity which all refer to as West.[69]

It is one of the recurring anachronisms of the Western perspective on Mediterranean history — and on history as a whole — that Aquinas prefigured the West which he in turn helped shape, but was not himself of the West except *a posteriori*; in the same way that Averroës belonged to the "Orient" (as we understand it today) only after the fact.

The Crusades contributed handsomely to the construction of this anachronism. More precisely, religious sectarianism made ample use of what Alphonse Dupront quite correctly defined as the "myth of the Crusade":

> The fact is that the Crusade survives the Crusades, so as to perpetuate an animating power such that, three centuries later, though the Crusades had ended, individual Crusaders continued to rise up, to depart, to dream....
>
> This historical tenacity is a sign, but an equivocal one. It signifies perhaps one of the modes of expression which the Christian West had sought, both at the moment of its birth and in its maturity, consciousness of itself and of its path forward toward unity.[70]

The West sought consciousness of itself, certainly, but above all it sought to repress that consciousness with the help of mythology. The Crusades can be understood as an attempt by "barbarian" Europe to draw closer to the centre of the world — the Mediterranean. The myth provided a way of magnifying the symbolic importance of the conflict, to create, after the fact, an imagined Mediterranean fissure. A fissure that was primarily, but not entirely, imagined. For it is also true that the encounter between northwestern Europe and Islam marked the beginning of a growing awareness, from the 11th to the 13th centuries, of what was to be, in the strict historical sense of the term, the destiny of the West. At the same time, it was a self-awareness defined through antagonism to the Other, a process in which religious fanaticism acted as a detonator. The Other, from the 11th through the 13th century, is clearly Islam. But not Islam alone: Byzantium, at least in cultural terms, also meets the definition. Which Islam, though? Less Islam-as-society than Islam-as-religion, which is to say, heresy. But heresy for whom? Again, for those regions of Europe geographically and sociologically farthest removed from Arab civilization, and for a Papal throne seeking the unitary ideology essential to the extension of its political power. But in the southern lands of Latin Christendom, in that age, the grip of religious fanaticism was tenuous, for Islam represented an at once identical and superior culture, with which coexistence was natural, desirable and beneficial — something the rare Christian intellectual elites, wherever they might be in Europe, were quick to understand.

In the South, relative tolerance prevailed. In the North, intolerance was the rule. Did not the cultural divide cut through Europe itself, rather than through the Mediterranean? The proof came in the form of another religious campaign which was contemporaneous with the expeditions to the Holy Land. This campaign — the so-called Albigensian Crusade — was no less violent and certainly more fanatical. It was, in fact, a war of repression waged upon the call of the Pope by the Burgundian, Norman, Flemish and German knightly orders against another heresy, that of the Catharans. The non-comprehension (read jealousy) of the North toward a more advanced, and brilliant society (despite the asceticism of the Catharans) which was more open, more free, more egalitarian than its own, found expression in the destructive violence of religious zeal. Catharan society was thoroughly Mediterranean, far removed from the feudalism of the North, open to the refinements of Arab civilization which still ruled the "Inland Sea." Europe, beneath the misleading aspect of a unifying faith, held within it more than one Christendom. True, self-confidence was slowly emerging through the fruitful contact of the intellectual elites with Muslim thought, science and art. But disparate Europe was quite incapable of conceiving of itself, in its generality, as historically and socially distinct from the Orient whose milk it had long suckled through its southernmost mouths. Nor, until the beginning of the 16th century, did the Mediterranean become the locus of East/West separation to which we have grown accustomed to assign it, in which we delight in imagining the clash of two irreconcilably hostile, foreign worlds.

The tensions and conflicts which periodically set Islam against Christendom created neither a sharp rift nor cultural incompatibility. What was true for the 13th century Mediterranean would hold equally true for 19th and 20th century Europe. Despite the wars of religion and the national conflicts which have bloodied the continent until 1945, no one has challenged the pertinence of the concept of Europe as a way of expressing, beyond conflicts and contrasts, a common historical trajectory, a shared civilization or community of thought, if only on the elite level. So too, at a similar level but also in terms of trade, was the Mediterranean until the end of the 15th century: a melting pot for the inhabitants of its shores, with whom Latin Christendom was able to maintain uneven contact. It was in this shared crucible of human experience that Latin Christendom came to know Islamic civilization, albeit in a highly irregular manner, and to transform the encounter into a stimulus for its own development.

It remains to be explained why the positive aspects of this encounter were almost systematically overshadowed, and masked by the dimension of conflict. We must acknowledge that of the two, admiration for Arab science and anti-Muslim racism, the second left the deepest, longest lasting imprint on the collective mind-set of the West, while in the 13th century, religious rejection generated no such sense of superiority over the Muslim world. Quite the opposite was true, in fact. But while the Arab enlightenment touched only a learned minority, the Church's calumnies against Mahomet and his imposture constituted the illiterate common people's sole source of information about Islam. Malicious misinformation on the heretical nature and the stupidity of the Muslim religion was perpetuated in Europe, seemingly by force of habit and not always, alas, by its lesser spirits. So it was that while he "exempted Avicenna, Averroës and Saladin from hell and assigned them instead to limbo"[71] along with Hector, Aeneas, Abraham, Socrates, Plato and Aristotle, the great Dante did not hesitate to condemn "Maometto" to the torments of the 8th circle of Hell.

NOTES

1. See Chapter 1.
2. The judicial inferiority attached to the status of *dhimmi* cannot be ascribed to any particular desire on the part of the Muslim leaders to proselytize. Conversion, by force if necessary, of the pagans of Arabia may have been necessary to consolidate the power of the new Muslim State; but it became undesirable with regard to monotheists of other confessions who, by virtue of the special taxes to which they were subject, contributed to the caliphate's treasury. However, the effect of the tax was to heighten the attraction of Islam to the subject populations and to hasten their conversion. The Umayyad caliphs, out of concern for their revenues, attempted to stem the tide of conversion and, when that failed, began treating these new, non-Arab converts as second class Muslims *(maula)* a discriminatory practice abolished by the Abassids in the next century.
3. *The Meaning of The Glorious Qur'an*, Verses II, 111: II, 82 and III, 67. Text and Explanatory Translation by Marmaduke Pickthall. Tehran, Salehi Publications, n.d.
4. The expression is from Jean-Jacques Waardenburg's *L'Islam dans le miroir de l'Occident*, Paris, Mouton, 1963, 2nd cd., p.144.
5. In Muslim tradition, another man took the place of Jesus on the cross at the last moment. Islam lays emphasis on the idea of a triumphant *(Pantokrator?)*, rather than a suffering Christ.
6. Sahas, Daniel J., *John of Damascus on Islam*, Leyden, E.J. Brill, 1972, p.27,43,127.
7. Daniel, Norman, *Islam and the West*, op. cit., p.4.
8. For Western borrowings from the Arab world, see Sigrid Hunke's *Le soleil d'Allah brille sur l'Occident, notre héritage arabe*, Paris, Albin Michel, 1963. There is no lack of works on the encounter between Islam and Christendom (or between the Orient and the West) in the Middle Ages. See H.A.R. Gibb, "The influence of Islamic culture on medieval Europe," in *Bulletin of the John Rylands Library*, Manchester 38, 1 September, 1955, p.81-98; R.W. Southern, *Western Views of Islam in the Middle Ages*, Cambridge, Mass., Harvard University Press, 1962; Norman Daniel, *The Arabs and Medieval Europe*, London, Longmans, 1975.
9. *The Encyclopedia of Islam*, Edited by H.Th. Houtsma, Leyden, E.J. Brill, 1913-1936, Vol, II, p.127. "Dar al-Islam, the Land of Islam, or, more simply, in Muslim authors, daruna, 'our country', is the whole territory in which the law of Islam prevails." The concept embraces more than the Muslim community itself, since the *umma* also subsumes the members of other revealed religions (Jews, Christians and Zoroastrians) whose status is guaranteed by the *dhimma*.

Although such terms as Mohammedanism or Islamism can be encountered in English, there is no equivalent designation to "Christendom" applicable to Islam. In this translation, Islam is used interchangeably to designate both the religion and Islamic culture and civilization, the meaning arising from context.

10. Waardenburg, op. cit., p.292.
11. See Leonard Binder, "Area Studies: A Critical Reassessment" in *The Study of the Middle East*, New York, John Wiley and Sons, 1976, p.12. "We are all acquainted with standard works in the field which generalize about Muslims without qualifications as to time and place." In the same collection, see also Charles J. Adams, "Islamic Religious Tradition," p. 29-95.
12. Djait, Hichem, *Europe and Islam*, op. cit., p.20.
13. Cahen, Claude, *Orient et Occident aux temps des Croisades*, Paris, Aubier-Montaigne, 1983, p.69.
14. Cahen, op. cit., p.18. A notable exception was the persecution carried out by the Fatamid caliph al-Hakim at the beginning of the 11th century, and which provided "Crusader propaganda" with a perfect pretext. Steven Runciman, in *A History of the Crusades, Vol. 1, The First Crusade and the Kingdom of Jerusalem*, Cambridge, Cambridge University Press, 1962, p.37, draws the same conclusion: "In the middle of the eleventh century, the lot of the Christians in Palestine had seldom been so pleasant."
15. Cahen, op. cit., p.43.
16. Pernoud, Régine, *The Crusades*, translated by Enid McLeod, New York, Putnam, 1963.
17. Cahen, op. cit., p.29.
18. Ibid., p.33-41. See also Hilmar C. Krueger, "The Italian cities and the Arabs before 1905" in *A History of the Crusades, Vol. 1, The First Hundred Years*. Madison, University of Wisconsin Press, 1969, p.40-53.
19. Cahen, op. cit, p.68.
20. Halphen, Louis, *L'essor de l'Europe (XIe-XIII siècles)* Paris, Alcan, 1932. See also Steven Runciman, op. cit., p.89 on the war in Spain.
21. Urban II, Sermon at Clermont (1095) in August C. Krey, *The First Crusade*, the accounses and participants, Princeton, Princeton University Press, 1921, p.29.
22. The expression is Louis Halphen's. op. cit., p.62.
23. Oldenbourg, Zoe, *The Crusades*, translated by Anne Carter, New York, Pantheon Books, 1966. p.549.
24. Runciman, op. cit., Chapter II, "The German Crusade," p.134.
25. Ibid., p.116-117.
26. Runciman, op. cit., p.83.
27. Oldenbourg, op. cit., p.77.
28. Ibid., p.501.
29. Ibid., p.114-115 and Runciman, op. cit., p.37.
30. Runciman, op. cit., p.88.
31. Oldenbourg, op. cit., p.505.
32. Pernoud, op. cit., p.19.
33. Ibid., p.107.
34. Ibid., p. 179.
35. Ibid., p.185.
36. Ibid., p.104,108.
37. Perroy, Edouard, *Le Moyen Age*, Paris, P.U.F., 1955, p.269.
38. Perroy, op. cit., p.270. Maxime Rodinson *(Europe and the Mystique of Islam, op. cit.)* also believes that the Crusades contributed to the rise of transmediterranean trade.
39. Rodinson, op. cit.
40. Cahen, op. cit., p.139.
41. Rodinson, op. cit., p.10.
42. Ibid., p.22-23
43. Hunke, S., op. cit., p.219.

44. Pernoud, op. cit., p.19
45. Rodinson, op. cit.
46. Djait, op. cit., p.35-36.
47. Sartre, Jean-Paul, *Anti-Semite and Jew,* translated by George Becker, New York, Schocken Books, 1948.
48. Daniel, Norman, *Islam and the West,* op. cit. (Note 7.)
49. Rodinson, op. cit., p.13.
50. I do not intend to take up the rather petty debate over the Arab character of the science and culture produced under the Caliphates. My view is that of Sigrid Hunke (op. cit., p.11): one may speak of Arabs and of Arab civilization despite the fact that the creators of this civilization were not all citizens of the nation designated by Herodotus as Arabioi, but included Persians, Indians, Syrians, Egyptians, Berbers and Visigoths. All those peoples upon whom the Arabs imposed their domination were united as much by one common language and religion, the Arab language and religion, as by the deep imprint of the rigorous genius of the Arabs themselves. Arab not in the ethnic sense, but in the sense of the cultural synthesis which took place under the Arab aegis.
51. Legoff, Jacques, *La civilization de l'Occident médiéval,* Paris, Arthaud, 1964, p.191.
52. Quoted in Hunke, op. cit., p.123.
53. Jolivet, Jean, "La philosophie médiévale en Occident," *Histoire de la philosophie, Vol. 1,* Paris, Gallimard, Encyclopédie de la Pleiade, 1969, p.1269.
54. Jolivet, op. cit., p.1223,1229.
55. Bloch, Marc, *Feudal Society.* Translated by L.A. Manyan. Chicago, University of Chicago Press, 1961, p.41.
56. Ibid., p.82.
57. Ibid., p.82. Not only, adds Bloch, were "the parish clergy, taken as a whole,...intellectually as well as morally unfit for their task," but the "religious life was also nourished by a multitude of beliefs and practices" and "innumerable nature rites," "In short, never was theology less identified with the popular religion as it was felt and lived." (Ibid., p.82,83.)
58. Watt, W. Montgomery, loc. cit., p.141.
59. The expression is Edouard Perroy's, op. cit.
60. Rodinson, op. cit., p.17 (basing his argument on Norman Daniel).
61. Ibid., p.16. Rodinson here invokes Jean Jolivet's "Abélard et la philosophie." Revue de l'histoire des réligions, vol. 164,97 ss, pp.181-189. On Abelard, see *Historia Calamitatum. The story of Abelard's adversities.* A translation with notes on the Historia Calamitatum, translated by J.T. Muckle, Toronto, The Pontifical Institute of Medieval Studies, 1954.
62. Corbin, Henri, *History of Islamic Philosophy,* translated by Liadain Sherrard, London, Kegan Paul International, 1991.
63. Ibid.
64. As Sigrid Hunke does in *Le Soleil d'Allah,* op. cit., p.266.
65. Ibid., p.269.
66. Dufeil, Michel-Marie, *"Oriens apud Tomam" Images et signes de l'Orient dans l'Occident médiéval,* p. 173.
67. Corbin, op. cit., p.1168-1176.
68. Corbin, op. cit., p.1192.
69. Dufeil, op. cit., p.173.
70. Dupront, Alphonse, *Le mythe de croisade.* Etude de sociologie réligieuse, thèse non publiée. Faculté des lettres, Sorbonne, 1956, Vol. 1, p.3-4.
71. Rodinson, op. cit., p.29.

III

The Genesis of Division

The Mediterranean Orient has long been Europe's nearest yet most bitterly-fought alterity and its unparalleled Other, contiguous both by geography and by imagination: mysterious and threatening, seductive and repugnant, at once empty and teeming, barbarous and refined, now violent, now indolent; locus of enchantment, of repulsion or exasperation — omnipresent, and ever otherly. Whether reflecting our inverted self-image like a mirror or acting as a foil, this nearest, most familiar — but least understood — Orient has, more than any other region of the world, nurtured the antinomy through which the West has repeatedly defined itself. The process of self-definition may be one of appropriation of the past or of present-day opposition, but the Orient, and particularly the Mediterranean Orient, has served the conscience of the West as a reference point of endlessly fluctuating shape and hue, contradictory in its attributes, shifting with the winds of circumstance but constant in its polarizing function.

How and when in history did the Mediterranean Orient begin to emerge as a systematic alterity in the consciousness of the West? It would be tempting to reply that there has always been opposition between the Orient and the West. But as I hope to have shown in the two preceding chapters, the eurocentric vision of history which traces this cultural (and civilizational) antagonism back to the age of the Crusades, or farther still, to Greek antiquity, is the projection into the past of a dichotomy which was to appear much later; certainly not before the end of what we call the Middle Ages.

Conversely, closer to home, the West's progress toward industrial society radically distanced it from other cultures. From the 19th century onward, the alterity of the Orient bursts into literature. But as an idea it dates back much farther: already we can find it at work in the preceding centuries. As the advent of heavy industry stands at the end point of a long evolutionary process which was as much social as technical, so the Oriental alterity which so unreservedly expresses itself from the 19th century onward had much deeper roots in the past. It could even be claimed that the expression of this fundamental difference began with the emergence of the West as consciousness of self. The history of the myth of the Orient, as a concept stamped with political and cultural significance (and not only as mystical symbol) would then be little more than one of the pathways along which we can hark back to the beginnings of Western consciousness.

Most historians concur in situating these beginnings, which were also the wellsprings of what came to be known as modernity, in the Renaissance — that period which began at the end of the 15th century with the great discoveries. In discovering the world, Europe discovered itself. What role did the Orient play in this process of discovery, how, in the eyes of European intellectuals and humanists, was it defined? This is the question which has shaped my inquiry.

Where can we first capture this representation of self, of the Other? In the written sources, of course: in accounts of voyages, in descriptions of the Turks, in debates on the advisability of conciliation or combat (as in Erasmus' *Consultation de bello Turcis inferendo*), in considerations of the respective merits of diverse religions (as in certain passages of Montaigne's *Apologie de Raimond Sebond*). First, however, we must look to the political motives which underlay the emergence of the first politico-social (and not strictly religious) vision of an Orient equated with the Ottoman empire. The way in which three authors in particular — Machiavelli, Postel and Bodin — apprehend the Orient represents a certain modernity. How was each the embodiment of his age, or in advance of it, in his understanding of the Other, here taken to mean the Turk? How, and to what extent did their thinking lay the groundwork for a new way of looking at the Orient? For though the phenomenon was a new one, it hardly arose overnight. Appropriate precautions are thus in order; in fact, any attempt to draw up a historical time-table would be a perilous exercise.

As we begin our investigation, one thing seems clear: at the end of the 16th century there existed, among certain European intellectual elites, a loosely articulated perception of the Orient (or, at least, of the Turk) as a social and political entity.

Such a perception, which, one and one half centuries earlier did not exist, must be seen in the perspective of a renascent structure of intellectual inquiry, and in the broader context of material (economic, military) relations in the Mediterranean. But neither of these two factors arose as if by magic at the beginning of the 16th century. The first stirrings of the Renaissance can already be detected in European thought of the 14th and 15th centuries. We must also understand the distinguishing features of Mediterranean world prior to the end of the 15th century in order to appreciate how the ensuing century was to transform it. For in this symbiotic world a new fissure was opening, a fissure almost certainly linked to the emergence of Western self-awareness.

RIFT OR EQUILIBRIUM IN THE MEDITERRANEAN?

Ottoman threat and closure

The overriding political fact of the historical evolution of the eastern Mediterranean from the 14th through the 15th centuries was the steady emergence of Ottoman power, which reached its zenith in the first half of the 15th, during the reigns of Selim I and Suleiman II, the Magnificent. Turkish hegemony, which by then extended from the Balkans to the Maghreb, brought together under one sole authority virtually the whole of Mediterranean Islam.[1] The expansion of the Ottoman Empire re-opened — in Western eyes — the rift which the Arab invasions of the 7th century had allegedly inflicted on the Mediterranean, and made it irreversible. The irreversibility of the caesura wrought by Muslim settlement of the eastern and southern shores of the Mediterranean is abundantly clear to us today as we begin to realize that, instead of being weakened by the brutal contact of Western domination and colonization, Islam has tapped a wellspring of ideological revival. But the clarity of today tells us nothing of the perception of 15th and 16th century Europeans: how, in fact, did they view the Ottoman Empire?

As a formidable power, certainly; a power which made itself felt principally in the Balkans, the power base of the Anatolian Osmanli State which, by the end of the 14th century, had reduced the Byzantine Empire to Constantinople and its immediate surroundings.

The infidel thrust into Europe ought to have rekindled the Crusader spirit which Pope Clement VI vainly sought to resuscitate in 1344. If the deliverance of Jerusalem no longer aroused great ardour, perhaps the safeguarding of Constantinople and the protection of the Christian brethren of the Balkans would. This was Urban V's aim when he issued his call for the unification of the Christian forces of the West in 1362. The result was meagre indeed: only the Count of Savoy was to respond, three years later, with hopelessly inadequate forces. Then came the expedition which ended in the defeat of Nikopolis, in 1396, when a large contingent of primarily French and German Crusaders joined forces with the Hungarians. The abortive Crusade came to nothing. Western Europe made no serious attempt to stiffen the Slavic peoples' resistance to the surging Ottomans or stave off the fall of Constantinople. Final proof came in 1400 with Byzantine "emperor" Manuel II's sad, hopeless quest from one European court to another in search of reinforcements, declaring that he was "prepared to give over Constantinople to whomever would swear to defend it."[2] So profound was the Western princes' indifference to Byzantium that none among them even attempted to capitalize upon the unexpected lull when, in 1402, the Ottoman Empire faced incipient dissolution under the onslaught of Timur (Tamerlane). Today their indifference seems so incomprehensible as to cause some contemporary historians acute embarrassment.

Absence of concern did not mean sudden tolerance for Islam. It expressed, instead, the division between Greek and Latin Christendom which was already latent at the time of the first Crusade.[3] But it also exemplified the substantial change which took place during the second. The Crusade "myth" (to use Dupront's expression) may not have been dead, but its ultimate objective could no longer unite hearts and mobilize energies. If the Papacy proved powerless to remedy the situation, it was because Germano-Latin Christendom had lost what had once made it a community capable of acting in common cause.

From the 14th century onward, and perhaps earlier, feudal society and along with it Christendom in a specific form, had begun a slow process of decay, giving way to, and under the influence of, the emerging monarchical states now arrayed one against another. The process was accompanied by the expansion of independent cities and republics (primarily in Italy, and slightly later, in Flanders and Germany), whose principal connection with the Muslim world was commerce. In any event, the city-states of Europe were too busy fighting amongst themselves to be concerned with fighting Infidels. Even Venice, shortly before the fall of Constantinople, an eventuality which posed a direct threat to its interests, was slow in dispatching even the most paltry assistance — which arrived, in the event, too late. It must be noted that Islam, rife with political division, was no threat to the maritime cities which then ruled the seas. On a religious level, thinkers like Roger Bacon held the view that Islam would soon enter into decline, having completed its historical mission (to bring monotheism to the pagans in the cause of unity — meaning Christian unity).[4] There was no sense of urgency in confronting the forces of Islam, which were generally on the defensive in the Mediterranean until the beginning of the 15th century.

The Ottomans held sway in the Balkans from the 14th century onward, but it was not until the end of the 15th that they began to impinge upon Europe as a full-fledged Mediterranean power. By conquering Byzantium (1453), Syria, Egypt (1516-1517) and Iraq (1534), then transforming North Africa as far as Algiers into its vassal, the Ottoman Empire greatly simplified the map of the "Inner Sea." The forces of Islam had been reconstituted and a major land and sea power had emerged; a power which would now represent, in European eyes, a serious threat.

Europe was never to provide a unified response. At the moment of greatest Turkish presence in the Mediterranean, François I began a rapprochement with Suleiman II (1535) and persuaded Venice to abandon the alliance with Genoa under Charles V against the Ottoman fleet (1540), opening the door to Turkish naval supremacy which was to last beyond the celebrated battle of Lepanto (1571) until 1580.[5] The "Christian" triumph at Lepanto was the victory of a coalition which now included Venice (as well as its arch-rival Genoa). But the coalition hardly outlived the victory: eighteen months later, the city of the Doges concluded a separate peace with the Sultan.[6]

Succinctly put, opposition to the Ottoman Empire was little more than a figure of speech. And a feeble one at that, since it never involved more than a part of Christendom (Spain under Philip II, allied with Austria and Genoa), whose main enemy was not always the Turk. It would be far more accurate to say that the Ottomans took part in the intrigues of the European powers of the day, playing off one against another exactly as the Europeans played Persia against the Sultan and the Sultan against their Christian adversaries. For Istanbul's actions were not restricted to the European theatre alone: in 1578, the Ottomans undertook a debilitating war against Persia which turned them away from the Mediterranean — just as Spain was turning its attentions toward the Atlantic. As Braudel summarizes:

> ...the Hispanic bloc and the Ottoman bloc, so long locked together in a struggle for the Mediterranean, at last disengaged their forces and at a stroke, the inland sea was freed from that international war which had from 1550-1580 been its major feature.[7]

The Turkish threat gradually diminished. It had loomed over certain coastal regions, certain countries of Eastern Europe, but never over the entire continent. While blocking Spain's hegemonic ambitions, it aided those of Spain's adversaries. Shaped by time and place, the Turkish threat ebbed and flowed; any attempt to chart a curve of European fears would be an exercise in futility. Certainly, the victory of Lepanto was hailed with great relief by the Christian populations of the Mediterranean littoral. It brought an end to the period of recurring fear: the Turk was not, after all, invincible.[8] Generally speaking, from the end of the century, and later, with the Austro-Ottoman peace of 1606, the Turkish threat began to wane. We should not forget, however, that the second siege of Vienna took place at the end of the 17th century (1683) — a surprising achievement for an Empire which most European historians today consider to have begun its decline at the end of the previous century: an easy judgement in hindsight. For the contemporaneous, the decline only became clearer in the 18th century. Before then Europe's behaviour toward Ottoman power was as contradictory as were its impressions. But it is also true that, as early as the 16th century, attentive observers noticed that Ottoman power was due more to European division than to the intrinsic strength of the Empire, no matter how impressive it might be.

The closer the balance of forces in the Mediterranean is observed, the more subtle it appears, the more intricate the cut and thrust of power politics. But we can still derive several general propositions: there was no doubt that Islam, under Turkish leadership, had reversed an unfavourable trend, and was able to exercise domination for three or four decades, until Spain and its allies could mount a counter-offensive; a new balance then emerged, primarily because the Mediterranean had ceased to be the central political issue for the two main powers involved.

So much for the military threat. There remained the matter of economic closure. This thesis, much favoured by Western historians, of whom Pirenne is the most vocal advocate, goes as follows:

> Things changed in the middle of the 15th century. The closing off of the roads to Asia and the eastern Mediterranean by the Turkish conquests forced Europe to search for ways of protecting its economic equilibrium in new directions. The Mediterranean ceased being the great trading artery it had been since Antiquity.[9]

According to this thesis, Turkish expansionism not only consummated but reinforced the Islamic breach of Mediterranean unity by closing off the Orient to European trade, which in turn caused the economic decline of the Mediterranean. But for the thesis to withstand scrutiny, the "new directions" which Europe had been supposedly constrained to explore (so claims Pirenne) could only have emerged after the mid-point of the 15th century — and only if that date is accepted as marking the point when the Ottomans became truly capable of interdicting the eastern shores of the Mediterranean to the fleets of Europe, an estimate which seems to me to be a good half-century in advance of reality. Pirenne himself affirms that the "crusade" against Ceuta (1415-1417) constituted the "mystical beginning of the astonishing epic which was to end in a commercial enterprise."[10] Which is another way of saying that this epic has nothing to do with Ottoman expansion (limited until the beginning of the 16th century to Anatolia and the Balkans) and everything to do with the African ambitions of Henry the Navigator, prince of Portugal, who explored the west coast of Africa with the goal of "discovering an arm of the sea" via which he could attack Morocco from the south, but which became the setting-off point for the circumnavigation of the continent.

> "There was no longer any doubt" adds Pirenne, "that it would be enough to circumnavigate the black continent to

reach those marvellous lands whence the Venetians acquired their spices, by way of Egypt.[11]

How could it have been more eloquently put? Egypt remained accessible to Italian traders both before and after the Ottoman expansion. Vasco de Gama opened the route around the Cape of Good Hope (1497) not to outflank a nonexistent Ottoman blockade, but to compete with Venice. The competition strained Venice almost to the breaking point,[12] but the city of Saint Mark took its revenge: "The old spice route was indeed once again busy and prosperous by the middle of the century."[13] The old route passed through Syria, Egypt, the Red Sea and the Persian Gulf, all regions which had come under the control of Istanbul since 1517 (the Gulf since 1534). Still, the Ottoman presence did not restrict Mediterranean trade. On the contrary, trade thrived. As Braudel explains:

> What is quite clear is that the Mediterranean had captured a large portion of the pepper trade, indeed the lion's share. Trade with the Levant was flourishing, supplied by numerous caravans, some from the Persian Gulf, others from the Red Sea. And at the end of these routes, looking onto the Mediterranean, two double cities owed their prosperity to this trade: to the north, Aleppo and the active quays of Tripoli, to the south, Cairo and its port Alexandria... To the West the renewal of the spice trade brought most benefit to the Venetians, the grand masters of trade, alongside whom the merchants of Marseilles and Ragusa cut a very modest figure. Venetian merchants even, rather curiously, moved inland...The Mediterranean was recapturing the treasures of the Indian Ocean...
>
> Any number of documents will testify to this revival. But since the opposite view has generally been accepted, let me warn that some details can be misleading. To avoid confusion, it must be realized that the two routes leading to Cairo and Aleppo had always been in competition.[14]

All the evidence militates against the closure thesis: the contradictions in which Pirenne becomes entangled, and Braudel's painstaking, detailed reconstruction which demonstrates that, after 1550, "the difficult gateway to the Red Sea stood wide open, and a huge volume of trade flowed through."[15] Even so, certain specialists in Near Eastern history persist in presenting the closing of Egypt (from 1525 onward) as so self-evident as to beggar demonstration. Furthermore, the closing was limited neither to Egypt nor to the ebb and flow of economic activity:

It is...certain that at the end of the 15th century(sic), the East closed in upon itself: its economy, social structures, political systems — all seemed irrevocably frozen.[16]

...So tenaciously rooted was the presumption that from the earliest days of Ottoman domination the Orient had somehow become ossified, and that this ossification expressed its fundamental alterity. But even if we were to accept the disputable premise of stagnation,[17] the process is claimed to begin at least a half century, if not one and one-half centuries, too soon.

Braudel strives to correct these generally accepted ideas. On both the socioeconomic and politico-military levels, he notes significant areas of resemblance throughout the Mediterranean in the 14th century: banditry, a weak bourgeoisie, an unstable nobility, a vigorous slave trade; economic growth and problems of State finance, corruption and venality.[18] One and the same crisis touched both Europe and Islam:

> There can be no doubt that society was tending to polarize into, on the one hand, a rich and vigorous nobility reconstituted into powerful dynasties owning vast properties, and on the other, the great a growing mass of the poor and disinherited, 'caterpillars and grubs', human insects, alas too many...In England, France, Italy, Spain, and Islam, society was undermined by this dramatic upheaval, the full horror of which was to be revealed in the 17th century.[19]

Two radically distinct Mediterraneans no more existed in the 15th and 16th centuries than in the Middle Ages: there were at once one, and several — just as there were several Europes: Mediterranean and Atlantic, Catholic and Protestant, Western and Eastern. The fault lines were multiple, and convergent. Two, in particular, were more significant than the others — one cut across the Mediterranean, another was the result of a sharp shift in the European centre of gravity.

Division in the Mediterranean; rift in the Atlantic

Parallel to the sea's horizontal axis lay "the ancient borders of the Roman Empire," a line of demarcation between Nordic and Mediterranean Europe.[20] But there also existed a vertical scar which, argues Braudel, closely followed the European boundary of the Ottoman Empire:

> ...The most extraordinary division in the Mediterranean was the one which separated East from West; that immutable

barrier which runs between Zagreb and Belgrade, rebounds from the Adriatic at Lesh (Allessio) at the mouth of the Drin and the angle of the Dalmatian and Albanian coastline, then passes through the ancient cities of Naissus, Remesiana and Ratiana to the Danube.[21]

"Immutable barrier" between the Orient and the West? Look more closely at the map: the line hugs the ancient boundary of the Roman Empire, which in turn corresponds approximately to the western-most continental limits of the Macedonian Empire and of Hellenism. Whether or not the Romans had consciously respected a historic stopping point, or whether they were acting out of simple administrative pragmatism in dividing their empire into western and eastern sections, it certainly appears significant that the Ottomans, heirs of Byzantium, stabilized their European dominions at the same longitude. But what does all this mean? Above all, it means that the division is not the result of a wound inflicted by Islam nor by the Turks. Still, it marks the point where they ended their advance. The coincidence is a troubling one: the western frontier of the Greek world was confirmed by Rome, Byzantium and finally Istanbul, as the eternal line of demarcation between the Orient and the West...

But we must be wary of the appearance of immutability which can cause confusion rooted in semantic anachronism. The term "Orient" (here applied to the eastern Mediterranean) has undergone a shift in meaning over the centuries: the Orient of Greco-Roman antiquity no longer has any relationship to ours. One conclusive indication is that most Westerners today — abusively, in the event — identify ancient Greece with the West, even though it lies to the east of that enigmatic line. In reality, history has bequeathed to the northern Mediterranean a geopolitical boundary which, with the emergence of Western modernity, was to take on quite another meaning. Once historical, the dividing line became, over time, one of "cultural" demarcation in the deepest sense of opposition between the modern West and the traditional Orient. It cannot be attributed either to Islam or Turkey, but draws its contemporary meaning from our own modernity, which began, in the 16th century, to assume its contemporary shape and identity.

The rift which sprang up in the Mediterranean was less the work of the Ottomans than the effect of a transformation which both impacted upon and divided Europe. From the end of the 15th century and perhaps even before, Europe had reached a turning point which the Turks — like so many other peoples — were not to reach.

Curiously, though all appear to speak of it, few view this turning point in the same manner, or place it at the same historical moment. What is the rift to which it leads? How can the rift itself be defined? The question is an immense one, with countless ramifications which I cannot pretend to answer here. Is the image of rift adequate as a descriptive tool? In certain respects yes; in other ways, no. In reality, there were several turning points, at different levels and at different times. There are, above all, points of continuity: certain circumstances hardly changed. Breakups coexisted with ongoing relationships, evolving together, often conflictingly. But there remains one indisputable item of evidence: something happened in 16th century Europe which was to leave its imprint on society as a whole, something which happened nowhere else. Clichés abound: the great discoveries, the rise of mercantile capitalism, "a profusion of industrial, military, nautical, economic, financial and political inventions," "a thirst for the good things of this world,"[22] the birth of individualism, humanism, a return to the roots (to the Greeks, to Scripture) and many other formulas only marginally less charged with ambiguity and passion, the Renaissance being far from the least misleading (if we are to speak of Renaissance at all, it did not belong exclusively to the 16th century, which in turn did not accomplish the renewal often attributed to it, particularly in outlook and thought).

What most interests us about Europe's turning point is the impulse which redirected it toward the Atlantic and which, by the end of the 16th century, was to cost the Mediterranean its predominance, though its economic importance remained substantial. The forces which were to fashion the modern West arose along the Atlantic shore. It was a progressive emergence which masked the political and military ups and downs of the two empires (Spanish and Turkish) which were locked in combat for control of the Mediterranean. The resulting peace — or better, the stand-off — which brought the confrontation to an end might well create an impression of symmetry. But the symmetry was illusory. To the west, the receding power of Spain was partially compensated by the rise of the Dutch, the French and the English, which went unmatched in the eastern Mediterranean. To the east, neither Persia nor Egypt was in a position to supplant the Ottoman Empire. Secure in its military might, Istanbul seemed captive of its size and centralized structure. Ottoman power devoted the bulk of its energies to the maintenance of its enormous realm. Meanwhile, pluralist Europe was bubbling with political rivalries, locked in fierce economic competition which drove the most dynamic of its States and cities to conquer other continents in search of new markets. Behind the military confrontation between Islam and Europe lurked an economic conflict which, despite the latter's constant payment deficit,[23] the Turkish empire was losing. If we are to believe Braudel, the process was already well underway.

> Since the 13th century the East had gradually lost one by one
> her supremacy in various fields: the refinements of material

civilization, technical advance, large industry, banking, and the supply of gold and silver. The 16th century saw her final defeat in the course of an unprecedented economic upheaval when the opening up of the Atlantic destroyed the age-old privilege of the Levant which for a time had been the sole repository of the riches of the 'Indies'.[24]

If a "rift," which was hardly apparent to the people of the day, had indeed sprung open in the Mediterranean, it originated in the West, and paved the way for the supremacy of Atlantic over Mediterranean Europe. For Europe, the axis of the world gradually shifted west. This shift could not but have influenced the European vision of the Orient.

AWARENESS OF SELF AND IMAGES OF THE OTHER

Evolving views

Such were the material conditions which governed the gradual evolution of mentalities. But the "stuff" of societies cannot be transformed without work, particularly without the work of the spirit — which simultaneously precedes and lags behind its time. It is not the least of paradoxes that the age of great discoveries and of the renewal of intellectual inquiry, when measured against medieval philosophy, remains "more heir than innovator."[25]

In tracing the contours of what he terms "the archeology of knowledge," Foucault clearly demonstrates the limitations of Western *episteme* prior to the classical age (which he dates at the beginning of the 17th century). The "prose of the world," which remained that of the 16th century, did not yet clearly distinguish between word and thing. Unlike classical representation, it sought meaning in resemblances and analogies. It was fundamentally accretive knowledge, which was "proceeded by the infinite accumulation of confirmations." It was "limitless" knowledge because of its "plethoric" structure, and thus, ultimately, impoverished.[26] But if "the learning of that period appears structurally weak," it nonetheless evidences "an already awakened awareness of that sovereign rationality in which we recognize ourselves."[27] The crossing of the oceans, and in more general terms, the "conquest of space" with the appearance of Mercator's first "true" maps, could not but modify the European vision of the world, and of the Orient in particular. Neither the meaning of the voyage nor the manner of seeing remained what they had been before. Contact with the Other stimulated sharper interest, in both senses of the word: as curiosity and as calculation. And religious antagonism no longer played the role it once had.

The rise of what we have come to call rationalism did not have the effect of lessening the religious spirit (as Lucien Febvre[28] has demonstrated) but of loosening religion's grip on thought. Thomas Aquinas, in the 13th century, had already blazed the trail: "his rationalist cosmology laid the foundations for the scientific age."[29] But Acquinas was still obliged to reconcile faith and reason, in the manner of the Muslim masters. In the next century, following in the footsteps of Duns Scotus, Guillaume d'Occam (1300-1350) went one step further; armed with his celebrated "razor," he separated as cleanly as possible that which proceeds from science and that which belongs to theology. Though his intent was to shield the divine from metaphysical speculation, Occam's constructive skepticism contrived to secrete a "corrosive power" which caused even his contemporaries to regard him as "the initiator of the 'modern method' (*via moderna*)."[30] The distance tolerated between science and philosophy on the one hand and religion on the other (though better to protect the dominion of faith) fostered a critical attitude toward the Church and had the effect of framing doctrinal conflicts in a context of relativism. Already, in the 14th century, a handful of rare, audacious spirits dared to direct toward the Church of Rome the same criticisms they had levelled against Mohammed, for both Catholicism and Islam adopted or rejected whatever they wished from Scripture.[31] Neither rite nor dogma mattered, only the relationship with God. The trend gained strength in the 15th century among thinkers like John of Segovia and Nicolas de Cues, precursors of the religious humanism and free thought which later emerged full-blown with Rabelais or Montaigne. Islam, too, was approached with both greater moderation and greater intellectual rigor, with a view to establishing full-fledged communication — even though, as we shall see, this attempt at *rapprochement* was restricted, and not unrelated, to the desire for conversion.

By the 16th century, however, an increasingly large number of thinkers no longer took institutional religion as the central point of reference from which to judge peoples. In like manner, the march toward the Levant was motivated by more than piety alone. In earlier times the journey to the Orient had almost always been linked with the act of pilgrimage. In an article entitled *Outremer, la terre sainte et l'Orient vus par les pèlerins du XVI siècle*, Alain-Julien Surdel demonstrates how the guide-books of the time focused exclusively on biblical anecdote, while totally ignoring the living realities which awaited the voyagers themselves. "They discuss not an existing country, but mythical lands," for the pilgrims "were not simple visitors to Palestine in the 15th century; they were undertaking a mystical voyage into a sacred region."[32]

At the same time, the great expeditions portended another mentality. In 1432, a half-century before Arnold von Harff (considered a pioneer),[33] Bertrandon de la Broquière, counsellor to Philip the Good (Duke of Burgundy) set out on an entirely different kind of pilgrimage, the account of which he was to publish 20 years later. With good reason: under the pilgrim's cloak he had undertaken a mission of observation — today we would call it espionage — whose secret objective was to evaluate Ottoman power. The approach was a novel one, in that the voyage had nothing to do with either trade or piety; its only aims were to observe and note down (which was not true of the Polo family's celebrated voyages to the Far East of in the 13th century, even though their accounts might suggest otherwise).[34]

Observing the Other

Though not necessarily driven by specific considerations, voyages to the Orient in search of information multiplied in the 16th century (and even more in the 17th). The object was no longer the search for paradise, which had been relocated to the New World, but to gather the maximum amount of information on the manners and customs of the inhabitants, as well as on the flora and fauna of the region.

From 1546 to 1549, the naturalist Pierre Belon of Mans travelled throughout the Levant on what was, for all intents and purposes, just such a scientific mission. The results were published in 1554 as *Les Observations de plusieurs singularités et choses mémorables trouvées en Grèce, Asie, Judée, Egypte, Arabie & autres pays étranges, rédigées en trois livres.*[35] In justification of his enterprise Belon argues for a general and disinterested overview. He propounds something resembling a theory of objectivity: the inevitable subjectivity of the traveller, he explains, is deforming enough without adding those specific distortions caused by the pursuit of precise objectives, particularly among those who "travel on business."[36] Two of the three books are devoted to Greece (ancient and contemporary), to the ruins of Troy (extensively) and other "illustrious cities of Asia" (Jerusalem, Constantinople), and to Sinai. Classical and biblical mythology still shape the traveller's vision, but they do not obscure the present: "The third will deal with the modern manner of living of the Turks."[37] We must not forget that Belon was, first and foremost, a naturalist; listing plant and animal species occupies the major part of his work. The manners and customs of the Turks receive but scant attention. But quantity is of secondary concern. What is essential to our purposes is that he employs the same tone, the same detachment in describing manners and customs as in cataloguing the essential oils of Asia Minor. And when he hazards the odd comparison with Europe, it is without passion, as in this passage on slavery:

> The fortune which befalls the slaves in Turkey might well be compared to that of the servants in our Europe: for they partake in felicity according to that master which they serve.[38]

Or this, on women:

> Their only burden is that of the children, and to live in peace, which is quite the contrary of the Latin manner, where women assume not only the administration of goods and chattels, but also authority and absolute power over their entire body, and are often the mistress.[39]

And also this more severe judgement:

> To repudiate one's wife in that land is almost like discharging one's chamber-maid in France.[40]

Of all the Turkish sciences, Belon seems most interested in medicine. He notes that the Turks have good physicians, and more remedies than in Europe, while deploring that "for all that, they exhibit too few of the other qualifications of a good physician," without explaining what these qualities are.[41] But on the whole, Belon's assessment is not particularly negative.

Only when he turns to the "Particular discourse on the beginnings of the origin of the laws of the Turks" does Belon unconditionally surrender to the deprecatory stereotypes of the traditional Christian vision of the Qur'an and its "false prophet Mahomet."[42] The critique is all the more startling in its sharp contrast with the serenity which permeates the remainder of the work. In fact, his execrations of the Qur'an and its "impostor" are more ritual, more linguistic automatism than carefully reasoned judgement. Nor are they accompanied by the slightest deprecation of Ottoman attitudes or religious practices. On the contrary, Belon pays homage to their spirit of tolerance:

> For the Turks oblige no man to live in the Turkish manner, and thus is it permitted for each to live according to his law.[43]

Though a little-known figure, Belon evidences the studious yet relatively unmethodical (from our point of view) way in which the observation of the Turkish Empire was undertaken. More than the world of Islam or the "Orient" (a term, like Levant, found nowhere in Belon's work) it is the Empire itself — and particularly the success of the Ottomans — that interests, fascinates or disturbs. No longer is the combat against heresy (only mentioned in passing) essential; borrowings from Islamic science have fallen from favour to become integrated into the "universalizing" knowledge of the West.[44] The aim has become to learn about the Turks in their daily life, and, above all, the organization of their social lives, their State and their army; particularly the army, object of almost unanimous admiration in Europe. Still, the Ottoman Empire only occupies a tiny fraction of the immense catalogue compiled by the 16th century's inexhaustible curiosity. Was it a one-way curiosity? All indications are that this was so; if nothing else the Ottomans lacked the means to disseminate the pictures and impressions their own travellers may have brought back from Europe.[45] Europe's curiosity was that of an equal, neither disdainful nor condescending; a mixture of respect and fear for this remarkably well-regulated State which was still seen, rightly or wrongly, as the most powerful in the Mediterranean world.

Machiavelli's political judgement

The army, not merely as instrument of foreign policy and conquest, but as the principal, indeed the sole pillar of the Sultan's internal authority, is what struck Machiavelli, that most modern of observers:

> Therefore, if then a ruler was forced to please the soldiers rather than the people, because the soldiers were stronger than the people, now all princes, except the Turk and the Soldan, are forced to please the people rather than the soldiers because the people are stronger. From this I except the Turk, who always keeps around him twelve thousand infantry and fifteen thousand cavalry, on whom depend the security and strength of the kingdom; hence, setting aside all other considerations, that lord must maintain the friendship of these troops.[46]

Why quote Machiavelli when he shows such scant interest in the Turks? Except for a ringing call for Christian unity against the "cruel enemy" who "grinds his weapons and seems to be all burning with desire to overrun your pleasant fields" failing which "your accustomed strength will be forbidden to you by Heaven, since your religious zeal is exhausted,"[47] they are hardly mentioned. We should pay scant attention; his exhortations are little more than florid turns of phrase (Machiavelli's faith is not his greatest strength, but, despite his modernity, he belongs very much to his time, to a "century that wanted to believe,"[48] as Lucien Febvre puts it). The Turkish Empire is also cited as a descendent of those "nations where men lived excellently."[49] Aside from these passages, and two or three minor references in the *Prince*, there is nothing else.

Then why Machiavelli? Because he compares political institutions, and because the institution being compared ("The Grand Turk") is far from fortuitous. The reference to Ottoman power is, in the strictest sense, central to his method. Let us examine how Machiavelli, in the *Prince*, develops his ideas on the "praetorian" nature of power. Outlining the dichotomy he seeks to construct, Machiavelli declares that "all princedoms of which we have record are governed in two different ways: in one there is a prince, and all the others are as servants...In the other, there is a prince, with barons..."

> Examples of these two different methods of governing in our times are the Turks and the King of France. The whole monarchy of the Turk is governed by one ruler; the others are his servants; dividing his kingdom into sanjaks, he sends them various administrators and changes and varies these as he likes. But the King of France is placed amidst a long established multitude of lords acknowledged by their own subjects and loved by them; such lords have their vested rights; these the King cannot take from them without danger to himself. On considering, then, both of these countries, you see that there will be difficulty in governing the Turk's country, but, when it is conquered, great ease in holding it. So, on the contrary, you can see that in some respects the country of France can be more easily occupied but that it can be held only with great difficulty.[50]

Well and good. But is Turkey not simply one among many? The first reference, which describes the Turkish political system as a notable exception, rules out any such innocuous interpretation. Machiavelli does more than synthesize prevailing educated opinion on Turkey, utilizing familiar material, and examples which best support his thesis; he creates a non-traditional dichotomy. The classical Aristotelian distinction between the three possible political regimes and their respective perversions (aristocracy-oligarchy, monarchy-tyranny, democracy-demagogy) gives way to a dual vision in which the Other emerges in all his singularity and difference. No longer are we dealing with the traditional opposition between Mohammedans and Christians, but with a purely political differences unrelated to religion. Machiavelli paved the way for the model which was to become dominant in the classification of political regimes, and would later nourish the concept of Oriental despotism — though it seems clear that it never occurred to the Florentine to disparage the Ottoman system. Machiavelli's dichotomy is significant as an advance warning of the fissure between the Orient and the West, a chilling sense of political awareness of both self (France here standing for Europe) and of the Other.

This self-awareness was strengthened by a sense of particular European destiny. Machiavelli compares Europe with ancient Greece, where the same political division and diversity produced a profusion of great men. With the return to the Ancients invoked by the thinkers of the 16th century, Machiavelli begins to articulate the appropriation of the Hellenic heritage by Europe's intellectual elite, combined with the mythical idea of an immemorial confrontation between Asia and Europe reaching back to the Persian wars. The opposition between the Orient and the West which Europe had begun to construct no longer rested entirely on religious differences, but also, and increasingly, on political ones whose confirmation and justification could be found in history.

In a concise, almost seminal way, Machiavelli makes manifest the political birth of the West in and for itself, via a vision of the Other. But this was not the central object of his intellectual exercise. The *Prince* brings us to the beginning of the 16th century. Later, with Postel, then Bodin, expression of this self-awareness becomes more complex and (primarily with Postel), more ambiguous.

Postel's universal integration

The 16th century was not the century of non-belief. Even among the intelligentsia the religious spirit still prevailed. But it had become diversified in its manifestations, and found expression in new sensibilities, enlivened by the debates which absorbed reformers and humanists (one thinks immediately of the dialogue between Erasmus and Luther); it neither forbade the exploration of the world of the senses, nor an opening to the Other.

A case in point is Guillaume Postel. Far from stifling his curiosity, religious fervour stimulated him to deeper study of the world of Islam, its social reality (*Description de la Syrie*, 1542; *De la République des Turcs*, 1560), its religion (*Le livre de la concorde entre le Coran et les Evangiles*, 1553), and its language (Arabic, which remained culturally dominant). Underlying his studies was the desire to bring about a reconciliation between Islam and Christianity which even today can cause an enthusiast for Islamo-Christian dialogue to exclaim that Postel's vision "has no equal in our times except in the luminous transports of a Louis Massignon." But Postel did not manage to escape the "spirit of systematic denigration" of the Qur'an and its prophet which persisted, unchanged, in his era:[51]

> To undertake...the explication of the perverse argument of
> the Alcoran, I have not relied on the Latin texts...but on the

Arabic texts themselves…I have not judged that those things which are satisfactory in these laws should be kept in mind, but instead the fortuitous manner in which Mahomet arrived at the clever stratagem of obtaining such rapid acceptance for his doctrines. I have noted down with great care all having to do with his life…all the misfortunes, in short, which he has visited upon the world. Finally, I have demonstrated…how unfortunate is such a great number of peoples, under the sway of his disastrous dogmas.[52]

The meaning of "conciliation" as preached by Postel appears in a stark light, as do the terms of his investigation. Little is new except for the method: whether the intent is to convince or to attack, the kernel of the Postelian message can be found in the imperious necessity to go to the sources, to know the Other in his own language. Go to the sources, to his country: nothing can replace direct contact with reality. There could be no other way to correct the negative stereotypes of the Turks, then widespread in Europe.

…For all those who have written [about the Turks] are merely speaking & more often than not by way of books or unknown persons, or yet proved adversaries, odious things & vices, without mention of virtue: that which no people, universally, even though Barbarian, can be.[53]

Knowing the Other through his fundamental texts and customs would lead to clear-headed judgements about the lives of peoples and the doctrine which governs them. The doctrine may be "perverse" or edifying; the ideological struggle, waged with full knowledge, must not distort the "facts." Was, as Simon Jargy claims, this new attitude toward the world of Islam (rather than toward Islam-as-religion) "a true permutation in relations between the Orient and the West"?[54]

Leaving the question open for the moment, let us examine how this precursor of Orientalism uses his science. Postel's erudition went well beyond simple curiosity in its objectives. Behind the thinker and the visionary, the mystic is at work. Postel the "cosmopolitan" (as he describes himself) meant to lay the ideological groundwork for a universal republic which would unite Catholics, Orthodox, Reformers and Muslims in one common faith.[55] The sharpest resistance to his plans would come from Islam, of this much he was certain. Impressed by Muslim wisdom, and much taken by the Turks, Postel still believed that a "regenerated Christianity" might "transform them into friends." Force, after all, could always be employed in the event of a setback. And if the West was unable to regenerate itself, if it failed in its duty? It would then fall to the Turks themselves to compensate for the failure of the Christian princes to act, and to bring about universal concord under their governance.

Such an eventuality was purely rhetorical: the Grand Turk as ultimate expedient seems totally implausible, if only because it presupposed the ideological unity which Postel proposed to bring about. No matter — his chimerical vision makes it possible for us to understand the ambiguity of the Postelian outlook toward the Orient, and toward relations between Christendom and Islam. In the spirit of symmetry which underlies his conciliatory ambitions, Postel set up a double opposition. He compared the dogmas and scriptures of the two religions; here Christianity triumphs easily over heresy as "true guardian of the divine edicts & the divine laws...sole and legitimate princess of this world, in things spiritual and things temporal."[56] Islam could be looked upon only as a lesser evil, a passing stage: introducing pagans as yet untouched by Christianity to monotheism, immunizing them against the "Greek fables."[57] However, in matters of behaviour, Postel reversed the order: the Muslims, by their devotion and piety, could show the Christians a thing or two, particularly since their ignorance of true revelation has made them "less sinful in the eyes of God."[58] Better still, their successes had transformed them into a salutary "whip, or rod" for reawakening both the Christians and their faith.[59]

Despite its pernicious origins and alterations, Islam had a doubly positive historical function: its conquests of idolatry would make straight the way for the coming of authentic revelation, while its threat would force Christendom to mend its ways. Here Postel shared common ground with Luther and Erasmus. Both, like many before them, had pondered what could be done in the face of the "scourge of God." The Turks had not been sent without reason: their coming was God's warning to Christianity that it must regenerate itself from within. But Postel went farther still, and invested the process of regeneration with a conquering, universalizing perspective. For Luther, the fate of Christianity depended upon its capacity for repentance and reform. Erasmus, who, for all his negative prejudices toward the Turks, remained hostile to even the notion of Crusade, contemplated a kind of peaceful coexistence. But the more impulsive Postel set out to persuade the Turks and, if necessary, to defeat them "either by reason, or by authority."[60] Islam could have no meaning until, its task accomplished, it dissolved itself in a reborn Christian universalism.

It was an arduous undertaking: the Cosmopolitan could hardly have been unaware that "the Mohammedan or Arabic peoples," which he also considered to be a hereditary enemy, were a redoubtable power. This was precisely why the Christians should "know their greatest rivals exactly as they are," in all their qualities and their defects, so that the princes of the West might "bring humanity into a state of perfect concord."[61]

Is this the "veritable permutation in relations between Orient and Occident" which Jargy purports to recognize in Postel? If we are to speak of permutations, surely they are of the methodological variety. The notion of "concord" is not a new one: already, in 1460, Nicholas de Cues, known for his open-mindedness, had written to Mohammed II on behalf of Pius II a letter celebrated as a "masterwork of humanism and arrogance," in which he directed the Sultan to convert both himself and his people to the only religion worthy of them. Postel simply carried farther his knowledge of the Other, who must now be understood within the context of his own concrete social reality, ideological conflict notwithstanding. The conflict was not to be forgotten, of course. But the objective was to circumscribe ideology (here, religion) within the social field as a whole, the better to identify the obstacles to be overcome in the struggle against it. But his approach was ill-understood by the Church. She mistrusted his reformer's zeal and his sympathy for the adversary, and did everything it could do to obstruct him. Today, four centuries later, the spirit of Vatican II has indirectly rehabilitated Postel. Rome's "ecumenical" opening to other religions, and to Islam in particular, has a distinctly Postelian look, particularly in its desire to subsume differences in a universal, catholic harmony (if I may be forgiven the redundancy). In retrospect, Postel appears as a link between traditional Christian thought and the Roman hierarchy's current attempts to broaden its horizons. The Cosmopolite, in his unequivocal condemnation of the "foul beastliness & blasphemies which are to be found in the Alcoran,"[62] remained a staunch traditionalist. But in his attempt to understand the Other the better to assimilate him, he both innovated and anticipated. In this regard, over and above religious matters, Postel was a precursor of European Orientalism: the Other is now seen as matter to be devoured, then digested.

Bodin and the sense of history

"One sole fold, or political state in this world..."[63] Postel's enterprise becomes more sharply defined in the light of the contemplations — different yet related — of Jean Bodin, his junior. Bodin, too, flirted with the idea of a "universal republic." His construct was not a blueprint, but a simple representation of the world — that most classical of exercises, performed many times over by the Ancients. But the exercise is a fascinating one. Beneath a traditional, even archaic exterior which today only makes us smile, Bodin's allegory of the world may well be one of the first modern manifestations of what we have come to call eurocentrism. Bodin was by no means Postel's equal as a specialist in Turkish and Islamic matters, but his wide-ranging knowledge encompassed them. The place assigned to the Orient — that which the Orient would become — in his vision of universal order is equally illuminating, a revelatory and representative vision, belonging to a pivotal moment in the Occident's consciousness of itself. As such, it well justifies examination.

At first glance, the sole object of Bodin's political cosmogony is to set up a system of classification. The author of *La Méthode de l'histoire* and *La République* makes no attempt to preach the gospel, nor to win converts to his cause. We have further proof in another of his works, *Heptaplomeres*, a work which was never distributed during Bodin's lifetime (clandestine copies continued to circulate for many years), and was finally published only in the 19th century! This book displays a genuine and profound spirit of tolerance which would have been the envy of Voltaire. Respect for the Other is purer, in fact, than in the philosopher of the Enlightenment.

Cast as a discussion between seven learned men of various beliefs (a Catholic, two Protestants, a Muslim, a Jew, a believer in natural religion and an eclectic), the *Heptaplomeres* presents the protagonists' doctrines and positions in the form of a brisk yet amicable intellectual exchange. The upshot is that none of the religions debated fares any better or any worse than the other, and that the diversity of approaches to God is itself a source of enrichment. Religious conformity and uniformity are as unattractive as monody in music. The seven finally agree to prefer polyphony, with its harmonies and dissonances — the reason for which "the Turks and the Persians admit every kind of religion in the state."[64] The colloquium ends on a note of greater mutual understanding: "Henceforth, they nourished their piety in remarkable harmony and their integrity of life in common pursuits and intimacy. However, afterwards, they held no other conversation about religions although each one defended his own religion with the supreme sanctity of his life."[65] Bodin, it should be further noted, displays an excellent understanding of Islam, and places telling arguments in the mouth of its representative, reflecting his deliberate wish to counterbalance the multifarious rubbish that continued to circulate with regard to the Qur'an and its Messenger.[66] Here was proof positive that his age still suffered from the affliction, but also an indication of the desire of the freest thinkers of the day to distance themselves from the dogmas and interminable controversies created by rival interpretations. Was it not the futility of religious disputation that led Montaigne to say:

> We are Christians by the same title that we are Perigordians or Germans.[67]

We become aware, in the author of the *Heptaplomeres*, of a genuine sense of openness to the Other, and particularly to the supreme Other which is Islam. Rather than reduce the alterity to his own scale of values, rather than neutralize it under a universal republic, Bodin accepts and respects it as an enriching difference. This difference has, of course, a place in a "system of the world," but without universalist, normative intentions. Contrary to Postel's republic, Bodin devises, in a purely allegorical construct, the most coherent and suggestive way in which to classify the diversity of the peoples of the world. The world is here taken to mean those regions falling between the Atlantic and the boundaries of Persia, which would indicate that the Mediterranean still functioned as the centre, determining geographical definition, of oneself and of the Other. It is this defining process, formulated just as the Mediterranean's thousand year preponderance had begun to ebb, which commands our attention.

In his *Méthode de l'histoire*,[68] Bodin distinguishes three geographical zones and the three human types which correspond closely to them: in cold, dry climes of the north, under the sign of Mars (and, secondarily, of the Moon), live the large, strong, attractive, rugged Northern peoples — the Germans, the English and above all, the Scythians, ancestors of the Turks; in the heat and humidity of the south, under the sign of Saturn, live the weak, small-bodied Southern peoples, prone to contemplation, philosophy and calculation, such as the Egyptians, the Greeks, the Italians and the Spaniards; in the temperate centre, finally, under the sign of Jupiter, live the Central peoples, quick-witted and politically minded men of action, of right and justice, whose number fortuitously includes, without Bodin even having to mention it, the French. His classification system is borrowed from Aristotle, but promptly skewed a half-turn to the right to make it palatable for his time and country. East-West typology gives way to a North-South scale which consigns the Greeks, driven from their median perfection by the French, to the position of a Southern people. Up until this point, Bodin's chart betrays not the slightest dichotomy between the Orient and the West — Europe itself is divided into three zones, while the Turks (or at least their ancestors) belong to the same group as the English and the Germans.

But the image is one of stasis. It must now be brought to life, invested with a human form. "Now let us consider this only as far as it concerns the republic of the world, and the nature of peoples; if it can be done, let us set up this world like a man, in its proper position."[69] Which meant ascertaining in which direction the individual/world should naturally turn its gaze. Here, Bodin follows neither Aristotle nor Pythagoras, nor Averroës, all of whom "placed the right side of this world...to the East, the left to the West,"[70] which remains to this day the classic vantage point of Western cartography. Nor does he adopt the Christian habit which literally "orients" the world by turning its churches and prayers toward the East, in the direction of Jerusalem. None of this "orientation" for Bodin; he prefers "occidentation."

> Moses turned the left side of the sanctuary to the south; the right to the north, This was for the best of reasons — because motion is rapid from the east toward the west, but the tread of man is forward, not backward or sideways. Hence Lucan said 'Wondering that the shadows of the grove do not fall to the left.'[71]

When we realize that Bodin was an "adversary of Copernicus,"[72] his meaning immediately becomes clear: the progress of the world becomes one with the (apparent) course of the sun; the allegorical individual who incarnates the universe looks and moves in a westerly direction. Here is Bodin, using his own theory to confirm the validity of his views:

> Now we have assumed that the northerners were more robust, the southerners weaker. But the left hand of the man is the weaker, the right hand the stronger...The we have made plain that the Scythians are reddish in colouring and abound in blood, while the southerners are bloodless and full of black bile. Now on the right side is the liver; on the left the spleen. The latter is the receptacle of black bile, the former of blood. We have shown also that the Scythians are intemperate and wrathful, and that they are driven to vengeance by impulse; but the southerners, only after premeditation. The former traits, of course, suited to the right side, the latter to the left. Then this black bile makes men quiet, and the gall bladder, wrathful, the liver immoderate. The result is therefore, that in this republic of the world, we should place the Scythians, like soldiers and manual workers, on the right side, the southerners on the left, and men of the middle region in the heart, like officials in the middle of the city. For the heart is between the brain and the liver, as well as between the liver and the spleen.[73]

As Bodin's "system of the world" comes into sharper focus, so do the functions of its parts: a great body which holds the sword in its right hand, science in its left, and whose will urges it westward under the political guidance of the centre, meaning temperate Europe (France in particular). Thus a significant East/West nexus is added to the North/South classification. Contrary to Pierre Mesnard's claim, this is more than a "weakened response" to the original dichotomy. Bodin has gone well beyond a theory of climates; now he introduces to his vast canvas an historical dimension, the arrow of time. It is, in fact, the most innovative aspect of his cosmogony. The new perspective enables him to further refine his ethnic typology, for "now that the latitudes have become known it has been discovered that in one and the same quarter of the heavens the people who dwell in the West are pre-eminent for strength of body; the Easterners for talent," and that "the West has a great affinity with the North; the East with the South."[74] Seen in this light, the peoples of the Northwest (such as the Scots) are doubly brave and ferocious, and those of the Southeast (like the Egyptians) doubly indolent and clever. The French, meanwhile, again find themselves advantageously situated, their western situation tempered by their southern contacts. To be at the westernmost extremity of the world is far from a handicap; it is, in fact, to be at the forefront of the action, in the vanguard of the movement of history, for the progression of history itself is toward the West.

We need not follow Bodin through his convoluted reasoning in order to grasp, beyond his contradictions, the deeper meaning of his allegory of the world. It is of less concern that the allegory itself be unsound, that it borrow from irrelevant notions: our search is not for objective truth nor even a globally coherent system, but rather the reflection — though it may be invisible to the mirror which reflects it — of a new awareness of Western Europe's place in the world. Bodin projects a gripping image of a vigorous West, aware of itself as the avant-garde of history, leading the world, coordinating the science of one group with the power of another as it goes. Land of religion and philosophy, both characteristics of old age, the Orient (which, let us remember, has affinities with the South) is cast as the direction whence we have come: it is already the past. Confirmation comes from Bodin's breakdown of history: after six millennia of the "elemental world," "As they say that in six thousand years the period of the elemental world will be complete, from the prophecy of Elia, a certain Rabbi, so for two thousand years men excelled in religion and wisdom and studied zealously the motion of the celestial stars and the universal power of nature. Likewise, in the next two thousand years they were occupied in establishing states, in enacting laws, and in leading colonies."[75] But this wisdom could not endure as a mode of government, for philosophy, which "has nothing in common with civil or military affairs,"[76] must ultimately succumb to force. It has political utility only in the employ of the magistrate represented by the West. In this regard, the Orient has left behind it an inestimable legacy, but its future lies solely in the hands of those rational yet enterprising souls, the inhabitants of the West. Bodin's scheme, though not quite so starkly expressed, represents the first stirrings of a sense of history in which we distantly though still nebulously, and in an altogether different language, detect an almost Hegelian resonance.

Where do the Turks fit into this scheme? Do they belong to the southern Orient (or oriental South)? Not in the slightest. Bodin hardly speaks of them in his *Méthode de l'histoire*, except to place them alongside the peoples of the North, alongside the Germans who, like them, constitute a "branch of the Scythian race." Like them, the Turks are impetuous, warlike, versatile, "without ruse nor shrewdness" — as Tacitus describes the Germans. As an illustration of the "quickness of spirit" that sets them apart, Bodin cites their rapid conversion to Islam.

> The Turks,…as soon as they invaded Asia, were converted to the Arabian faith.[77]

The Turks do not belong "genetically" to Asia, and even less so to Africa, which they conquered. They are a young people, remote from the philosophy and religion of old age. Following Bodin's logic, one might well argue that their geographical situation in the northeast (the Orient offsetting the crudeness of the North) makes them more like the peoples of the centre, though Bodin does not say as much. Is this because of lack of knowledge of the Ottoman Empire? On the contrary. Bodin justifies the brevity of a chapter entitled "The type of government in states," containing a section on "changes in the Empire of the Turks," by the fact that "many men have written many things about the state of the Turks, it is enough for me to touch lightly upon them,"[78] (while complaining that the history of the Arabs "is obscure and full of fables, which our men have put into writing,"[79] despite the scope of their power).

Bodin appears to attribute the success of the Ottoman Empire to its system of land recompense for its soldiers, the granting of "fiefs" but not of money: "This system makes the State invincible,"[80] he concludes. Furthermore, in his classification of political systems, he identifies two kinds of "monarchical governments" (excluding tyranny). In the first category are those sovereigns who submit to no law, among whose number are to be found the Turk, the Persian, the Scythian and the Roman Emperors: "those kings whom Aristotle calls lords." The second includes "those who conform" [to the law]: "like the Christian sovereigns, with few exceptions, and the Carthaginians."[81] The dichotomy recalls Machiavelli's earlier distinction, but is much less clear. It is, above all, a dichotomy that corresponds to no clear-cut opposition between the Turkish Orient and the Christian West, and which makes no pejorative judgement on Ottoman power. Bodin, in fact, compares it favourably to the Holy Roman Empire.

> Turning to foreign nations, what has Germany to oppose to the Sultan of the Turks? Or which state can more aptly be

called a monarchy? This fact is obvious to everyone — if there is anywhere in the world any majesty of empire and of true monarchy, it must radiate from the Sultan. He owns the richest parts of Asia, Africa and Europe, and he rules far and wide over the entire Mediterranean and all but a few of his islands. Moreover, in armed forces and strength he is such that he alone is the equal of almost all the princes, since he drove the armies of the Persians and the Muscovites far beyond the boundaries of the Empire.[82]

This power and magnificence, which Bodin returns to, however briefly, in *Les Six livres de la République* is far from synonymous with despotism (in its pejorative sense). The Sultan, in fact, is cited as an example of freedom of conscience.

The King of Turks, who rules over as great part of Europe, safeguards the rites of religion as well as any prince in this world. Yet he constrains no one, but on the contrary permits everyone to live according as his conscience dictates.[83]

Bodin's thought is not easily encapsulated. In it, self affirmation clearly outweighs definition of the Other, whose aspect is double. On the one hand the Orient, in its vagueness and vastness, is synonymous with the past. On the other hand, the Turkish State, as expression of the contemporary, is edifying in the efficiency of its institutions. Curiously enough, despite its familiar presence and its deep European roots, and despite its military superiority, its place in the course of history remains uncharted. Is the incontestable vitality of the Ottoman Empire fated to decline simply by virtue of its geographical position, or by the absorption of southern lands into its realm? Nothing allows us to draw such a conclusion. But it can be faintly apprehended in the logic of Bodin's "world system" which makes Europe the spearhead of the movement of history — and of the movement through which, at the same point in time, the idea of progress was to take root.

In this century, we have seen greater progress amongst our men of science than our ancestors would have witnessed throughout the fourteen preceding centuries.[84]

May we conclude?

In 1539, Jacques Signot, in *La Division du monde*, noted that, in accord with the Ancients, Asia was "the first & principal part of the world," and Europe the second:

> Europe...is not the greatest in the abundance of its lands, but
> in number of cities it is the strongest.[85]

Fifty years later, Bodin's Asia had faded away, retreated toward the past, where the "cosmogonic" status of the Turks, despite their present power, remained ambiguous. At the beginning of the century, Machiavelli had randomly ascribed "excellence" (*virtù*) to one people or another, from west to east, and from north to south.[86] By the end of the same century, Bodin had conferred upon it a single direction, as certain and irreversible as the progress of the sun.

A profound shift had taken place. On the humanist horizon loomed a new vision of the world suggested in the writings of Machiavelli, Postel and Bodin, a world in which the Mediterranean Orient was no longer the same. Machiavelli had charted the hairline political fracture between the Ottoman and European regimes which would be re-used and reinforced by European political thought in following centuries. Postel, in his positive "normality," described and ingested the Other, all the while brandishing it as a scourge intended to awaken the universal evangelical zeal of a Christendom threatened in its faith and in its spiritual unity, like a distant echo of the spirit of the Crusades, while at the same time employing the Other as material for investigation and for self deliberation. Bodin's Orient, though it had not yet acquired its antithetical quality, had already lost its mystery and its attraction. He had turned his back on it, neither out of contempt nor ignorance but because he had determined in which direction his century had begun to move: that direction was to be the Atlantic.

By the end of the 16th century, the symbolic duality of the Orient and the West as opposing socio-historical entities had not yet assumed clear-cut form, but the conditions — both intellectual and material — for its emergence were now in place. The Orient no longer exerted the same fascination as it had in the Middle Ages, but it had not yet become a vehicle for the exotic (as it was to become in the next century), while Islam-as-religion, despite its base origins, gradually lost its negative virulence and, considered in the light of its practice, even became respectable. Likewise the Mediterranean, while maintaining its cultural and economic predominance, was losing its centrality, slowly ceasing to be the symbiotic basin it had been until the end of the Middle Ages. At the same time the divisions which crisscrossed it, which were, in the centuries that followed to transform it into a locus of rift and cultural opposition, were reinforced.

Indeed, a deep socio-historical breach, of which its contemporaries were barely aware, had opened between the Southeast and the Northwest. Not because of some hypothetical closing off of the Mediterranean by the Turks, who, far from opening the fissure really only suffered from it. But because the western and northernmost region of Europe, as Bodin has sensed, was now ascendant over its Mediterranean flank.

NOTES

1. With the exception of Morocco. Islam here stands for the *dar-al-islam*, the land of Islam.
2. Grousset, *L'empire du Levant*, op. cit., p.614.
3. "Better behold the Turkish imperial turban than the Latin mitre in the center of the city," could he heard in Constantinople shortly before its capture by the Ottomans. Quoted (with no indication of source) in *Le miroir de l'Islam, Musulmans et Chrétiens d'Orient au Moyen Age (VII-XI siècle)*, textes présentés par A. Ducellier, Paris, Julliard, 1971., p.288.
4. Southern, R.W. *Western Views of Islam in the Middle Ages*, Cambridge, Mass., Harvard University Press, 1962, p.61.
5. Braudel, Fernand, *The Mediterranean and the Mediterranean World in the Age of Phillip II*, translated by S. Reynolds, New York, Harper and Rowe, 1972, Vol. 2, p.904-905.
6. Ibid., p.1125.
7. Ibid., p.1185.
8. Ibid., p.970-987 on Turkish supremacy; p.1102 on the resounding Christian victory at Lepanto.
9. Pirenne, Henri, *La fin du Moyen Age*, op. cit., p.143.
10. Pirenne, loc. cit., p.153.
11. Ibid., p.153-154.
12. Braudel, *The Mediterranean*, op. cit., Vol. 1, p.543-544.
13. Ibid., p.547.
14. Ibid., p.548-549.
15. Ibid., p.550.
16. Ducellier, A., Kaplan, M., and Martin,B. *Le proche Orient médiéval*. Paris, Hachette, 1978, p.243. The authors go on to add: "Nonetheless, the Orient was not dead; in its deep slumber, it was to go on nurturing a heritage which, particularly in the intellectual and artistic sphere, would break into brilliant bloom." Here we have the Orient as sleeping beauty.
17. The concept of stagnation did not exist in the 16th century. "Stagnant" and "stagnation" emerged in the figurative sense in the 18th century to convey the absence of progress.
18. Braudel, op. cit., Vol. 2, p.704-755.
19. Ibid., p.755.
20. Ibid., p.771.
21. Ibid., p.771.
22. Mousnier, Roland, *Les XVI et XVII siècles*. Paris, P.U.F., 1954. (Vol. IV of *l'Histoire générale des civilizations*), p. 3,2.
23. Braudel, Fernand, *Civilization and Capitalism, 15th-18th century*. Translated by S. Reynolds. New York, Harper and Row, 1982. Vol. II, p.208: "Only one trade balance seems to have been stuck in the same position; from the Roman Empire to the nineteenth century trade with the Levant always left Europe with a negative balance."
24. Braudel, op. cit., Vol. I, p.137. Turkish naval failure in the Indian Ocean contributed strongly to confining the Ottomans to their land empire, Ibid., pp.1175, 1176, Vol. II.

25. de Gandillac, *Histoire de la philosophie*, Paris, Gallimard, Pléiade, Vol.2, 1973, p.5. See also Lucien Febvre, *The problem of unbelief in the 16th century, the religion of Rabelais*. Translated by Beatrice Gottliels, Cambridge, Mass., Harvard University Press, 1982, p.355-370.
26. Foucault, Michel, *The order of things, an archaeology of the human sciences*. London, Tavistock Publications, 1970, p.29-30.
27. Ibid., p.32.
28. Febvre, op. cit.
29. Dufeil, op. cit., p.167.
30. *Histoire de la philosophie*, Vol. I, p.1506.
31. Southern, op. cit., p.78-84. The person in question is John Wycliff (1320-1384).
32. *Images et signes de l'Orient dans l'Occident médiéval*, op. cit., p.323-339.
33. Rodinson, *Europe and the mystique of Islam*, op. cit.
34. The younger Marco Polo was motivated primarily by curiosity and the taste for adventure. But the voyages of his father and uncle (including those in which Marco participated) were the result of commercial and political considerations. Observation was only to come later, in an account written by Marco Polo's cell-mate during a lengthy stay in the prisons of Genoa. But the entire undertaking was exceptional for the day, so much so that his contemporaries believed that he had fabricated his descriptions of the Mongol Empire.
35. Paris, chez Hierofine de Marnef et la eufve Guilamme Canellat, 1588.
36. Belon, op. cit., p.2.
37. Ibid., preface, n.p.
38. Ibid., p.426.
39. Ibid., p.409.
40. Ibid., p.394.
41. Ibid., p.401.
42. Ibid., p.378-379.
43. Ibid., p. 398.
44. *Histoire de la philosophie*, op. cit., Vol. II, p.17. The "universalizing" character of Western knowledge is not at issue. It need only so define itself, right or wrong — an elegant way of sidestepping its borrowings from Arab science.
45. The Turks discovered printing only at the beginning of the 18th century, in the course of a voyage by Mehmed Effendi to France, in 1720. On the absence of information on Europe in Turkey, see Bernard Lewis, *The Muslim Discovery of Europe*, New York, Norton, 1982.
46. Machiavelli, Niccolo, *The Prince*, in "Chief Works and Others." Translated by Alan Gilbert, Duke University Press, 1965, Vol. I, p.76.
47. Machiavelli, Niccolo, *By the blessed spirit, Carnival Songs*, in "Chief Works," Vol. II, p.880.
48. Febre, op. cit., p.455.
49. Machiavelli, *Discourses on the first decade of Titus Livius*, in "Chief Works," Vol. I, p.323. Note the use of the past tense: "lived" (nations of noble lineage of which the Turkish empire was a part), as opposed to "today, the people of Germany." Is this an indication that the Turks are no longer what they once were? Perhaps, though doubtful at the beginning of the 16th century. More probably the problem is a grammatical one: the Turks still belong to those people recognized for their *virtu*.
50. Machiavelli, *The Prince*, in "Chief Works," Vol. I, p.20-21.
51. Simon Jargy, preface to Segesvary, Victor, *L'Islam et la Réforme*, p.9,7.
52. Postel, Guillaume, *Alcorani seu Legis Mahometi*, quoted (in translation) in Segesvary, op. cit., p.68.
53. Postel, Guillaume, *De la République des Turcs: & là ou (sic) l'occasion s'offrira, des meurs & loy de tous Muhamedistes*. A Poitiers, Par Enguilbert de Marnef, 1560., p.1.

54. Jargy, op. cit., p.7.
55. The project is outlined in *De orbis terrae concordia* (Basel, 1543), but permeates the whole of Postel's *oeuvre*, and particularly those works dealing with the Turks and the Orient.
56. Postel, Guillaume, *Des Histoires orientales et principalement des Turkes ou Turchiques et Schitiques ou Tartaresques et autres qui en sont descendus,* par Guillaume Postel, Cosmopolite deux fois de là (sic) retourné et véritablement informée. De l'imprimerie de Hierosme de Marnef et Guillaume Cavellat au mont S. Hilaire, 1575, p.372.
57. Postel, Guillaume, *Histoire et considération... op. cit., p.45.*
58. Ibid., p.50.
59. Ibid., p.44.
60. Postel, *Des Histoires orientales*, op. cit., p.373.
61. Postel, *Histoires et considérations*, op. cit., p.4.
62. Postel, *De la République des Turcs*, op. cit., p.76.
63. Postel, *Des Histoires orientales*, op. cit., p.372.
64. Bodin, Jean, *Colloquium of the seven about secrets of the sublime.* Translated by Marion Leathers Daniels, Princeton, Princeton University Press, 1975. p.151.
65. Ibid., p.471.
66. Ibid., p.208-232.
67. Montaigne, Michel de, *The Complete Essays.* Translated by Donald M. Frame. Stanford, Stanford University Press, 1965. Book II, Chapter 12, p.325.
68. Bodin, Jean, *Method for easy comprehension of history.* Translated by Beatrice Reynolds, New York, Columbia University Press, 1945, p.111.
69. Ibid., p.117.
70. Ibid., p.117.
71. Ibid., p.118.
72. *Histoire de la philosophie*, op. cit., Vol. II, p.291.
73. Bodin, Jean, *Method*, op. cit., p.119.
74. Ibid., p.132,133.
75. Ibid., p.122.
76. Ibid., p.117.
77. Ibid., p.126. Bodin earlier described the Scythians thus: "In general, it has been so arranged by nature that Scythians, who have less reason, but more strength, should place the height of all virtues in military glory." (p.115)
78. Ibid., p.262. In Chapter X, Bodin notes, between 1490 and 1550, seven works on the Turks (including that of Postel) as against only one on the Arabs and Africa, and, by comparison, nine on Spain, demonstrating that Turkey was a subject as frequently dealt with as the various states of Europe.
79. Ibid., p.261.
80. Ibid., p.263.
81. Ibid., p.204. In his *Six Books of the Commonwealth*, Bodin distinguishes between "Royal, or Legitimate Monarchy" and "Despotic Monarchy...in which the prince is lord and master of both the possessions and the persons of his subjects by right of conquest in a just war; he governs his subjects as absolutely as the head of a household governs his slaves. Tyrannical monarchy is one in which the laws of nature are set at naught, free subjects oppressed as if they were slaves, and their property treated as if it belonged to the tyrant." (p.56-57)
82. Ibid., p.292.
83. Bodin, Jean, *Six Books of the Commonwealth.* Translated by M.J. Tooley, Oxford, Blackwell, 1967, p.143.
84. Quoted by Mousnier, op. cit., p.9.
85. *La division du monde, contenant la déclaration des provinces et régions d'Asie, Europe & Aphrique (etc.)* A Lyon, par Benoît Rigaud & Jean Saugrain, MDLV (1555) (1st edition, 1539) no author's name, but attributed to Jean Signot, p.17.29.

86. Machiavelli, Niccolo, *Discourses on the first decade of Titus Lavius*, in "Chief Works, Vol. I, p.322. "...whereas the world first placed excellence in Assyria, she later put in it Media, then in Persia, and finally it came to Italy and Rome. If the Roman Empire was not succeeded by any Empire that lasted and kept together the world's excellence, that excellence nevertheless was scattered among many nations where men lived excellently, such as the Kingdom of the French, the Kingdom of the Turks, and that of the Soldan, and today the people of Germany, and earlier that Saracen tribe that did such great things and took so much of the world after it destroyed the Eastern Roman Empire."

IV

The Faraway Orient

How did 17th and 18th-century Europeans visualize the Mediterranean Orient; what was its utility? What remote globality — seen in a multiplicity of viewpoints and at a plurality of levels — did the concept of Orient stand for? What sense of curiosity and contemplation did it evoke?

Why this particular historical period in the first place? Why attempt to encompass two contrasting centuries within the same framework of investigation.

We can find justification enough in Foucault's discourse of "classical representation,"[1] which unearthed the unbroken epistemological thread running from the mid-17th to the end of the 18th century. Our overriding concern, after all, is how the Mediterranean Orient was represented; and how this representation evolved from classicism in the narrowest sense of the term (delineated by the reign of Louis XIV) up to the Enlightenment, through what Paul Hazard has defined as the "crisis of European consciousness" (1680-1715).[2] For this was the crisis which all but snapped Foucault's thread: the representation continued but its universe broadened out and became diversified, its motivations changed, presaging the epistemological course change which was to occur in the following century.

It can be argued that assigning events to historical periods is an arbitrary exercise. We might also criticize Foucault's perhaps excessively Gallo-centric purview. But if ever there existed an age in which the influence of French culture and intellectual life was felt beyond its borders, the era which stretched from Descartes to Diderot was the one. Embodying as it did a certain European universalism, the French viewpoint will be of primary interest to us here.[3]

Yet another problem arises, a more serious one: the length of the period under examination. How can we draw general conclusions without collapsing under the sheer burden of detail, how can we avoid the distortions inherent in an examination process spanning almost two centuries? When we realize how fertile, even prolix were the two centuries, with regard to the Orient, when their output is measured against the meagre production of the preceding century, the issue becomes particularly acute.

The very prolixity and diversity which helped shape the many faces of the Orient may well be the main distinguishing feature of an entire period of evolution. If the previous century, the "long" 16th, produced little on the Orient aside from the abusively generalizing concept itself, it was because Europe was so deeply caught up in the physical exploration of the planet and in the affirmation of its own identity. As I have attempted to indicate earlier, this endeavour redirected Christendom from its fascination with the mystical Orient (seat of Paradise), the profane Orient ("Mahometan" heresy) or the wise Orient (Arabo-Muslim science and philosophy).

Classical Europe, as heir to the conquests of the 16th century could turn with greater intellectual openness to an Orient which it might henceforth contemplate at leisure, and name as difference. Atlantic Europe had supplanted Mediterranean Europe. As sovereign of the seas it faced no serious threat, and anticipated even less (though Mediterranean trade remained substantial) from the Ottoman Empire, which it now looked upon with greater serenity and detachment. Part of this sense of detachment came from being as yet unengaged — covetousness aside perhaps — in the colonial enterprise. The Mediterranean Orient, uncolonized still, represented the essence of the Other at the historical moment when Europe had become fully aware of being the centre (an idea already expressed by Jean Bodin, in his fashion[4]).

It was, one might argue, a natural enough tendency for any civilization. The Turks, after all, considered themselves to be at the pinnacle of the world's mightiest empire. But the inner conviction of superiority cannot alone suffice to appropriate the material universe. The Turks were to appropriate nothing beyond the confines of their empire; certainly nothing significant. The contrast with the Europeans was enormous: the transoceanic expeditions, the conquest of the Americas, the slave trade (not to mention the wealth which poured into metropolitan coffers) had far-reaching consequences. Not only was the West laying the foundations of its economic supremacy; it was also beginning to view the world in a different way. The Other became reified as it was conquered, subjugated, sold, exploited, or merely explored.

The Orient — still sovereign, still imposing — was to escape neither exploration nor reification. It became, in its own manner, an object of curiosity, of knowledge, of enticement (exoticism), and of reprobation (despotism). Then it became the subject matter of comparison and consideration, both window and mirror. Domination — to the extent it existed — was structural and intellectual: Europe had long enjoyed its commercial outposts in the Orient, its traders, its ambassadors and consuls, its travellers and spies, and soon, its learned men (the specialists). Edward Saïd,[5] whose survey focuses primarily on the 19th century, may claim otherwise, but Orientalism predated Europe's first Levantine incursion since the Crusades — the Napoleonic expedition to Egypt — by at least one and one-half centuries. Later, though, Orientalism was to accompany, sustain and in turn draw sustenance from the imperial adventure.

Time has now come to define that which, despite wide diversity, unified one hundred and fifty years of contemplation of the Orient. Europe now possessed a sense of self-certainty, and curiosity about the Other; it was at peace, both in terms of ideas and of arms, with that which it contemplated as it rarely had before, and was never to do again.[6] The period was one of seminal importance.

These were the formative years for the idea of the Mediterranean Orient as intrinsic political, social and cultural alterity. So closely interrelated are these three terms that they can be subsumed under the general heading of culture, in the sense of a hierarchy of values governing the lives of groups and individuals as well as the place and the function of social and political institutions. Culture and the cultural will thus be employed in this general sense, and used to characterize the overall differences between civilizations (or groups of societies), even though the same words were not employed in this way during the age I propose to examine. Indeed, awareness of the sweeping difference between the Orient and the West emerged with progressively greater clarity over the course of the 17th and 18th centuries.

For the sake of convenience, but also to illustrate the development of mentalities from the century of Louis XIV to that of the Enlightenment, I have divided — without attempting to compartmentalize — my examination of the period into two sections: the first, underscoring curiosity (with its undercurrent of covetousness), the second concentrating on the thinking and the debate stimulated by the object of that curiosity.

THE CLASSICIST'S ORIENT

The century of "classical representation" witnessed the insatiable exploration of the planet; grand designs and world planning schemes proliferated, accounts of voyages and descriptions of non-European lands were published. The principal focus of this activity was the Turkish Empire. Though it may have lost its significance as a threat, it still formed a hard core of resistance, at once familiar and ill-suited, to Western projects for the ordering of the known universe, as well as an undesirable observer — and potential beneficiary — of inter-European rivalries.

Rather, some reasoned, than offer the Infidel this pathetic spectacle should not the princes of Europe unite in a common undertaking against him? But the quality of Infidel had, perhaps inevitably, become devalued; it subsisted only as reflex, as ingrained habit. Beyond the old litanies of woe against the Qur'an and its prophet, religion was no longer truly at issue. Perhaps it still sustained a stereotype, or justified negative judgement. Still, it remained a convenient stereotype, a way of representing the eternal adversary (or so it was believed) becoming an ideal, almost fictitious enemy. At this level, the Turk fulfilled an almost mythical political function, that of catalyst for European federation. Union could only be achieved through the dismemberment of the great, still-living Ottoman corpse.

Projects for peace and for the apportionment of the remains proliferated. The process itself became something of a parlour game. But there was no unanimity in choosing Turkey as the designated victim of the peace. Some, like the obscure pacifist Crucé, wanted to involve the Ottoman Empire in the peace process. Immediately below the Pope in his Senate of Nations sat the Sultan "whereas he holds the seat of the Eastern empire" (the listing includes "the kings of Persia, China, Prester John, the Precop of Tartary and the Grand Duke of Muscovy").[7] But his openness was the exception. More often, as in the case of both Sully and Père Joseph, Richelieu's "eminence grise" and author of an interminable *Turciade*, peace must be made at the expense of the Ottomans.[8] So much for the slackening of the Crusader spirit.

Political reality was quite another matter. The monarchs of Europe were locked in a battle of wits as each attempted to negotiate with the Porte the establishment or renewal of the most favourable possible capitulations[9] for his country's traders. Aside from the regional alliance formed by Austria, Poland, Venice and Russia to block the last Turkish offensive in central Europe (Vienna was besieged for the last time in 1683), never did there exist even a hint that the great schemes might come to pass. But though these plans and projects remained moribund, they revealed a predatory mentality, as we will see when we examine Liebniz's Egyptian proposal. The Ottoman Empire had become the stuff of speculation, the subject of studies and political exercises, on paper at least.

Voyages to the Orient

The coveted object exerted an attraction that went beyond political fiction. European curiosity penetrated the Orient in other ways. Commercial considerations were constant, of course. But there was also plain and simple interest, and its accompanying diversification. The Turks were no longer the only inhabitants of the West's imaginary world. Persia became an object of interest, as did the nationalities who formed a part of the population of each of these empires. But this diversity was in turn a component of the universality named Orient, or Levant. These imprecise definitions of geographical space (the first could well lead all the way to China) became charged, on the socio-cultural level, with increasingly apparent antithetical meaning: the social and cultural universality they designated was, geographically speaking, close at hand.

Commerce aside, curiosity remained the principal means of penetration and appropriation of this nearby, but still untamed Orient. This meant travel, accompanied by pillage of the intellectual variety: travellers were soon to return carrying texts in their baggage, as later they were to pry loose the stones themselves: the sculptures, the bas-reliefs, the obelisks. But above all, they produced accounts of their own making, "relations" as they were then called, which became the raw material from which an Orient could be manufactured, then enriched with works on the history of its peoples (Arabs and Turks above all), which later led to attempted assemblages of the knowledge about the Orient. One of the earliest among them was the celebrated *"Bibliothèque Orientale* or Universal Dictionary herein containing All Things relating to the Knowledge of the Peoples of the Orient, their veritable Histories and Traditions, sects and politics, their Sciences and their Arts...by Monsieur d'Herbelot," an encyclopedic compendium of the 17th century's output on the Orient first published in 1697.

Stéphane Yerasimos has estimated that more than two hundred "voyages" to the Orient were published in the 17th century.[10] Most were "private," but some were underwritten or undertaken at the behest of the state, like that of Pitton de Tournefort, who, in the introduction to the first volume of his relation, sets forth the intent of his enterprise:

> My lord the Comte de Pontchartrain, Secretary of State, charged with the vouchsafing of the Academies & ever attentive to those things which may endow the sciences with greater perfection, proposed to His Majesty in the end of the year 1699 to dispatch to foreign lands persons capable of observation, not only of natural History & upon ancient and modern Geography, but yet of matters regarding Commerce, Religion and the Customs of the diverse peoples who inhabit them.[11]

Gathering information on the foreigner had become an important State concern; so important, in fact, that the State undertook to finance its own observers, despite the abundance of already existing accounts.

Not only were these accounts abundant; coming at five, ten or twenty year intervals, they were numbingly repetitive. It would be useless and tedious to review even a twentieth of them. Especially when we have, in Jean Thévenot, the near-archetypical traveller who borrowed wholesale from his predecessors, and was in turn shamelessly pirated by his successors. Thévenot, however, stood apart from most of his contemporaries in his devotion to detail and truth, which lends his account an "ethnographic character."[12]

Not unlike Belon du Mans in the preceding century, Thévenot, between 1655 and 1659, travelled for travel's sake, with no other concern than seeing and telling. Aside from his deprecatory ritual doggerel about Mahomet, "a man without science," and the Qur'an, "full of fables and follies,"[13] he treated the Turks with the respect due an equal. He stressed their piety, their spirit of tolerance and charity, noting that "they gladly assist the destitute without consideration for religion, whether Turk, Christian or Jew."[14] Thévenot even found it necessary to correct the European prejudices of the day, which he had shared before his departure.

> Many in Christendom believe that the Turks are great devils, barbarians and faithless people, but those who have known them and conversed with them have a different sentiment; for it is certain that the Turks are good people, who well obey the commandment made upon us by nature, to wit, not to do to one's neighbour what one would not wish done to oneself …The native-born Turks [in contrast with those renegades who have espoused Islam] are honest people, who esteem honesty in others, be they Turks, Christians or Jews.
>
> I know that I may be asked: 'Why do they so scorn the Franks?' But we may be certain that they are driven to do so by the Christians and the Jews.[15]

The passage is instructive in that it points to the perpetual gap between direct contact in the field and preconception, indicating how rarely, as Hélène Desmet-Grégoire[16] has observed, the traveller's message is received. The best knowledge available about the Other — itself at best a half-measure — touches only a tiny minority, and has virtually no effect on the clichés which inhabit the collective imagination.

Curiously, even a model observer like Thévenot could not escape the perverse effects of stereotype when he departed Turkey for Egypt. The contrast was too striking for him not to attempt an explanation. Of course, like all others, the Turks were not without their faults; their virtues were simply the other side of the coin.

> And in regard to their vices, they [the Turks] are supremely arrogant, esteeming themselves above all other nations; they believe themselves the most valiant on earth, and that the world has been made for them alone: thus they show scorn, in general, toward all other nations, and principally those

which do not follow their law, such as the Christians and the
Jews, and they commonly call the Christians dogs.

And:

The Turks are little inclined toward the sciences.

And again:

They are strongly inclined to love, but of a brutal nature
indeed; for they are great sodomites, and it is a very common
vice amongst them.[17]

Last epithet aside, there is nothing terribly offensive in our traveller's
catalogue: the Turks are a proud people, conscious of their strength and
valour. In short, the conqueror and ruler must be respected (there is only
one potential weakness, science, to which we will return). This respect in
turn throws light on the contrast which he attempts to explain. We may
judge for ourselves from Thévenot's approach to the Egyptians.

The inhabitants of this land generally, both Muslims and
Christians, are of dark complexion, they are the most spiteful
rascals, cowards, ne'er do wells, hypocrites, great pederasts;
thieving, treacherous, avaricious, quite capable of killing a
man for a trifle; they are, withal, perfect in all vices, poltroons
in the ultimate degree, falling easy prey to anger and recon-
ciling as rapidly.

What had the poor Egyptians done to merit such indignity, particularly
from an observer known for his moderation and honesty? Let us read on:

These miserable people are held by the Turks as slaves, or
rather as dogs, for they [the Turks] govern stave in hand.
...As well, the Egyptians are of such abject nature that they
desire to be beaten, esteeming all the more those who abuse
them, in the manner of dogs and serve well indeed when
they are well chastened, and are instead insupportable and
wish to do nothing when they are well treated.[18]

The slave, by his "abject nature," has willingly brought upon himself the
state of servility he so richly merits — and so willingly endures. How better
to exonerate the master, with whom Thévenot seems to have identified
with scant remorse. Perhaps his experiences in Cairo had been unpleasant

(a common European complaint at the time). Perhaps he realized that he stood on conquered terrain, in a land reduced to subject status. Nothing any longer blocked out what can only be described as outright racism. But it was racism expressed in a new way: no longer based on religious affiliation (Thévenot lumps Christians and Muslims together uncritically), but on skin colour (swarthy) and alleged character traits (laziness, spinelessness, servility, bullying, pederasty). A more sombre picture would be hard to visualize.

Was our Frenchman merely giving voice to the feelings of the Ottoman rulers toward their Egyptian subjects? Possibly. But he was surely exaggerating: such contempt by the Turks toward fellow Muslims is hard to believe.[19] On the other hand, it is difficult not to draw a direct connection between his degrading language and that which was to be employed later by the colonialists, the slave traders and settlers of the Americas to justify their excesses. What white eyes saw as laziness and indolence has always served to legitimize the violence inflicted upon people of colour. Domination, as we well know, is among the master's greatest services to his slave. Thévenot strained to admit the "indignities" inflicted on the "Franks who live in Egypt," which he explored in detail, while remaining silent on the open antagonism of the French of Cairo toward those of Alexandria.[20] His capacity for indignation is selective indeed: shocked by the ill-treatment of his compatriots, he contrived to describe the slave market — and the "circumcision" of girls — with lofty serenity.

> The Moors circumcise their girls in excising a tiny piece of that which is called the nympha, and the act of circumcision is performed by the women. The Turks do not do this whatsoever; they circumcise only the boys.[21]

He then moves on, unperturbed, to a wordy description of the "little saints" — the whirling dervishes whose practices he examines at length, the better to vituperate. The mutilation of young girls warrants not a comment, but the incantatory vertigo of the dervishes disturbs the order of the world.

Thévenot never visited Persia. But on that empire we have the classic relations of Jean-Baptiste Tavernier, and of Chevalier Chardin[22] after him. These two authors can be placed at the approximate midpoint between benevolence and condescension — which would have consigned Persia to a place somewhere between Turkey and Egypt (probably closer to the former than the latter) on Thévenot's scale of values. In the event, the appreciation corresponded, in general terms, with political reality. As heirs to an ancient culture, the Persians enjoyed greater prestige in European eyes than did the Turks; but they were, at the same time, less respected politically — Europeans had never had cause to fear them, and had long considered them to be in decline and on the defensive, despite several outbursts of renewed vigour against their Ottoman adversaries.

Tavernier describes a Persia at once indulgent and unflattering, where luxurious decadence and depravity prevailed at the court of a neglected country, in an "ill-built and dreary capital, Isphahan." The author takes particular pains to incriminate "the sloth of men who prefer to live poorly rather than work," in explaining the cultural backwardness afflicting "entire regions."[23] There is no comparison with the Turks that does not diminish the Persians, who are said to suffer from despotism, corruption and superstition.[24] They surpass Europe in one field only, health, though here too Tavernier hastens to add that "the Persians themselves admit that medicine is practised without great method & agree that only the Franks have a true understanding of it"[25] (which would have made Molière glad...). In the final analysis, the Persians owe their good health to the climate; by their own admission, Europe surpasses them even where they excel. How better to reinforce one's own self-esteem?

Chardin's palette is richer, his sense of observation sharper. He concurs with his precursor's negative judgements, but not without having first recognized in the Persians a profusion of "natural parts," particularly their "kindness towards strangers," their hospitality and their tolerance. But, though they "are born with as good *natural Parts* as any other people...few abuse them so much as they do."[26] Such people have "an eager bent to Voluptuousness, Luxury, Extravagancy and Profuseness," qualifiers which we earlier encountered almost word for word in Tavernier. The two observers also conclude that the Persians are "ignorant of Frugality and Trade."

> Their aversion to *Labour* is one of the most common occasions
> of their Poverty.[27]

We are not far distant from Thévenot's assessment of the Egyptians: for all in the Near East that is not Turkish, idleness constitutes the common denominator. Here too the explanation is a racist one, more developed than in Thévenot:

> The *Persian Blood* is of its nature crude. This can be observed
> amongst the Parsees, who are the descendents of the ancient
> Persians. They are *ugly, ill-formed, heavy,* of *coarse complexion*
> and *dark in colour.*

Their crude nature ill matches Chardin's catalog of the "natural" talents of the Persians. Whence do they then derive such qualities? Here is the answer:

But in other Parts of the Kingdom, the *Persian* Blood is now grown clearer, by the mixture of the *Georgian* and *Circassian* Blood, which is certainly the People of the World which Nature favours most, both upon the Account of the Shape and Complexion, and of the *Boldness* and *Courage*; they are likewise *Sprightly*, *Courtly* and *Amourous.*[28.]

A Frenchman could have hardly described his own "race" more eloquently. It is difficult not to conclude that a European would naturally be more inclined to identify with the Christian peoples of Georgia and Circassia than with the Parsees; or that this sense of identity is the sole foundation upon which Chardin has constructed his theory.[29]

It is our good fortune that Chardin did not restrict himself solely to the observation of manners and customs. The sciences, along with political and religious institutions, also attracted his attention, and provided him with fascinating fodder for comparison with Europe. He explains the "Persian genius" for the sciences: "after the Christians of Europe, they are the most learned people in the world, without excepting the Chinese."[30]

They have a ready disposition to Sciences, as distinguished and as extensive as do we, excepting of the modern Systems & the discoveries of our Europe, which they do not know; this is not, however, so considerable as we might imagine, several *Theorems* being found in *Persian* and *Arab* books, though more obscurely, are presented in our country as new discoveries.[31]

All the fine reverence for Persian wisdom conceals a condescension which soon rises to the surface. After noting their "excellent disposition for study" and their progress, Chardin adds:

But their achievements would be much greater had they the excellent methods of our *Europe*, were they to apply themselves to only one *Discipline* at a time, were books available to them as cheaply as *Printing* makes them for us....[32]

Method. The specialization of knowledge. Here we come to the crux of the matter. We can recall that the only major weakness which Thévenot attributed to the Turks was of a similar nature:

The Turks are not drawn to the sciences; but they have their doctors of law.[33]

Chardin's and Thévenot's remarks are mutually illuminating. The peoples of the Orient possessed both knowledge and aptitudes in numerous fields (in law, but also in astrology and poetry, as Thévenot mentions). But something was missing: new sciences, and "modern systems" — precisely those things which, in the West, were in the process of becoming science itself, with all the "fine methods" and the compartmentalization that implies. We must not forget that in the classical age, the term "science" had a comprehensive meaning, covering a wide range of knowledge and talent (philosophy, poetry, etc.) and was not yet clearly distinguished from "art." But the imprecise use of language (by 20th century standards) did not deprive European travellers of a sense of being in the forefront. Something new had happened: observations on the Orientals' lack of method would have been simply inconceivable a century before. Europe had begun to consider itself "modern" with respect to the Orient. Beyond all other differences, beyond even the medieval religious anathema, the factor which cast the Oriental (including now the Turk) into "another world"[34] was quite precisely the awareness (though still unexplicit) of modernity.

Henceforth, everything could be marshalled for the confirmation and reinforcement of this alterity. The transformation into near-ironclad principals of the political observations of Machiavelli, Bodin and others on the Ottoman Empire, formulated a century before, should not surprise us. As with the Turks, the Persian despot's absolute, personal and arbitrary power, resting as it did exclusively upon military force, contrasted utterly with that of "these happy Lands of Europe where the authority of law guarantees the life and goods of all against violence of all kinds,"[35] wrote Chardin without batting an eyelid when, in his own country, the king could, on a whim, imprison any person indefinitely without trial. Thus was laid the groundwork for the debate over the question of "oriental despotism" launched by Montesquieu — to which we will return in due course.

Let us, for the moment, attempt to weigh the impact of these voyages, or rather, illustrate the novelty of the questions they raised — perhaps unbeknownst to their authors.

On the proper use of the Orient

We may well be unable to identify what constitutes "true" knowledge of the Other, to do more than enter into the subjectivity of the traveller and the group he represents, but these voyages pose the fundamental question of distance and difference (with all the prejudices they imply) and, as through an unalterable prism, the question of their use. Meaning, ultimately, the use of a flimsily constructed Orient.

Any voyage worthy of the name is, in a certain sense, a search for self. But the voyages which we are discussing here fulfill a well-defined collective function which goes far beyond the individual. I cannot hope to fathom Chardin's or Thévenot's personal motivations; I wish only to know what kind of generalized thirst their relations, of which their contemporaries seemed particularly fond, were intended to satisfy.

For a European of the 17th century, the "voyage to the Orient" (that which was undertaken physically, but primarily and far more frequently, that which he held in his hands) was almost consciously intended to confirm his own identity, here understood in a collective sense. To do so, one must travel toward difference, abolish physical distance the better to consolidate cultural distance, ascertain whether that distance would be favourable to the civilization which had invented it,[36] the better to certify that Europe was at the vanguard of the march of history; that it was, in a word, modern.

> ...Asia is not like our Europe," Chardin warns, "where what are called *Modes*, be they for Vestments or for Buildings, or for any other things [as we have seen him demonstrate in the case of science]. In the *Orient*, this is not so. All, in everything and everywhere, is constant.

Little has changed in the last two thousand years, he adds, with the exception of religion, "which is not greatly substantial."[37]

Europe thus validated its own vitality by travelling to an unvarying world which incarnated the past, which was the near and visible presence of the past.

This mind-set casts the question of bias in a new light. Though some set out on their journey intent on removing the blinders from their eyes, or felt the enchantment of having them fall away in the course of a journey, the fundamental aim of the voyage was to consolidate existing values and convictions. And what applied to authors applied doubly to readers. The Orientals might well have been revealed as good, generous, charitable, pious, poetic, gifted with no end of hidden qualities; one could even claim, in good faith, that they were being unfairly treated — but this was not the heart of the matter. The crux of the issue was that they were different. To be so, it was enough that they belonged to another age.

In his preface to *Bajazet*, Racine explains how he uses the Orient in the theatre:

> The distance in place makes up in some sort for the too great nearness in time. For ordinary folk treat in much the same way what is, so to speak, a thousand years from them and what is a thousand leagues away. This is what ensures us, for

example, that Turkish characters, however modern they may be, have dignity on our stage. They are looked upon as ancients. Their manners and customs are so different. We have so few points of contact with the princes and other persons who live in the Seraglio, that we regard them, as it were, as people who live in a different age from ours.[38]

The passage is remarkable (particularly for us as we read it in the light of our own concerns), and typical of the highly revelatory debate — already well underway by then — on the use of the Orient in literature. At the heart of the debate was the question of "local colour" which, in and for itself, foreshadowed the rise of the Orient as a source of the exotic. For Racine the debate was a specious one, though he had helped launch it when he affirmed in his first preface:

The main thing I was concerned with was not to alter any-thing in the manners or customs of the nation.[39]

It was an unfortunate sentence, which Racine deleted from the third preface. With good reason: contrary to what Pierre Martino[40] (whose analysis is adopted by Maxime Rodinson) appears to believe, Racine sought less to bring local colour to life than to establish distance, which he so masterfully explained in the previous passage. This passage, later added to his second preface, was the one which was retained. Let us re-read it attentively, in the knowledge that Racine had made a careful study of Turkey, and particularly that he had consulted Sir Paul Rycault's *The Present State of the Ottoman Empire*,[41] one of the most oft-consulted and most disparaging sources of information then available on the subject. In it, the ever cautious Racine avoids the pitfalls of biased information, taking pains not to judge Turkish society. He mistrusts the knowledge available to his contemporaries, and ultimately grounds the distance essential to his dramatic purposes upon what he knows to be the general view of the Turks then prevailing in France, that of "people who inhabit another century." Racine says, in essence, that Turkey belongs to the landscape in the same way as do the An-cients. In both instances, the distance he seeks to establish rests on ignorance of their daily reality; only mythical personages could possess the "dignity" with which he wishes to endow them. Ignorance thus became a source of respect for those whom we do not know.

With Molière, as opposed to Racine, ignorance was cause for mockery — in the *turqueries* offered to Monsieur Jourdain in the last act of the *Bourgeois gentilhomme*. But who was being mocked? The Turks or the French who, in their fascination with "local colour" are prepared to believe the moon is made of green cheese? Though diametrically opposed in desired effect (levity versus solemnity), these two stage images of the Turk partook of the same process: the use of the Other toward ends utterly unconnected with him. Turkey was in fashion[42] — that was enough: fashion which, in all its futility, entrapped Racine in the debate over local colour; fashion whose spread literature (literary fiction, and not only travel chronicles) was to encourage from the last quarter of the century on. The new literary infatuation with the Orient, which grew wider spread still in the following century, is well documented. For our purposes, suffice it to say that the Orient had become the stuff of diversion. It's use as exotica[43] had begun.

Significant though it may be, this relatively insubstantial use was of limited importance. Or, put more precisely (as we shall see in our discussion of the 18th century), its meaning derived from its political resonance.

Leibniz's venture into the political

The image of the Other was most fraught with consequence at the political level. Not only in the sense that failure to understand the Other could lead to diplomatic errors (as recounted in Chardin's account of the blunders of several of Louis XIV's ambassadors to the Sultan[44]), but because the image fuelled inordinate ambition or projects totally removed from real possibility.

One such project was the proposed expedition to Egypt devised by Leibniz for Louis XIV in 1672.[45] It was a curious undertaking, conceived in circumstances never entirely elucidated; a "grand design" of classic proportions, an amalgam of real knowledge and stereotypes dredged up from the depths of traditional Catholicism, propounding a scheme for conquest that harked back to Saint Louis and prefigured Napoleon. A full century ahead of its time, it marked the abortive debut of the Eastern Question.

Was this painstakingly elaborate venture taken seriously by those for whom it was designed? Some claim it was, but most remain sceptical: there is no evidence that Louis XIV was ever aware of the scheme. Advised by his ambassador to Mainz that an attempt was afoot to direct France's martial energies "against the infidels," Arnaud de Pomponne (Louis XIV's foreign minister) replied:

> I shall say nothing of these proposals for a holy war; for you well know that they ceased being the fashion after Saint Louis.[46]

The Crusader spirit is not the only target of Leibniz's fierce humour. But beneath the "Christian" ideological discourse used to justify the enterprise lie a resolutely modern resonance and logic. Whatever the motives of those who commissioned the study, the spirit in which it was conceived was among the most open minded of the day. But for us, the most compelling aspect of the affair was the political use made by the brilliant young Leibniz (he was only 26 at the time) of knowledge then available on the Orient, and on the Ottomans in particular. What was the significance of the enterprise he so ardently promoted?

In Leibniz's view the Orient must be treated sternly. For him, it was little more than a hunter's prey — and a considerable asset for the European prince who would be first to capture it. Egypt, in particular:

> It is the link, the gateway, the barrier, the key, the only possible entry point into two parts of the world, Asia and Africa. It is the place where contact is made, the common market of India, on the one hand, and Europe on the other.[47]

So much for considerations of the first order: the strategic and the economic. The second order was political and social, and here Leibniz postulated the success of his venture on a harsh judgement of Turkey, its manners and customs, its institutions and its techniques. While his intent may well have been to demonstrate that the Ottomans were incapable of defending Egypt, the ease of the enterprise alone could not fully explain either Leibniz's tone or relentlessness in describing the "undisputable (sic) decline of Turkey," whose military weakness he needed only prove.

> The state of the Empire is unknown even to the [Turkish] ministers themselves; the most simple notions of history and geography are utterly foreign to them; ignorance and barbarism everywhere rule. You will find aboard Turkish vessels not a single marine map upon which the bravest pilot would dare rely. It is, as it were, the homeland of darkness and barbarism; and the Sultan, himself thrust deep in ignorance, clings to his throne, in the midst of women and eunuchs, clothed in the robes of Sardanapalus.[48]

Leibniz's gloomy canvas contradicted not only Thévenot, but also Chardin, whose appreciation of the Porte's political sophistication covered the period ending the very year of the composition of the *Concillium* (1672) — a period of recovery which had followed a phase of decline and instability in Ottoman power. But the vestiges of this unfavourable phase alone did not explain Leibniz's harshness; his analysis was based on more than short-term considerations.

Egypt and Turkey will change. It is certain that the Turks, and first among them the Grand Vizier, will utilize all the forces at their avail to carry out a general reform. They have already learned our military arts...Are the Turks' heads not similar to our own?[49]

Perhaps the aim was to transmit a sense of urgency, lest the propitious moment might pass. But, come time to develop his thought on the transfer of knowledge Leibniz proved to be altogether more cautious over Turkish like-mindedness:

Though they [the Turks] be the dullest-witted of men, there are to be found a considerable number of renegades [Christians] who might easily instruct them in all the divine and human sciences in which the Christians are versed. All for which the Turks want is to apply themselves, and a strong will; and who can assure that they will always be wanting for these?[50]

Leibniz was not, strictly speaking, a racist (the Turks' incapacity was not genetic, but social). Still, the scope of his evaluation far exceeded short-term considerations; he was passing judgement on an entire civilization over the long term:

That one would be hard-put to encounter in the deserts of today the ancient populations of Asia and Greece, is a point upon which it would be pedantic to insist. ...Arts are not honoured; the inhabitants make no effort to improve cultivation of the land, nor do they attempt to build structures that might endure.[51]

The Orient was not simply neglected (by those who inhabited it as well as by those who governed it); it was not simply backward or immobile on the scale of progress: it had been stripped of its past, stripped of the dignity which Racine was, at that very moment, in search of. The Other was no longer an antinomy, hardly even an adversary; its existence, if it could be said to exist, was nebulous:

In one word, life in that country is as unbridled as a dream and has all the appearances of a play. Most of its inhabitants, like mushrooms sprung from the earth, know neither family nor friend; they live from day to day, not knowing what they seek or desire.[52]

Here the insolence of Leibniz's approach, which contrives to ignore the much more moderate accounts of the most reliable travellers, soars to delirious heights quite untypical of the Classical Age. The immoderation, the boundless contempt — in the image of the undertaking itself — seems to echo with the colonialist arrogance of the 19th century. Witness how much at ease Foucher de Careil, in his commentary on the *Concillium* two centuries later (1864), feels with the grand design, and with its guiding spirit:

> When Leibniz, in some of his finest pages, showed us 'the Constitution of the Turkish Empire, that motherland of barbarian shades, that prison of slaves ruled over by the son of a slave [followed by a long litany of quotations from Leibniz]', one might well ask if Leibniz had not been much more attuned to the question, and a part of that great historical current culminating in the final elimination of the Turkish race and the ceasing of this scandal of Ottoman power than court poets like Racine who, in his preface to Bajazet, fluttered with ecstasy over the pomp of oriental despotism...[53]

In this sense, Leibniz was undeniably a precursor, not of the Enlightenment, but of the century which was to follow. But he was also profoundly of his "classical"[54] age in certain aspects of his method and approach. His imperialist *realpolitik* was ever mindful that it must adopt the ideology underlying royal absolutism, the law which justified not only the king's power within the realm but legitimized any conquest he might undertake beyond the boundaries of Christendom in its name.

Leibniz exhorted Louis XIV to expand "the empire of the Savior from Egypt to the remotest nations of the earth."[55] But beneath the gilt and baroque ornament, divine right on a world scale was being propounded. The goal — unmistakably — was no longer to liberate the Holy Places from the infidel, but to establish the primacy of Christian Europe throughout the world. This was quite precisely the meaning of Bossuet's *Discours sur l'histoire universelle:* the divinely-inspired mission of Catholic Christendom was to achieve universality, to make the world, including its cradle, the Orient, its own.[56] The sense of appropriation, with regard to Egypt, found its most concrete possible expression in Bossuet:

> Now that the King's name is penetrating into the remotest corners of the earth, and that His Majesty is extending far and wide the researches he has ordered to be made for all that is fairest in Nature and in Art, would it not be a worthy object of this lofty curiosity to seek to lay bare the beauties

which lie buried in the deserts of the Thebaid and to enrich
the splendours of our buildings with all that ancient Egypt
can supply?[57]

European self-representation placed itself at the centre of the world,
giving order — if only intellectually — to all that surrounded it. Trapped in
the past, the Orient stood as hierarchical second in this well-ordered
representation. But its past had nothing in common with Antiquity, of
which the peoples of the Orient had been dispossessed. Henceforth Antiquity belonged to the West. For classical Europe not only gave order to the
space around it, but to history as well. Even though Europe lacked a
homogeneous, unified vision of the Orient, the Orient existed as a global,
unifying representation; an unblinking mirror at whose feet European
classicism had come to lay its certitudes.

In disturbing those certitudes, the 18th century threatened to shatter
the mirror. Once an object of contemplation, the Orient was to become an
object of debate, the raw-material of reflection.

THE ORIENT OF ENLIGHTENMENT

As an expression, "Orient of Enlightenment" is as attractive in its double
luminosity (*ex Oriente Lux*) as it is seductive in its ambiguity. Who, after all,
enlightens whom?

At first glance, the question may appear superfluous. The European
17th century sought enlightenment in the East less than it did the reflection
of its own splendour; the following century was little different. Still, in the
course of what Paul Hazard[58] has termed Europe's "crisis of consciousness"
between 1680 and 1715, mentalities had evolved, and with them the
European vision of the world. The "representation" was to continue, but its
universe had expanded and diversified, with the destabilization wrought
by expansion. Classical metaphysics retreated under the onslaught of a
"sceptical rationalism" more concerned with the concrete universe, and
more inclined to call its own explanations into question.[59]

Was this constructive scepticism not proof of a genuine opening to
the world? Would the birth of anthropology as a discipline distinct from
history and philosophy not lead to better understanding of the Other,
or would it lead merely to a more elaborate classification of peoples on
the civilizational scale? Where on this scale did the Mediterranean
stand? High indeed, say those who are inclined to view the Enlightenment as a kind of golden age of the European view of the region. Thus,
for Maxime Rodinson:

The 18th century saw the Muslim East through fraternal and understanding eyes.[60]

And Hichem Djaït adds:

Even the 20th century liberal critique of colonialism and imperialism has failed to reach the level of disinterestedness attained by the 18th.[61]

We will return later, with greater overall understanding, to the pertinence of this judgement. First we must ascertain what part of the Muslim Orient is being discussed. Are we talking about perceptions of the Muslim religion, or the perception of what could be termed the general state of affairs of the lands of the Mediterranean Orient? For the philosophers of the Enlightenment did not treat these two aspects of the Orient in the same way. On the one hand stood Islam-as-religion, and the history of its founding people; on the other, the political and social situation of the contemporary Orient.

Islam and its founding people: a sociology of religion

The Enlightenment's relative benevolence toward Islam was directed primarily toward religion. The speed and sweep of its initial success and the breath-taking grandeur of Arab civilization touched off a new curiosity about the circumstances of its birth, and about its founding people, in a century when heresy was no longer a matter of widespread concern. The reawakening of interest in Islam and in the Arabs marked the convergence of two distinct currents: the critical study of the historical and social foundations of religion, in which case the content of Islam was less dangerous than that of Christianity; and the rise of a taste for "Arab" literature as part of a broader literary fascination with Oriental settings and adventures.

We no longer need demonstrate that from the end of the 17th century on, the "oriental" taste had invaded virtually every form of literary expression. Complete with its inevitable fluctuations of taste, the vogue which was to cross pollinate almost the whole of the 18th century was given great impetus by the publication in Paris, in 1704, of the tales of *The Thousand and One Nights*, translated and presented by Antoine Galland. According to the translator, these fables demonstrated "how greatly the Arabs surpassed the other Nations in this manner of composition," a literary genre in which "nothing so beautiful has been beheld up until the present day in any Tongue." But above all they offered readers of both sexes an "Orient in the pure state," delivered to their door:

These [tales] must as well be pleasing in their description of the customs and the manners of the Orientals, of the ceremony of their Religion, the pagan and the Mahometan; all things are better exposed than in the Authors who have written of those things, and in the Relations of Travellers. All the Orientals, Persians, Tartars and Indians, can be clearly distinguished, and appear herein as they truly are, from the Sovereign ruler to the persons of basest condition. Thus, without having to incur the fatigue of seeking out these Peoples in their Lands, the Reader will encounter herein the pleasure of seeing them going about their daily lives, and of hearing them speak. Care has been taken to conserve their characters, not to depart from their expressions and sentiments; we have not strayed from the text but when proper decorum did not permit us to follow it closely.[62]

Galland's Orient was well adapted to the tastes of his century, which in turn was one of the keys to its success. For Europe he was more than convincing; he created the basic recipe for the literary Orient. But at the same time, the The Thousand and One Nights restored the reputation of the Arabs, and delivered them from centuries of oblivion.

European specialists in Arabic and the study of the Arab world had never completely vanished; but, from the early 14th century onward the influence of Arabo-Islamic culture in Europe had ebbed (leaving in its wake a vast alluvium whose origins Europeans had increasingly forgotten). It was only in the 18th century that a certain section of the intelligentsia rediscovered not so much Islam's contribution to Europe as the history of the Arabs themselves.[63] The discovery was a timely one, coinciding with a radical renewal of the approach to religion in general, and to Islam in particular.

From the 16th century (and even before, among extremely open minds), the religious polemic with Islam had ceased to be one of Europe's primary oriental concerns. Its themes simply persisted, repeating an earlier motif, this time as setting for discourse on the Turks. The following century differed only slightly: not only did the usual negative clichés rear their insistent heads whenever the subject of the Qur'an and Mahomet arose; religion, as we have observed in both Leibniz and Bossuet, had returned in another guise, as the ideology of European world supremacy. This ideology, in its religious, Christian, and particularly Catholic aspects, was to be rejected by the "enlightened" 18th century. The authoritarian use of religion became incompatible with the belated triumph of the ideas of Spinoza. As Cassirer summarizes:

Henceforth, religion is not to be a matter of mere receptivity;
it is to originate from, and to be chiefly characterized by,
activity. Man is not merely seized and overwhelmed by this
activity as by a strange power, but he in turn influences and
shapes activity from within. It is not supernatural power nor
divine grace which produces religious conviction of man; he
himself must rise to and maintain it.[64]

'Moral conscience' henceforth prevailed over Scripture to such a degree
that all holy writ could and must henceforth be studied critically, whatever
its origin: the Bible contained no fewer "fables" than did the Qur'an.

One of the pioneers, Richard Simon, in his *Histoire critique de la Créance
& des Coutûmes des Nations du Levant* (1684), inveighs against the very
notion of heresy, both within Christendom and without. Not only were
"the major portion of the Heresies which are ascribed to the Peoples of the
Levant without substance";[65] Islam itself was but a variant of the same
great faith, "hardly more than a combination of the religions of the Jews
and the Christians" — the burden being upon the Muslims to admit that
their belief "is beholden to the Jews and the Christians for all the good that
it contains."[66] Since the Mahometans "speak so well of God & of His
perfections," it was no longer necessary to make their prophet out to be an
impostor. Mahomet became a clever man "obliged to don the mantle of
Emissary of God"[67] to transmit his message.

But Simon's message was soon to encounter problems of its own. Ten
years later Pierre Bayle's *Dictionnaire historique et critique,*[68] under the entry
"Mahomet," faintly praised Simon's book while describing the founder of
Islam in the most insulting terms. On the one hand, "this infamous impostor swiftly inundated with his false dogmas a vast number of provinces,"
and on the other, added Bayle, "I cannot understand in whatsoever manner
this false prophet has departed from the Moral of the Gospel," none of
which stopped him from retelling "the impertinent lies which have been
uttered regarding Mahomet."[69]

Old clichés die hard. But still, the viewpoint had shifted. Islam was no
longer condemned *a priori*, nor was it spared the critical process which had
begun to scrutinize the historical origins and anthropological foundations
of religion. Quite the contrary. Seen in this light Islam became an ideal
testing ground, simultaneously close to Christianity and yet without
danger, as the use to which it was put by Boulainvilliers and Voltaire was
to indicate.

Boulainvilliers, along with Ockley in England and Reland in Holland,
was one of the main contributors to the reversal of the negative image of
Islam and of Mohammed in Europe, and to the rehabilitation of the Arabs
in history. For Boulainvilliers, the Prophet could not be understood apart

from his people, nor apart from the historical circumstances of its unification. His *Life of Mahomet*[70] was a "modern" approach to the history of the Arabs, as well as a rudimentary attempt to construct a sociology of religion. But there was more to his book than an attempt to rehabilitate; it had a critical dimension, often quite lively in tone, which contrived even to reinforce some of the most negative clichés about the Orient and the Arabs.

Islam as cataclysm and fanaticism

Boulainvilliers could well acknowledge that the Arabs were "an ingenious People, generous, open, brave, wise and free from those untamable passions which the irregularity of the seasons infuse into the rugged breasts of the Northern nations."[71] But, though the "Arab Nation, solitary, dispersed in the Desert & so long unknown to the rest of the world, had never been without qualities,"

> ...yet when they issued from their profound retreats, and providence called them, in their turn, to govern the world, they betrayed several enormous vices; which roused against them all whom they did not immediately subdue, which rendered their name odious and detestable, as well as terrible; and which wold not allow the least notice to be taken of their virtues ...I speak of that hardness of heart attributed to them; the necessary result of their constitution, and of that solitary life to which they are accustomed from their tender years...of that barbarous scorn for all those things which are the object of other peoples' affection and esteem...of that inflexible cruelty which transported them to cut off from the rest of the earth one half of its inhabitants, and therefore the residue of all that learning which mankind had treasured up by long and painful experience.[72]

From his first pages Boulainvilliers sets out his method of incessant alternation between best and worst. He begins with a paradox shaped around a comparison between the barbarian invasions of the Western Roman Empire and the Arab conquests of the first century of the Muslim era. Though they were "spiritual, generous, disinterested, courageous and prudent," quite the opposite of the Germanic barbarians, the Arabs brought more misfortune upon the world, more indolence and ignorance. The reason? "Seiz'd with a religious enthusiasm, they were all at once excited to so cruel a conduct as it were by enchantment; an enthusiasm founded upon the high estimation which they had conceived of that book, wherein their religion is contained, which they assert to be the sublimest effect of the Divine Wisdom, as it contains the eternal truths which GOD himself was pleased to reveal to men...."[73]

The term "fanaticism"[74] made its first appearance in French around 1688; it had previously appeared in Simon Ockley,[75] source of many of Boulainvilliers' borrowings. It was a new word, not even a part of the traditional "Mahometan" discourse, even as an adjective. The cruelty for which Europeans reproached the Saracens and Turks was not generally represented as an inevitable consequence of their religion, which numerous Christian observers had characterized as tolerant. In religious terms, as we know all too well, falsehood, heresy, imposture, absurdity and even lewdness were the attributes traditionally associated with the image of the Muslim — the very stereotypes against which Boulainvilliers felt obliged to militate, and whose presence he deplored in Ockley's work, despite the Englishman's reputation for objectivity and seriousness.[76]

Neither the Arabs nor their history,were without qualities. But both suffered from extremes. Mahomed was not so much a lewd impostor as a leader of men, an Alexander or a more virtuous Caesar[77] invested with a historical mission — which even Bossuet might have found acceptable (I maintain) — as had been many Christians before him. The Prophet, Boulainvilliers asserts, was ultimately the instrument of God: he confounded the dissolute and corrupt Christians of the Orient, overthrew the remains of Greco-Roman paganism, subjugated the Persians, thus spreading "the knowledge of the unity of God from India to Spain, and to suppress every other worship besides his own."[78] In so doing he also raised up the Arab peoples which he had united, conferring on them a strong, unitary identity in the face of outside pressure.[79] A "sociological" explanation of certain traits of the Muslim religion (dietary laws, ablutions, circumcision, etc.) follows: Boulainvilliers demonstrates that nothing is arbitrary, that Islam's prescriptions, including matters involving the "plurality of women,"[80] are dictated by its human and physical circumstances.

Islam, then, was the instrument of a universal will and of a national destiny: this double mission suggested to Boulainvilliers that both Oriental and Western society contribute to the universal, toward which they converge along different paths. Nothing found in Islam fundamentally contradicted Christianity.[81] But caution is nonetheless in order: this convergence had little to do with Postel's Christian universalism, and even less with 20th century ecumenism. The aim was not to "repossess" the Other, but to respect or, at least, accept its difference — without the slightest hint of subservience. I have difficulty understanding how Maxime Rodinson can describe *La Vie de Mahomed* as "apologetic."[82] Boulainvilliers' attitude, on the contrary (and at the risk of seeming violently contradictory), keeps the Other at a distance. Despite the Arab contribution to world history, whole areas of their historical accomplishment are brutally condemned as "...the utter extirpation of arts, sciences and learning from the face of the earth, by a people, who defacing every monument and burning every library, declar'd their intent to abolish the very memorial of all former generations."[83] The excessiveness of the untruth reflects one of the greatest and most enduring obsessions of the Western view of the Muslim Orient: Islam as historical cataclysm. Despite the empathy which informs his efforts, the Orient, for Boulainvilliers, was the product of a radical rift, born of Islamic expansion. The rift was inevitable, and from the Arab standpoint, desirable — but Boulainvilliers in his virulence condemned it as irreparable; proof of how "GOD is pleas'd sometimes to humble wisdom with an apparent folly, of which we should never have had any notion unless we had seen the success of events."[84]

Was this the expression of a new sensibility, under which cultures and civilizations would have no choice but to tolerate one another without necessarily understanding one another? Perhaps. What seems to me less uncertain is that Boulainvilliers' two contradictory appreciations — of the Arabs and the beginnings of Islam — partook of the same desire for tolerance, as if to say: "Behold what intolerance has done; be then tolerant enough to recognize the greatness of those who were its instrument!" In the final analysis, The Life of Mahomet may well have been part pretext for a discourse on intolerance of whatever source; its subject, ostensibly the ardour of the first Muslims, may well have been the fanaticism at work in the Christian Church — or Churches.

What was probable with Boulainvilliers becomes unmistakable with Voltaire, though the way in which the author of *Candide* used Islam was determined by the capriciousness of his moods and tailored to fit his adversaries. In a thesis entitled *Voltaire et l'Islam*, Javad Hadidi attempts to arrange the philosopher's contradictory judgements on Islam in a chronologically coherent progression from the negative to the positive.[85] From his stormy "first encounter" with the Muslim religion (particularly the tragedy *Mahomet*, written in 1741), through his "essay on the true knowledge of Islam" (in *Essai sur les moeurs*, 1756), Voltaire eventually came to admire Mahomet, and to declare himself "for Mahometism against Christianity" — a praiseworthy attempt to recon-cile Voltarian progressivism and tolerance of spirit with a generous vision of the Other. But Voltaire's view of Islam and of the Arabs did not follow a steadily ascending curve. As we shall see, it was in a state of constant flux.

Never was the great polemicist to be as disparaging as in *Le Fanatisme, ou Mahomet le prophète*, a tragedy in which the eponymous protagonist manipulates the religious ardour which inspires him to have one of his zealous acolytes kill a rival in love:

Mahomet: ...those who reason are not oft prone to believe; thy part is to obey....

Seid: It is the voice of God that speaks in Mahomet; command, and I obey.[86]

Here Mahomet is, put bluntly, a despicable character. Voltaire's aim was certainly not to use an imagined intrigue to establish the historical verity of his protagonist. The stage prophet bodies forth violence, treachery and lasciviousness the better to allow the dramatist to inveigh against sectarianism and religious fanaticism, irrespective of origin, and particularly of the Christian variety. But the image selected both to mask and to represent this object was no casual choice: Voltaire relied on the centuries-long disparagement of the Prophet in the Christian imagination as a means of sidestepping reprisals from the Church — a telling commentary on the respectful use of the Other who, as such, counts for nothing.

We should have been surprised to find the pen of the historian and philosopher less acid. Taken from *Essai sur les moeurs et l'esprit des nations*, an historical portrait of peoples and civilizations through which Voltaire aspired to establish progress in human evolution, his judgement on Mahomet can be well summarized in this striking passage:

Most probably Mahomet, like all enthusiasts, violently taken with his ideas, poured them forth in good faith, fortifying them with his reveries, deceived himself whilst deceiving others, and came finally, through the necessary deceits, to espouse a doctrine which he believed to be good.[87]

But eight years later, in his *Dictionnaire philosophique portatif* (1764), the philosopher contended that Mahomet "...feigned revelations, he uttered predictions; he gained credit with his own family, which was perhaps the most difficult part of his enterprise."[88] His view of the Qur'an likewise fluctuated.

We have imputed to the Koran a great number of foolish things which it never contained (and to rehabilitate, specifically, its image of women)... Still, his Koran is a collection of ridiculous revelations and vague and incoherent practices combined with laws that were very good for the country in which he lived. ...This tedious book is, nevertheless, said to be a very fine production, at least by the Arabs, who assert that it is written with an elegance and purity that no later work has equalled.[89]

Voltaire cheerfully praises the Arabs themselves ("extraordinary generosities which lift up the soul," "hospitality," "clemency," "liberality") particularly to contrast them with the Hebrews, "that atrocious nation," "enemy of the Human race."[90] But above all, he recognizes that "from the second century of the hegira, the Arabs become the preceptors of Europe in science and the arts, though their Law would seem to have been the enemy of the arts,"[91] and attacks the widespread idea (which has some currency even today) of Islam propagated by force of arms: "it was by their enthusiasm, by their persuasion and, primarily by the example of the victors, which held such power over the vanquished."[92] But this did not inhibit him from remarking derisively:

> In vain does the Count de Boulainvilliers, who had some respect for Mahomet, extol the Arabs. Notwithstanding all his boastings, they were a nation of bandits.[93]

A nation of bandits who accomplished great things, who were themselves the bearers of an upsurge of civilization all too brief, alas, for inclusion in the annals of the "four happy ages" of the human spirit:[94]

> The Arabs brought their refinements upon Asia, Africa and part of Spain until they were subjugated in turn by the Turks, and, finally, expelled by the Spanish; then ignorance covered all those beautiful regions of the earth; harsh and sombre manners made rude the human race from Baghdad to Rome.[95]

Ultimately, praiseworthiness for Voltaire, as for Boulainvilliers, seems to have depended on the antiquity of the object being observed. Historical distance allowed him to view the Arab adventure, long over, as a brilliant feat. "I have accommodated my style to the humour of the people of whom I write," Simon Ockley had earlier written. "To write of men in their circumstances, who were all humorists, bigots and enthusiasts, in the same style as becomes the sedateness and gravity of the Greeks and Romans, would be most unsuitable and unnatural."[96] To each people his own style: the history of the Other (the Greeks and the Romans belong to us) became a kind of preparatory course in differentiation, which forbade anything resembling preconceptions. "What we find in them to laugh at is the difference of their manners. But this is but a childish reason, and the very same which makes ignorants laugh at scholars," adds Ockley.[97] It had become possible to appreciate the finer qualities of the Arabs, and at the same time to deplore the devastation wrought by their fanaticism. The condemnation of commonplaces — in the manner of Ockley, Boulainvilliers and Voltaire — might well have proved the best way to affirm the truth of their vision, and make Arab fanaticism all the more real. Similarly, the benevolence with which the past had now been illuminated[98] — clear evidence of objectivity — became a qualification for judging the present and extolling the Arabs, the better to censure those who had "subjugated" them and who loomed still before our gates: the Other, the Turk.

The same stratagem could equally be applied to Islam. The religion of Mahomet might well be partially rehabilitated in terms of its origins and its fundamentals — making of it a legitimate expression of faith — but it could be severely judged on its visible, contemporary effects. The prophet was no longer a heretic, the Qur'an no longer a compendium of nonsensicalness, but "this book, governing with despotic sway the whole of northern Africa, from Mount Atlas to the desert of Barca, the whole of Egypt."[99] The use of the term "despotic" was hardly fortuitous: it formed an integral part of one of the 18th century's central polemics — the issue of despotism — with the Orient as living evidence.

The Orient of the despot

In the 18th century despotism, far more than fanaticism, carried on the hoary tradition of prejudice against Islam. Mahometanism, meanwhile, had become all but obscured by the broader concept of the Orient, of which it remained an important but not the sole component. A transfer from religious sectarianism to political criticism had taken place.

The process had begun in the 16th century with Machiavelli and Bodin. The Florentine had differentiated, without normative intent, between the solitary power vested in the Grand Turk by his army (the Janissary corps) and that exercised by the French monarchy in conjunction with, or in opposition to, the nobility which it could neither dominate nor destroy.[100] Bodin was later to define this form of government as a "ruled" or "royal" monarchy, as "legitimate," and "most excellent" in contrast to the "despotic monarchy" exemplified by the Ottomans, "in which the prince is lord and master of both the possessions and the persons of his subjects by right of conquest in a just war; he governs his subjects as absolutely as the head of a household governs his slaves."[101] It was this paternal quality which distinguished the lord from the tyrant, an outlaw whose illegitimate power was the worst possible. The Turkish despotic regime stood at the midpoint on the scale of values, a respectable place which reflected the image of the Ottoman Empire, whose power still commanded respect.

The 18th century political thinker who made the greatest contribution to propagating the idea of "oriental despotism" had read his Bodin well. His name was Montesquieu. During the one and one half centuries which separated *L'esprit des lois* from *La République*, the prestige and relative influence of the Porte in international affairs had steadily declined. The trend was reflected in political thought on the Orient. Bodin's carefully graduated scale gave way to radical antinomy: despotic power, the hallmark of the Orient, emerged as the antithesis of the power of moderation, as epitomized by Europe. The coupling of Orient and Occident had assumed a general political form. Though neither definitive nor complete in the historical context of the western view, this form was fundamentally modern, a socio-cultural opposition which had outstripped mere institutional difference. Henceforth the notion of despotism was to form the axis around which the image of the Other would revolve, discovering its principal function as it went.

Montesquieu was central to this construct, though the question hardly exhausted his immense verbal energy — but that is not our concern here. Montesquieu correlated, constructed, and explained as he went, marshalling and integrating scattered fragments of oriental despotism drawn from the accounts of travel and other works on the Orient published during the century before him. The notion of despotism lent shape and polarity to a significant part of his examination of climate and power. The matter of despotism had infiltrated the novelistic structure of his *Persian Letters* even before the publication of *L'esprit des lois.*. Voltaire, his contemporary Anquetil-Duperron, and in our day, Alain Grosrichard and Karl Wittfogel,[102] have thoroughly enough analyzed what can be called the theory of oriental despotism in Montesquieu that we need not go back over the same ground. But we would do well to appreciate its significance.

If we are to judge by the stir caused by the *Persian Letters* and by the reputation for objectivity and levelheadedness enjoyed by *L'esprit des lois* — despite the weaknesses which were quickly identified — that significance was considerable. "I have not drawn my principles from my prejudices, but from the nature of things," Montesquieu asserts, and then adds: "I write not to censure that which is found in any country."[103] More than mere rhetorical precaution (we must not forget that *L'esprit des lois* was placed on the Index in 1751), this was Montesquieu's claim to impartiality: the author's assessments of oriental societies and regimes (among others) flowed from the "nature of things," not from his observational vantage point.

Montesquieu was far from insensitive to the question of vantage point. Did the *Persian Letters* not represent an audacious role reversal, a lesson in social relativity? A blow to the navel-gazing of classicism, another world's view of Europe? Perhaps, but they were more representative still of a literary genre which had already proven its worth; Montesquieu's letter writers are as Persian as the protagonists of *Bajazet* were Turkish; Usbek is more the precursor of "Rameau's Nephew" than the bearer of tidings from Isphahan. But at the same time he *represents* his country; he *is* the

Occident's Orient. It is a classic case of double identity: a Frenchman scrutinizing France from his perch on Sirius, and an imaginary Persian fretting over his harem from afar. But in addition to the rapidly apparent duality of his character, Usbek fulfils a third function, assumes a third viewpoint, which allows the reader to approach the Orient from the east. On his way to a Europe which he has never seen, Usbek happens upon Turkey. We encounter this incongruous observation:

> While the other nations of Europe are every day growing more polished, these people remain in their former ignorance.[104]

What extraordinary clairvoyance from a man who was to declare twelve letters later, upon his first confrontation with Europe: "I am beginning to come out from behind the clouds that covered my eyes in the land of my birth."[105] Montesquieu had no fear of contradicting the logic of his own narrative structure to conjure up two distinct Orients. One was superior, and more distant, because of its receptivity to the illumination of the West, and because of its ability to anticipate that receptivity in order to pass judgement on its Ottoman neighbour. The other was inferior: the neighbour to be justly condemned for his ignorance, a prisoner of intellectual inertia. There was nothing gratuitous about this coupling: while of the Orient, by virtue of its despotic system, Persia was presented as a possible advance post of Europe in Asia. Fantastic though the idea might have been, it allowed the Orient to be turned against itself, and confirmed, through that Orient which could grasp it and against that Orient which could not, the European Enlightenment's universality and self-evidence. That the former was Persian and the latter Turkish made little difference; but the choice had the effect of designating the Ottoman Empire as a corpse, a geopolitical obstacle to the communication of culture and meaning, to the spread of Western ideas. There is no evidence that Montesquieu deliberately wished to transmit this specific image: what is at work here is primarily the unconscious. But it is difficult not to read his work as a precursor of Western theses on the closing off of the Mediterranean by Ottoman power. In any case, the dualist Orient of the *Persian Letters* justified both the interest shown it, and the objections it provoked. Its function was both that of mirror and of foil.

Such, too, was the double function of oriental despotism: to illuminate and to intimidate. To illuminate the despotic potentiality of the western monarchies; and to intimidate by displaying despotism in its most perfect, most odious form. Present though totally foreign, despotism was the Europe's domestic Orient, a model of monstrosity and a timely warning, a threat to be averted; but at the same time, it was the European self,

half-consciously travestied through the Other, a flagrant misappropria-
tion. Voltaire was not mistaken; in taking the opposing view he defended
neither the Orient nor the Turks, but the absolutism of Louis XIV and his
attempts to bring the nobility into line. Montesquieu, he suspected, wished
to see noble privilege reestablished. The Orient and oriental despotism
thus became the subject of a debate internal to the West, having little
connection with the reality of Turkish or Persian power. Even so, despite
the flagrant impertinence of the concept which Montesquieu made
fashionable, oriental despotism, later relabelled as "totalitarianism," was to
be used down to our day to assail the Other, using a terrifying portrait of it
to divert attention from our own problems.[106]

Oriental despotism posed more than the question of its use in
western political thought. An entire vision of the Orient, and of its place
in history, hung in the balance. For the author of *L'esprit des lois*,
despotism corresponded to a profound and immutable reality, that of the
Orient. It was not (contrary to Voltaire's claims) a perversion of monarchical power, but the very form of power in the Orient. Even today it has
been asserted without even a hint of irony that Montesquieu provides
"the rare example of an advocate of tolerance who does not condemn
persecution, but painstakingly explains how it can take place."[107] The
ethnocentrism which is here voiced with such self-assurance (two centuries later) perfectly epitomizes Montesquieu's mind-set. Far be it from
him to pass judgement. He merely explains. So well, in fact, that
despotism seems as inevitable as the weather. In Book XVII of *L'esprit des
lois* , we learn that "we ought not...to be astonished that the effeminacy
of the people in hot climates has almost always rendered them slaves;
and that the bravery of those in cold climates has enabled them to maintain their liberties. This is an effect which springs from natural
causes."[108] Bodin and Aristotle revisited! But Montesquieu had surpassed
his masters, concluding, after a long discursion on the climate of Asia,
that "power in Asia ought, then, to be always despotic," where "there
reigns...a servile spirit."[109] So imperious was the necessity, that any attempt to do something about it would be ill-advised.

> It is a capital maxim, that the manners and customs of a
> despotic empire ought never to be changed; for nothing
> would more speedily produce a revolution.[110]

What could have been more tolerant than a "natural" explanation which
would excuse everything, while prudently suggesting that the Orient be
left to huddle in its servitude and millennia-long stagnation... What would
have been personally intolerable was tolerated in the Other, who was
destined by nature to remain what it had always been. The antinomic

image of the servile Orient — ignorant and beyond the redemption of the Enlightenment — was thenceforth frozen, as was Asia itself.

Though Voltaire confessed to loathing the Turks "as tyrants of women and foes of the arts,"[111] he inveighed against the "calumnies" to which they were subjected. Nor did he hesitate to heap ridicule on Montesquieu's precious theory of climate. But his polemics were motivated more by a concern for method than by the desire to rehabilitate the peoples of Asia. "We should take great care how general propositions escape us,"[112] he concluded, having shown how poorly the climatic principals of *L'esprit des lois* apply to the Arabs. Though Voltaire rejected every form of determinism, and, more important, every form of *a priori* disdain, he and Montesquieu converged at that point where the Orient and the West were placed in mutual perspective:

> In short, of whatever civilized people of Asia we make mention, we may say this — they have gone before us, and we have surpassed them.[113]

Progress exists; Europe is the proof.

Anquetil-Duperron was one of the rare authors to have systematically rejected the dominant 18th century view of the Orient, and to have illustrated the inanity of the concept of despotism. Though his attempts to politically rehabilitate the Orient had little impact beyond a small erudite circle, they merit mention: not simply because of their exceptional quality, but because Anquetil-Duperron was one of the pioneers of learned Orientalism; and because this specialized branch of Western learning today stands accused — not without justification — of having perpetuated and sheltered by its scientific authority an image which, for all its intellectual refinement, remains profoundly disparaging toward the Orient.[114] The man who introduced to Europe the *Avesta* of the Zorastrians and the *Upanishads* of the Hindus, also took up the defense of Ottoman and Persian political institutions in his study of *Législation orientale*.[115] Such legislation, which rulers were bound to respect, did exist as did private property. European observers had abusively generalized the transgressions common to other governments into an arbitrary, typically oriental system: "that which must justly be reproached" in the behaviour of the rulers of the Orient were "those abuses of authority recognized by the princes themselves, and by their subjects."[116] In a display of honesty rare even in the relative openness and tolerance of the 18th century, Anquetil-Duperron went to considerable pains to adopt the self-image of the Other. And the Other had proved capable of looking upon himself with a critical eye. It was a simple reminder, but its impact was striking, almost explosive: the object, the Orient, had, for a brief instant, become a subject, instead of nature's plaything it had become the responsible creator of its own history.[117] Instead of transforming those things which they recognized as qualities in themselves into faults in the Other (what in Europe might be dismissed as political cleverness was seen in the Orient as deceit), Europeans might well learn from the Orientals in such fields as private law and certain aspects of public administration.

Beyond his critique of the concept of oriental despotism, Anquetil-Duperron issued a more generalized warning about Europe's view of other peoples. The terminology which condemned them to barbarism must be discarded, and "presumptuous science" must be mistrusted. It was almost as though he had been able to see where the reification of the Other was to lead, and how the theory of despotism would come to be used: as justification for the conduct of Europeans who "believe they are, in some manner, conforming to the established order in these lands by imitating the rapacity and the cruelty of many Indian Commanders."[118] His voice both anticipated and disavowed the scientific arrogance of the white man, and — though isolated in its own century — rang out against the spirit of the era to come.

The Enlightenment witnessed the first stirrings of a sociology of the Mediterranean Orient. No longer was it enough to relate and compile; now rational causes must be sought in geography, in history, in institutions. The Orient would henceforth be explained in terms of its difference and its immobility, and assigned a place in history as an instant of progress, or rather as the vestige of a bygone age, in a spirit which prefigured Hegel, Marx and the inexhaustible controversy over the Asiatic mode of production.

To the extent that it can be described in its generality, the Enlightenment's view of the Orient contemporaneous to it was neither ill-intentioned nor systematically hostile. But it was by no means as fraternal as some have claimed. Admiration of the Orient was almost exclusively for its past, upon which the West would often draw. Rarely was it for the present, where occasional benevolence barely concealed a strongly condescending tone. The Western attitude could be best described as an absence of sharp aggressiveness and irrational fear. Europe looked upon the Orient with the lofty assurance of someone who felt neither threatened nor threatening. Its relative openness helped eliminate — if only provisionally — old biases (particularly from religious sources). But it also solidified others, this time casting them in the cement of reason — the reason of the West which seemed to itself to be the only reason possible.

For as Europe looked out upon the world, it was looked upon only by itself. The searchlight beams of the Enlightenment played unhindered across the continents. Conscious of its superiority, Europe made an act of faith toward science. Whatever self-doubts Europe might have avowed were quickly incorporated into the internal workings of reason. For

Europe, reason now constituted the bedrock of its superiority over other civilizations; its intellectual preeminence. But self-doubt only helped pave the way to self-mastery. In the best of hypotheses, the Other's greatest contribution was this: to force one to regard oneself more closely. Here lay the source of the century's "luminosity," with all the truth and illusion the word contains. The Other was not (as it had been, and was again to become) a mere target, an avenue of evasion, a release. Diversion, exoticism, and amusement, yes. But not flight from self. Far more than exoticism, the Orient was a prismatic loop transporting one back to oneself. The Orient was, in the hands of those who wielded it, an optical instrument: a lens, a mirror for examining oneself at a distance, from other angles (or simply for avoiding censorship). And, necessarily, an object: the Orient itself never questioned the West; never called it into question; it merely reflected or filtered those questions which Europe asked of itself.

Only this intellectual use of the Orient could explain the contradictory images which it aroused in the selfsame persons, and which it stimulated within a system of thought like Voltaire's. The detour by way of the Other was at once a source of strength and a source of stimulation for the West. The intellectuals of the Enlightenment were able to draw upon it intelligently, and inflict the least possible damage upon the peoples of the non-colonized Orient. In this sense, the Enlightenment view of the Orient was not an entirely negative one. But it contained the germ of the enormous misunderstanding which still burdens us today. Lacking consciousness of its true function, it believed that it could visualize the Other in its immutable reality, in its essence. The opening of minds to the outside world was thus accompanied by an illusion pregnant with denigration: the naive belief that the process of exploration would lead to knowledge of the Other. This knowledge would be true because it would be rational.

NOTES

1. Foucault, Michel, *The Order of Things,* op. cit., See also Ernst Cassirer's classic, *The Philosophy of Enlightenment.* Translated by F.C.A. Koelln and J.P. Pettegrove, Princeton, Princeton University Press, 1951. "...Thus it is evident that, if we compare the thought of the 18th century with that of the 17th, there is no real chasm anywhere separating the two periods. The new ideal of knowledge develops steadily and consistently from the pre-suppositions which the logic and the theory of knowledge of the 17th century — especially in the works of Descartes and Leibniz — had established." (p.22).
2. Hazard, Paul, *European Mind, 1680-1715.* Translated by Lewis May, London, Hollis and Carter, 1953.
3. Among all *European* cultures, that of France probably — even today — has the greatest pretensions to universality, much more than that of England.

4. Bodin, Jean, *Method,* op. cit., p.116.
5. Saïd, Edward, *Orientalism,* op. cit. p.40. "Knowledge of the Orient, because generated out of strength, in a sense *creates* the Orient, the Oriental and his world.
6. Above all in relation to the great Hispano-Turkish confrontation in the Mediterranean during the 16th century, and even though the struggle against the corsairs continued. But the peace affected only Western Europe: neither Austria nor Russia remained long at peace with their Ottoman neighbour.
7. De Rougemont, Denis, *Vingt-huit siècles d'Europe,* op. cit., p.91. A work to which I owe several of the above considerations.
8. Ibid.
9. It must be remembered that "capitulation" here means "chapter" (as in a treaty, or document).
10. Thévenot, Jean, *Voyage du Levant.* Introduction, choix de textes et notes de Stéphanie Yerasimos, Paris, FM/La Découverte, 1980, p.5.
11. Pitton de Tournefort, *Relations d'un voyage du Levant,* fait par order du Roy A Paris, de l'imprimerie Royale, 1717, p.1.
12. Thévenot, op. cit., p.9. (Commentary by S. Yerasimos, who underlines Thévenot's "honesty" and "great prudence": "his name is often encountered in the footnotes of later works on the Orient."
13. Ibid., p.88-89.
14. Ibid., p.112-113.
15. Ibid., p.128-129.
16. Desmet-Grégoire, Hélène, *Apports et influences du monde turco-ottoman en France au XVIII siècle,* Aix-en-Provence, Thèse de doctorat du 3e cycle, 1978, p.497.
17. Thévenot, op. cit. p.130-131. Note that the Turks' disregard for the Christian nations is compatible with their tolerance toward the non-Muslim communities of the Empire.
18. Ibid., p.295.
19. Turcologist Robert Mantran has assured me that as of this writing (1983), no source permits us to speculate on the Ottoman opinion of the Egyptians in the 17th century.
20. Ibid., p.302. In his introduction, Yerasimos describes the epic struggles between natives of Aix and Marseilles for control of the French consulate at Cairo, precisely at the time of Thévenot's visit.
21. Ibid., p.298.
22. Travernier, Jean-Baptiste, *Les six voyages de Jean-Baptiste Tavernier, chevalier baron d'Aubonne,* qu'il a fait en Turquie, en Perse et aux Indes (etc.) à Paris, chez Gervais Cloutier, 1682, nouvelle édition, revue, corrigée et augmentée; et Chardin, *Voyages de Monsieur le chevalier Chardin en Perse et autres lieux d'Orient,* à Amsterdam, chez Jean-Louis de Lorme, 1711 [Chardin, Sir John, *Sir John Chardin's Travels in Persia,* London, Argonaut Press, 1927.]
23. Tavernier, op. cit., p.1.
24. Ibid., p.523,565.
25. Ibid., p.575.
26. Chardin, *Travels in Persia,* op. cit., p.185.
27. Ibid., p.186.
28. Ibid., p.184.
29. Another indication is the disproportionate space Chardin allots to describe Mingrelia, or Colchide, a land of Christian tradition bordering Georgia (Chardin, op. cit.).
30. Chardin, op. cit., Vol.II [French original]. p.93-94.
31. Ibid., p.95.
32. Ibid., p.101
33. Thévenot, op. cit., p.84.

34. Chardin, op. cit., Vol.I, p.II (Chardin claims to "examine with greatest care all that which warrants the attention of our Europe, in relation to a great and vast Land which we may name as another World, both in its distance, and in the diversity of its Customs and Manners.")
35. Chardin, op. cit., Vol. II, p.212.
36. It can only be an invention. Outside the Western mentality there exists no universal scale against which human progress can be measured.
37. Chardin, op. cit., Vol. I, p.V.
38. Racine, Jean, *Complete Plays*, Translated by S. Solomon, New York Random House, 1967, Second Preface to Bajazet, p.5.
39. Racine, Jean, op. cit., First Preface, p.3.
40. Martino, Pierre, *L'Orient dans la littérature française au XVII et au XVIII siècle*, Paris, Hachette, 1906, p.194. Martino asserts that local colour can be found in Bajazet (which seems to me insupportable); see also Rodinson, op. cit. p.39.
41. Rycaut, Sir Paul, *The Present State of the Ottoman Empire*, New York, Arno Press, 1971. Rycaut was secretary to Charles II's extraordinary ambassador to England in company of the Sultan. Not strictly speaking a traveller, his viewpoint is that of a diplomat in contact with the Porte during one of its rather unstable phases. While tolerant in the religious sense, his political judgement is a negative one. He is critical of the flattery, arbitrariness and the servility which prevail everywhere. "It must be said, in a word, that this Empire is peopled by naught other than Slaves."
42. This fashion in the *Bourgeois Gentilhomme* corresponds with a specific event: the visit of the Sultan's ambassador to France the previous year (1669). Despite Martino's judgement (that the Turk is still "too powerful to be ridiculous," p.226), he was utilized more successfully for comic than for tragic ends. Fashion killed the distance which Racine sought to establish, which may partly explain the relative failure of Bajazet.
43. The word first appears in the 16th century, but only enters current usage in the 18th.
44. Chardin, op. cit., Chardin describes the misadventures which accompanied the renewal of the capitulation agreement between France and the Porte, a long series of unexpected turns (1655 to 1672) during which ambassadors from the Court of Louis XIV, in a rare display of mind-numbing arrogance and lack of comprehension, heaped one error on top of another.
45. Leibniz, *Projet d'expédition d'Egypt présenté à Louis XIV, 1672*, or *Concillium Aegyptiacum* (1672?). Oeuvres, tome cinquième, Paris, Firmin-Didot, 1864. The project is introduced and annotated in quite chauvinist fashion by A. Foucher de Careil, who, two centuries later, appears to regret that it was never put into execution.
46. Quoted by Leibniz, Project d'expédition d'Egypte... op. cit., p.359.
47. Leibniz, op. cit., p.47-48.
48. Ibid., p.124.
49. Ibid., p.27.
50. Ibid., p.256-257.
51. Ibid., p.124.
52. Ibid., p.154.
53. Ibid., p.XLII-XLIV.
54. Cassier, op. cit., p.7 sees Leibniz (1646-1716) as a man of the 17th century, in comparison to his contemporary, Newton, a man of the 18th.
55. Leibniz, op. cit., p.260.
56. Bossuet, Jacques Benigne, *Discourse on Universal History*, Chicago, University of Chicago Press, 1976. Bossuet claims the "clear victory" of the Catholic Church "over all sects," when he affirms: "Any sect that does not show its succession from the beginning of the world does not come from God." (which only the Catholic Church is able to do). Bossuet goes on to explain that "Mahomet" proved incapable, despite

his desire to do so, of producing "any previous evidence" (in Scripture) which "might have authorized his mission], p.289-290.

57. Bossuet, quoted in Hazard, op. cit., p. 15. Hazard also states that Bossuet wished that the Turk of Constantinople be driven from his throne. Leibniz, meanwhile, had attempted to open a dialogue with Bossuet on the union of the Christian churches, an initiative firmly rejected by Bossuet.

58. Hazard, op. cit., preface, p.xv.

59. Cassirer, op. cit.: What has changed is "the absolutism of the unity principal," (p.23). "The ideal of deduction is now confronted with the ideal of analysis." (p.52) He goes on to cite Newton, who no longer seeks "ultimate causes" (p.52) and considers his theory of gravitation as a "provisional point of rest." (p.52)

60. Rodinson, op. cit., p.48.

61. Djaït, op. cit., p.39.

62. Galland, Antoine, *Les mille et une nuit. Contes arabes.* 1ère édition complète 1717. Paris, Garnier, 1960. In the late 19th century, Sir Richard Burton was to write: "Our century of translations, popular and vernacular, from (Professor Antoine) Galland's delightful abbreviation and adaptation in no way represents the eastern original."

63. The Arabists of the 16th and 17th centuries were isolated. Aside from Postel, Edward Pococke (1604–1691) was the first professor of Arabic at Oxford, and author of a Specimen Historiae Arabum (1650) of which P.M. Holt (Studies in the History of the Near East, London, Frank Cass, 1973), p.11) notes: "Profoundly erudite in content and uncontroversial in tone, Pococke's notes show the emergence of the scholarly study of Islam from the distortions of medieval polemic."

64. Cassirer, op. cit., p.164.

65. Publiée par le Sr. de Moni, À Francfort, chez Frederic Arnaud, 1684, p.2.

66. Ibid., p.164.

67. Ibid., p.167, 164-165. With added detail: "Mahomet thus feigned that God had sent him…certain books of Scripture." (p.166) Here, Simon is in error; the Prophet transmitted his message orally; the Qur'an was written down 25 years after his death. But on the whole, Simon's presentation of Islam is moderate and generally sympathetic.

68. Bayle, Pierre, *Historical and critical dictionary selections.* Translated by Richard H. Popkin, Indianapolis, Bobbs-Merrill, 1965. The English edition does not include the entry entitled "Mahomet."

69. Bayle, Pierre, *Dictionnaire historique et critique, cinquième édition.* À Amsterdam, chez P. Brunel et al., 1740 (1ère édition 1696, 2ème éd. 1701), p.256-272. The entry on Mohamet is tortuous in the extreme, and full of contradictory notes, as if the entire subject still had to be treated with utmost caution. Bayle makes use of M. Prideaux's *Life of Mahomet,* translated into French in 1698, and then in wide use. "We there ascertain, says Bayle, that Mahomet was an Impostor and that he made use of his Imposture to serve his Cupidity," which does not appear to have influenced Maxime Rodinson's judgement that "The French philosopher Pierre Bayle, an admirer of Muslim tolerance, included in his *Dictionnaire historique et critique,* an objective biography of Muhammad." (Rodinson, op. cit., p.46).

70. Count of Boulainvilliers, *The Life of Mahomet.* Translated from the French original written by the Count of Boulainvilliers, author of *The Present State of France,* and of the *Historical Memoires* thereto subjoined. London, Printed for W. Hinchliffe, at Dryden's-Head under the Royal Exchange, 1731. Reprint by Darf, London, 1983.

71. Ibid., p.3.

72. Ibid., p.39-40.

73. Ibid., p.3-4.

74. In English, 'fanatic' first appears in the mid-16th century, applied to the Nonconformists. Oxford: "Affected by excessive and mistaken enthusiasm, especially in religious matters."

75. Ockley, Simon, *History of the Saracens*, London, Bohn, 1848. Ockley describes the Arabs as "men…who were bigots and enthusiasts" without the "sedateness and gravity of the Greeks and Romans," Introduction, p.xxii.

76. Boulainvilliers, op. cit., p.169, is sharply critical of Ockley for relying excessively on the work of Mr. Prideaux, "who, though a very judicious historian, has thought fit to adhere to the common notion, that makes of this false prophet an impostor as ignorant as contemptible."

77. Ibid., p.244.

78. Ibid., p.166. Boulainvilliers also suggests that Islam had brought to an end the apparent contradictions of the Trinity with the unity of God (p.138).

79. Ibid., p.166.

80. Ibid., p.169.

81. Ibid., p.243. "…In a word, with respect to the essential doctrines of religion, all that he [Mahomet] has laid down is true; but he has not laid down all that is true."

82. Rodinson, op. cit., p.47.

83. Boulainvilliers, op. cit.,p.2-3.

84. Ibid., p.165.

85. Hadidi, Javad, *Voltaire et l'Islam*, Paris, Publications orientalistes de France, 1974.

86. Voltaire, *Works*, a contemporary version, New York, E.R. Dumont, 1901. Scene VI, Act III, "Mahomet," Vol. 8, Part II, p.55-56. [The 1901 edition does not contain all Voltaire's works.] See also *Oeuvres complètes*, Paris, Garnier, 1878.

87. Voltaire, *Oeuvres complètes*, Vol. II, p.205.

88. Voltaire, *Works*, op. cit., Vol. 13, Part I, p.49.

89. Ibid., Vol. 3, Part 1, p.95, 98, 101.

90. Voltaire, *Essaie sure les moeurs. Oeuvres*, op. cit., Vol. 11, p.208-209.

91. Ibid., p.210.

92. Ibid., p.220-221.

93. Voltaire, *Works: A philosophical dictionary*, Vol. 3, Part I, p.104. Voltaire's appreciation is not far removed from that of Boulainvilliers'.

94. Voltaire, *Works*, The Age of Louis XIV, Vol. 12, Part I, p. 5.

95. Voltaire, "Essaie sur les moeurs," *Oeuvres*, op. cit., Vol. 13, p.176.

96. Ockley, Simon, op. cit., Introduction, p.xxii.

97. Ibid.

98. It is striking to note, in reading Paul Hazard (op. cit., p.14) to what extent the infatuation for the Orient (early 18th century) which he describes was focused on the peoples of the past. Perfection was to be found in pharaonic Egypt.

99. Voltaire, *Works: A Philosophical Dictionary*, Vol. 3, Part I, p.93.

100. Machiavelli, *The Prince*, op. cit., p.75, 21.

101. Bodin, *Six Books*, op. cit., p.56.

102. Wittfogel, Karl, *Oriental Despotism; a comparative study of total power*, New Haven, Yale University Press, 1957. See also Alain Grosrichard, *Structure du sérail*, La fiction du despotisme asiatique dans l'Occident classique, Paris, Seuil, 1979.

103. Montesquieu, *The Spirit of Laws*. Translated by Thomas Nungent, New York, The Colonial Press, 1900. Preface, p.xxxi.

104. Montesquieu, *The Persian Letters*. Translated by J.R. Loy. Meridian Books, World Publishing, New York, 1961. Letter XIX, p.72.

105. Ibid., Letter XXXI, p.89.

106. On this modern-day usage, see Karl Wittfogel, op. cit., p.1. Wittfogel, who attempts to establish a continuity of oriental despotism from Antiquity to contemporary totalitarianism in the former U.S.S.R. and China, hails Montesquieu as a pioneer: His "were extraordinary insights. They were, in fact, the starting point for a systematic and comparative study of total power."

107. Caillois, Roger, preface to Montesquieu, *Oeuvres complètes*, op. cit., Vol. I, p.xxxi.

108. Montesquieu, *The Spirit of Laws*, op. cit., Book XVII, Vol. 1, p.264.

109. Ibid., p.269.
110. Ibid., Book XIX, p.297.
111. Voltaire, *Dictionnaire philosophique...*, Vol. 20, p.20.
112. Ibid., p.6-7.
113. Voltaire, *Ancient and Modern History*, op. cit., Vol. 14, Part II, p.258.
114. The most recent of these critiques is Edward Saïd's *Orientalism*, op. cit.
115. Anquetil-Duperron, *Législation orientale.* Amsterdam, M.-M. Rey, 1778.
116. Ibid., p.vi.
117. Ibid., p.5,7. Montesquieu (The Spirit of Laws, Book VI, Vol. 1, p.73), on the other hand, could not imagine how one might learn anything at all from these "most ignorant of all nations."
118. Ibid., p.18.

V

The Orient of Modernity

The Orient of modernity is not the modern Orient. It is that Orient which, from the 19th century onward, was probed, prodded, pushed and ultimately absorbed by European modernity. It is at once a real Orient and an Orient of dreams, victim of power politics and product of imagination. A multi-faceted, undifferentiated Orient scrutinized by the same predatory eye: besieged by artillery, capital and Western fantasy.

Like the preceding centuries, the 19th represents less a clearly defined historical period than a state of mind from which we have not yet managed to escape. In many ways — particularly with regard to the Mediterranean Orient — the century our own has often described as "stupid" still hangs like a millstone around our necks. We cannot easily assign its modernity either a starting or an end date ("post-modernity"). After several centuries of gestation, modernity assumed, in the 19th century, its mature form with the industrial revolution and the acceleration of upheaval both in Europe and in Europe's relations with the outside world — particularly the Near East, whose observation and intellectual utilization by the West had begun in the 14th century. By the end of the 18th, a new, more brutal kind of use was in preparation. Two centuries later, we are still clearing away the debris.

WHITHER THE ORIENT?

The sword and the pen

> Sublime, il apparut aux tribus ébluies
> Comme un Mahomet d'Occident![1]

Though Napoleon's Egyptian expedition ultimately failed, it was a dramatic turning point in Orient-Occident relations in the Mediterranean — and the sudden manifestation of an underlying long-term shift. The shock caused by the penetration of Western arms and science into the heart of Mediterranean Islamic society was both military and cultural. The wall separating Europe and the Orient had been breached for the first time. Fifty years later, with the construction of the Suez Canal, the breach was consolidated.

Suddenly, and simultaneously, the Mediterranean Orient became an object to be coveted and conquered, a battleground for the European powers. With his invasion of Egypt, Napoleon had unconsciously set in motion the project Leibniz had devised for Louis XIV. Bonaparte's aim was not simply to strengthen French presence in the Levant, nor to lay the groundwork for a modern Eastern empire, but also to strike a blow at England. Indeed, this had been one of the expedition's main objectives from the outset. The main enemy was not the victim of attack: Egypt was simply the ground upon which the confrontation was to take place, but it soon became the object of the first attempt at European colonization in the region since the Crusades.

The ease with which Napoleon seized the valley of the Nile spoke volumes about the reversal in the balance of power between Europe and the Ottoman Empire. Recall that the shift to the detriment of the Porte, though not immediately visible in military terms, was already underway, on land at least. The Ottoman Empire's first reversals in Eastern Europe, in the 17th century, had little effect on its frontiers. Only after the defeats of the Russo-Turkish war of 1764 and the Treaty of Kutchuk-Kaïnarji (1774), was the Porte forced to relinquish territory. This was the event which orientalist chronology has generally accepted as the beginning of "the Eastern Question" — the question of the fate of the Ottoman Empire which was to become one of the most pressing preoccupations of the chancelleries of Europe.

What was to come of the Empire? Was it to fall into the hands of Russia, the nearest European power? Should it be divided it up, and if so, how? Or perhaps it should be helped to recover, to modernize? European capital (in the form of loans) was already active in the region; protecting that capital had become a concern. As early as 1776, voices were raised suggesting that France mount a military expedition to recover the Egyptian debt, which neither Mameluks nor Ottomans seemed inclined to repay. One of the creditors, a certain Baron de Tott, was dispatched to evaluate the project.[2]

Discussion of the nature and causes of despotism was no longer the order of the day; now Ottoman weakness and ineffectuality which placed European financial operations — and soon investments — in the Near East at risk were to be chastised. Well before any attempt at military conquest, Western finance's frustrated quest for wealth had posed the colonial question. From the early 19th century onward the combined pressure of Egyptian and Ottoman debt forced the Porte to accept European intervention in the management of its customs houses and finances. Persia followed suit. The West's view of the Orient was no longer that of an observer, but of a would-be possessor (which Leibniz already was) and school-master — who showed scant respect for the values and the culture which he had dislocated and which he held in contempt, no matter the exotic charms he might glean there.

Edward Saïd[3] has painstakingly demonstrated how this outlook drew upon already accumulated images and knowledge of the Orient. There is much truth in the demonstration. But his insistence in presenting the Western outlook as a continuum might also suggest that the outlook had always been a dominating one, an idea we know to be indefensible. From the Middle Ages onward there existed, in the European view of the Orient, only one constant: the perception within it, coupled with the production, beginning with it, of an alterity of widely varying substance (first religious, then socio-cultural). There also existed the attraction of mythical origins, the taste for "local colour" which subsisted, along with the ruins, as a vestige of the past. But it was not until the dawn of the 19th century that alterity became the stuff of intervention, that the question of domination was truly posed.

The invasion of Egypt in 1798 was "the keynote of the relationship [between] the Near East and Europe," which represented "in many ways the very model of a truly scientific appropriation of one culture by another, apparently stronger one."[4] A correlation exists between the construction of orientalism as a systematic, specialized science, and the European conquest of the Orient. What remains to be seen is whether, as Saïd notes, this science "justified in advance"[5] the colonial enterprise, and to what extent this assertion is compatible with another, which claims that knowledge of the Orient was "generated out of strength."[6]

There can be little doubt — as we shall see — that science was eagerly invoked in the service of colonialization, based on an estimate of the cultural, scientific or political inferiority of the countries to be colonized. But the pretention of knowing the Other might also serve as justification for non-intervention. Montesquieu maintained that the Orient should be abandoned to the despotism assigned it by nature. Irrespective of the ideology which may have employed it, knowledge, in its most concrete, most descriptive aspects, was of a purely practical utility. An officer of Napoleon's army described Volney's *Le voyage en Egypte* (1787) as the guidebook of the French in Egypt; it alone had "never deceived them."[7]

Conversely, science's debt to arms had rarely been more eloquently illustrated: the expedition to Egypt was that most exemplary of alliances: that of the sword and the pen. The enormous accomplishments of the diligent French engineers and draughtsmen who accompanied the army and later published the monumental *Déscription de l'Egypte* (a census of "all" Egypt past and present, its flora and fauna, its monuments, its population, economy, social and political institutions, etc.) constituted an unprecedented, perhaps even unequalled enterprise.[8] Still, Egyptology had not been delivered into the world by French bayonets; it had begun to flourish in England, at the beginning of the 18th century.[9] Narrow strategic considerations aside, what began with Napoleon was the conceit — so typically French — of bringing, in the wake of revolutionary messianism, enlightenment and liberty to a once mighty but now prostrate Orient which deserved a better fate:

> He (Bonaparte) instituted schools where the people might learn, military colleges where young Frenchmen, Copts and Arabs would instruct one another Arabic, French, geography, mathematics and the exact sciences: in a word, he created a nation; and, wielding the powerful motive force of enthusiasm he recalled to the Arabs the glory of their ancestors; showed them, in the French army, the miraculous instrument of the decrees of Providence which will reawaken the power of the ancient empire of the Arabs and deliver them from the yoke of the barbarous Osmalis, purify the law of the Prophet which has been debased by ignorant and unreligious men, and usher Asia into a new century of grandeur, science and glory.[10]

Force of arms thus placed itself at the service of science and of progress — the Other's science and progress. It was not so much knowledge of the Other that had been "generated out of strength," to use Saïd's expression, as the science imposed in the name of what was known of it and of its past. "Science" is here understood at two levels of justification: in a general sense, as the motor driving human progress; and, specifically, as knowledge of the Orient and of its past, thanks to which Europeans could authoritatively regenerate an Orient which they knew better than any Oriental[11] — pretending even to "purify the law of the Prophet." Such was the motivation underlying the colonialist discourse in its most candid, or most hypocritical form, depending on the mouth which spoke it: the marriage of Enlightenment and imperialism, wherein the husband never failed to subjugate the lovely wife to his basest designs.

Such, too, was the discourse which flowed from the pen of Volney, whose oriental investigations were too closely linked to the first modern Western incursion in the Mediterranean Orient to escape attention. It seemed to confirm suspicions that "Volney eyed the Near Orient as a likely place for the realization of French colonial ambition," and that his book on Egypt and Syria had been little more than preparation for France's invasion of the Levant.[12] Still, Volney's (perhaps too obvious) enthusiasm at Napoleon's successes in Egypt corresponded unfavourably with his pessimistic prediction, made ten years earlier, about the fate of such an enterprise. "This chimera will meet with total failure," he proclaimed.[13] He went on to provide a sociological explanation for the failure: even supposing that France succeeded in overcoming the three obstacles represented by the Mamelukes, the Turks and the English, the most difficult part still remained:

> These men must be governed, and we do not know their
> language, nor their manners and customs; misunderstand-
> ings will arise which will cause troubles and disorders at
> every turn. The character of the two nations, opposite in
> every way, will become reciprocally antipathetic: our sol-
> diers will scandalize the populace with their drunkenness,
> revolt it by their insolence toward women: this alone will
> have the most serious of consequences. Our officers will
> carry along with them that *flippant, singular, disparaging* tone
> which makes us intolerable to foreigners.[14]

The European's educational vocation and the generosity of the Enlightenment now seemed suddenly to give way to more classical strategic considerations: the Levant reverted to being a field of manoeuvre rather than
an entity to be emancipated. The contradictions which permeated Volney's
appreciation of the Egyptian expedition can be more readily understood by
reading his reservations, formulated *prior* to the French revolution, about
a colonial project in the Near East. Still, the most striking aspect of Volney's
observations was that he wrote his major work on Egypt and Syria at a time
when the idea of an armed intervention had stirred the European imagination, but before it could be realized. Volney probed the Orient and its
possibilities in a pre-colonial manner, some of whose elements still resonate
strongly today.

Probing the Orient: Volney's investigation

It is not clear what motivated Volney's voyage to the Levant. Perhaps
his intent, as Jean Gaulmier argues, was to develop arguments against an
eventual French military intervention in Egypt (openly supported by
Baron de Tott, for whom the banks of the Nile were inhabited by a "weak"
people "who have always submitted to the first slave who possessed the
will to command them").[15] Whatever its motives, his *Voyage en Egypte et en
Syrie* had all the hallmarks of a detailed investigation. In this respect it
differed from most earlier, and indeed subsequent, accounts of voyages.[16]

More than any other traveller of his era (with the exception of the
authors of *Description de l'Egypte*), Volney focused his attention on the
"political state" of the countries he visits. As in the best methods, their
"physical state" was described only to explain better the geographical
context of the societies examined (but without a hint of climatic determinism). But Volney did little more than tip his hat, or thumb his nose, at

the vestiges of Antiquity or the beauty of the sites he encountered. He mocked the temptation of the traveller to exaggerate the splendour of the places visited, in order that "the marvellousness of that which he has beheld reflect first of all upon himself," and then upon his reader.[17] Once the sense of exaltation had passed, even where the spectacle was as breathtaking as the pyramids of Giza, "one is overcome with indignation before the extravagance of the despots who caused these barbarous constructions to be erected." They were less a testimonial to the "genius of an opulent, art-loving people than to the servitude of a nation tormented by the capriciousness of its masters."[18] Then, as if to bring us back to the present: unquestionably, "if Egypt were to be possessed by a nation enamoured of the fine arts, we would discover resources for the knowledge of Antiquity which the rest of the world henceforth denies us," but "assuredly the interests of this people, more than the monuments, must dictate the desire to see Egypt pass into other hands."[19]

The land of the Nile was not in good hands. But before asking to whom Volney would have commended it, let us take a closer look at his diagnosis. The sickness was a familiar one: the patient was suffering from despotism. But contrary to the opinion of Montesquieu, the situation was not irreparable. Volney gave no credence to climatic theories, and sought the source of illness in society itself: "The morale of peoples, like those of individuals, depends first and foremost on the social situation in which they live."[20] The optimum solution for the antiquated and corrupt institutions of the Ottoman Empire was to sweep them aside: nothing could be salvaged from the "Turkish spirit," which consisted of "destroying the accomplishments of the past and the hopes of the future."[21] The tone of disparagement is difficult to reconcile with Volney's self-proclaimed lucidity ("not only must one fight the prejudices one encounters; those who carry such prejudices must be overcome: the heart is partial, the facts insidious and illusion comes easily"[22]). Volney, an accomplished ideologue, an admirer of republican ideals and convinced of the perfectibility of man, lashed out at the corruption and the ignorance of the mighty. His indulgence went instead to their victims, to the people in whom he, like other European observers of the day, recognized "a more human, more generous character, a more noble, polite simplicity, something more refined and open of spirit and manner than among the people even of our country."[23] This was particularly true of the Muslims, whose goodness, humanity and strength of character contrasted with the "Greek Christians, vile in their subservience" and "insolent in their good fortune" — differences which he attributed to the respective social situations of the two groups.[24]

But his praise of the Muslim did not stop him from assigning the Qur'an to the same fate as the institutions of the Ottomans. Ever the rationalist and anticleric, Volney was scarcely moved by the qualified, even positive appreciation of the holy book of Islam found in the work of Arab-speakers such as George Sale in England, or Claude Savary in France:

> The Muslims vainly claim that the Koran contains within it the seeds, and indeed the development of all legislative knowledge, of jurisprudence...Whoever should read the Koran will be obliged to admit that it presents not the slightest notion of the duties of men in society, nor of the formation of the political corpus, nor the principles of the art of government, nothing, in a word, that could constitute a legislative framework. The only laws which can be found can be reduced to four or five prescriptions relative to polygamy, divorce, slavery, the succession of close relations: and these prescriptions, which do not form a code of jurisprudence, are so contradictory that the doctors are still engaged in dispute in an effort to resolve them. All the rest is naught but a tissue of vague phrases, empty of meaning, an emphatic declamation of the attributes of God which have nothing to instruct any man; a collection of puerile stories, of ridiculous fables: in total, a composition so dull and uninteresting that no one is able to read it from beginning to end, despite the elegance of Savary's translation. If through the disorder of a perpetual delirium there does appear a spirit, a certain meaning, it is that of an ardent, unrelenting fanaticism...Behold the spirit of the Koran; it is apparent in the very first line: "In this book there is no doubt; it guides without error those who believe in it without doubting, who believe in that which they cannot see." And what is the consequence, if it is not to establish the most absolute of despotism in he who commands, through the blindest of devotion in he who obeys? Such was the design of Mahomet: he sought not to enlighten, but to rule; he sought not disciples, but subjects.[25]

We find not even a hint of intellectual curiosity about the Qur'an or about Islam from this admirer of Voltaire, who seems not to have outgrown the *Mahomet* of the regrettably notorious tragedy...This long passage perfectly reveals the ethnocentrism of the Western view: Islam, insofar as it helped maintain those very structures Volney felt compelled to analyze in order to understand what had impeded the progress of society, was seen as little more than an obstacle along the road to modernity. It was in this structural analysis that Volney produced his best work.

In examining the "causes of the despondency of the Egyptians," he propounded a veritable comparative sociology of the Orient and the West:

> In the European states, governments derive from the nations themselves the means of governing them, it is neither easy nor advantageous for them to abuse their power...the reason is that, over and above that multitude which is called the people, which though strong by virtue of its mass is always weakened by disunion, there exists an intermediate order, which, partaking of the qualities of the people and the government, creates a manner of balance between the one and the other. This order is that class of citizens of wealth and ease who, holding a diversity of positions in society, have a common interest in that the rights to security and to property which they enjoy are respected. In Egypt, conversely, there is no intermediate status, no numerous class of nobles, of persons of the legal profession or the church, of merchants, proprietors, etc., which might act as an intermediary between government and people. There, one may be but a military man or a man of the law, that is to say, a man of the government.[26]

Right or wrong, in so peremptorily denying the existence in Egypt of an "intermediate order," Volney posed, in his own fashion, the inexhaustible question of the bourgeoisie in the Near East, a question which is still hotly debated even today.[27] His ethnocentrism was quite "modern," really, free of preconceptions about the Orient, and of the archeologically oriented approach of many a learned orientalist after him. The Ottoman world was examined not as a predetermined, immutable Orient, but as Europe might have been. In this sense Volney can be considered — after Ibn-Khaldun — as one of the first true sociologists of the Mediterranean Orient.

The modernity of his view was not restricted to analysis of the inner workings of oriental society, but extended to its relations with the outside world, and particularly with Europe. The Orient's political and scientific inferiority, he asserted, had placed it in a position of commercial inequality. The observation, in itself, was hardly a new one. Montesquieu believed that the Ottomans were "incapable of carrying on commerce;"[28] likewise, Jean-François Melon attributed the weakness of the Turkish empire to its pursuit of the "spirit of conquest" to the detriment of the "spirit of trade."[29] But Volney went farther still. Inserting Ottoman commerce into a context of international trade, he demonstrated that this commerce was of "more harm than benefit" to the empire.

> In truth, as the objects exported by this State are raw, unfinished materials, it is deprived of all those advantages which it might obtain were they indeed to be finished by its

own citizens. In the second place, merchandises from Europe and India, being objects of luxury, only increase the pleasures of the wealthy class, the government, and only serve to render the conditions of the people and the tillers more difficult.[30]

Volney went on to illustrate the other side of those "exchanges in which all the advantage is ours; for, while we deliver to the Turks objects ready to be consumed, we take from them raw materials and products which the new advantages of manpower and industry have won for us."[31]

An absent "internal bourgeoisie," and raw materials traded for finished goods provided the basic components of underdevelopment (or dependence) and of unequal trade. All that was lacking was a general theoretical framework.

But Volney's concerns were of another order: the search for a solution to the famous Eastern Question favourable to France. What was to be done? Maintain the secular alliance with the Porte, attempt to reinforce his crumbling empire in the face of the ravenous rival European powers, particularly the Russians? Or allow the Tsars to impose their tutelage on the Ottoman Empire? Volney chose the second solution. His contempt for the Ottoman government, the "enemy of the human species,"[32] was so intense that he could not entertain even the possibility of supporting it. Hope of recovery was illusory: the Turks were "too cavalier to admit their weaknesses" and "too ignorant to understand the primacy of knowledge."[33] Meanwhile, the accelerating deterioration of the empire made it less and less desirable as a trading partner.[34] France would profit only if a "modern" power were to establish itself at Constantinople and take the development of the country in charge. Russia, being too sensible to promote rival manufacturers (and probably poorly placed to do so) was perfectly qualified; it's first task would be to reform agriculture, for the greater benefit of French trade.[35] Volney's political realism is admittedly less than dazzling — but the spirit of the project interests us, not its plausibility.

Why, indeed, did Volney not contemplate the role of tutelary power for his country? Why, instead, did he not warn against the temptation of overseas colonies?

It is in our homes, and not beyond the seas, that our Egypt and Antilles are to be found. What need have we of foreign land when one sixth of our own land remains untilled & and when the remainder has been tilled as it should? We should well look to improve our fortunes and not to expand them: we should know how to derive benefit from those riches

which are in our hands, & and not practice, beneath foreign
skies, a wisdom which we do not utilize at home.[36]

Volney's warnings of the misadventures which would befall any
expeditionary corps daring to occupy Egypt instantly come to mind.
Volney may well have read Melon who, before him, "many times over
emphasized the advantages to be had from establishment of commercial
enterprises in a country subjugated by a foreign power without having to
provide such administration as is incumbent upon a conquering nation."[37]
This would explain why Volney entrusted to Catherine II rather than
France the "noble ambition...of liberating the numerous peoples from the
yoke of fanaticism and tyranny, to return the sciences and the arts to their
the lands of their birth...and for the glory of the Orient reborn to efface the
glory of the ancient Orient!"[38] Still, awe-struck by Napoleon's first
successes in Egypt, he quickly transferred to the Proconsul the civilizing
mission which he had previously reserved for the Tsarina, as he exhorted
the hero of Italy to turn back toward Europe via Constantinople![39]

Volney's attitude was not without its ambiguities. But the shift in his
thinking toward a more interventionist approach may well have had less
to do with the Napoleonic expedition than with the French Revolution.
Did the revolution not warrant new aspirations for the entire world? Such
would seem to be the message of *Ruines*, or *Méditations sur les Révolutions
des Empires*, published in 1791, well before the Expedition to Egypt, as a
philosophical sequel to the *Voyage*.[40]

The site of his meditations was Palmyra — fabulous ruin *par excellence*.
The ruins were fabulous, too, in the literal sense of the word. Volney himself
had never visited the place, and knew of it only through his readings. The
site was both real and imagined — in the image of the mythical Orient.
There our author, troubled by the inexorable decline which appeared to be
the fate of even the most brilliant civilizations, suddenly received from an
all-powerful Genie the revelation of a new world, where "corps of free and
enlightened nations" coexist, in which "the communication of enlightenment by one portion will reach out from neighbour to neighbour, extending
to all. By the law of imitation, the example of the first portion will be followed by the others; they will adopt its spirit, its laws," until the "entire
species" becomes "a great society, one family governed by the same spirit,
by laws held in common, and enjoying all the felicity of which human nature is capable."[41] But, continued the Genie, the road would be a long one,
fraught with obstacles (inequality, servility, aggression, etc.); humanity
might travel this road only in liberty and equality.

No sooner had he spoken these words than an immense roar
resounded in the West; turning my head, I perceived, at the

far reaches of the Mediterranean, in one of the nations of
Europe, a prodigious upheaval.[42]

...Where it is impossible to mistake the events of 1789 here
"prefigured" *a posteriori*. For Volney and for so many others, the Revolution
would confer upon France, and upon all of Europe, a new role in the world.
The key element in the grandiose scheme of the *Ruines* is the specific
function attributed to each pole of the Mediterranean: in the Orient,
revelation; from the West, salvation. The gales of '89 had swept Europe
clean of the last vestiges of despotism and had draped the West with the
mantle of emancipator and liberator: the historiographers of the
Napoleonic expedition were later to claim that "the French armies
delivered rather than conquered Egypt."[43]

Volney, in his sociopolitical observation and his progressive ideology, was both precursor and witness to a turning point in relations between the Orient and the West. Though not himself a proponent of the
colonial adventure, and even less a promoter of "French colonial ambition,"[44] he helped prepare the ground for European interventionism and
colonialism in the Levant. Were I less concerned by the dangers of
anachronism, I would label him neocolonialist rather than colonialist.
Volney's objective was less to appropriate directly the riches of the Other
than to integrate it into a commercial system. But commercial concerns
alone do not exhaust the scope of his thought. We find, in Volney, a
desire to share European Enlightenment, as well as a sense of im-
patience, of dissatisfaction with the state of the Orient. As a man of
reason and progress, as a European imbued with the superiority of his
civilization, convinced that this superiority carried with it obligations
toward other peoples, Volney believed that the fallen Orient must be
restored, through the intercession of Western science, to a new
prosperity worthy of its ancient grandeur. Predictably, this very pretension — this sense of self-importance, if you will — suffuses the entire
justificative discourse of colonialism, just as the need for modernization
has thoroughly saturated the discourse of the bureaucratic elites in
power in most Near Eastern countries. In this way, Volney was very
much a precursor: the Orient was no longer simply that alterity which
we might examine with curiosity, with which we might amuse ourselves
intellectually. It had joined — in spite of itself — the fast-flowing current
of modern European history, and thus became a "responsibility" of the
West.

It was not a discourse "generated out of strength." Instead, it preceded,
anticipated, and sought to bring that strength to bear on objectives which
corresponded with the interests of France, and of those peoples bound by Ottoman shackles, without realizing the contradictions of this double ambi-

tion. Good intentions aside, the excessive and derogatory criticism of the Ottoman administration and of the Qur'an suggested that Oriental institutions, measured against those of the West, had no legitimacy. This delegitimization of the political and social structures of the Ottoman Empire was to prove useful to colonialists and interventionists of every size and shape. Contrary to Volney's intentions, it was used to accredit the most nefarious enterprises, the most contemptuous attitudes; knowledge had not so much offered its services to colonialism as colonialism had been quick to turn them to account. From this moment onward, our image of the Other was shaped neither by curiosity nor by the presumptuous desire to transform, but, in the rawest terms, by the European's power to dominate and to exploit.

THE ORIENT OF EVERYDAY COLONIALISM

Colonialism — the mentality which preceded and accompanied it, and gazed nostalgically back upon it when it had become inoperative — produced an inexhaustible compendium of rubbish about the Mediterranean Orient, to which many Westerners refer even today when they encounter the Arabo-muslim world. Despite the Western imagination's fascination with the Orient as exotica, 19th and 20th century Europe's images of the Orient were the worst yet concocted. Colonialist Europe, with its possessive stranglehold, simultaneously adored and despised an Orient which it could never entirely appropriate as it wished. Hence the multiplicity of images, the violence of the contrasts, the coexistence of the sordid and the naively idealistic.

Contempt and depreciation

No matter how elaborate the disguise, depreciation of the Other in all its forms, from subtle disdain to grotesque arrogance, was the hallmark of the 19th century, the century of European industrial colonialism. Colonialism was more than the outcome of conquest; it represented a particular form of seizure and domination. Conquerors had often adopted the culture of the conquered. Such was the fate of the Crusaders who occupied Palestine in the 11th and 12th centuries who, for all their fanaticism, never looked on their adversaries with contempt. No sense of cultural or racial superiority flowed from their religious convictions. Sixteenth century Europeans, regardless of their avowed hatred, respected the Turks. Only toward the end of the 17th century did a sense of superiority over the Orient appear, then turn to depreciation when it joined forces with a manifest thirst for domination as exemplified by Leibniz —

whose example was both exceptional and premonitory. Depreciation can be defined as a feeling of superiority in the service of domination, whatever its forms: it is impossible for the colonialist to escape it completely. At best, he may attempt to justify his acts by criticizing the process of which he is a part, or by sheltering his troubled conscience behind an often unfeigned generosity, or a desire for fraternity all the more acute for being perverted by the cold realities of power. For depreciation had become a collective attitude of which individuals might partake — and even find themselves doing so involuntarily.

In the West's general depreciation of the colonized peoples, the Mediterranean Orient held pride of place. This was a result of its proximity, certainly, but primarily it was because of the resonance struck by its faraway but prestigious past, whose heritage Europe, judging the modern Orient as unworthy, now claimed for itself. The apathy which it attributed to the Oriental peoples confirmed, as if confirmation were needed, that the great civilizations of western Asia belonged to the history of the western world, and that it fell to the West to reveal their full splendour, in the image of the monuments which Western archeology had discovered buried beneath the dust of ages.

While possession of high Antiquity was apparent, cultivated Europe was reluctant to cast itself as heir to the more recent Arabo-Muslim civilization, and was more inclined to minimize its legacy. It could not, of course, entirely close its eyes to the accomplishments of the Omayyad and Abbassid caliphates, nor resist the temptation of rescuing their remnants from Ottoman negligence. The trick was to place the accomplishments of Arabo-Muslim civilization in their "proper" perspective, a task to which Ernest Renan, among many, applied himself with singular skill.

While deprecating the scientific contribution of the Arabs, who "did little more than adopt the whole of the Greek encyclopedia which the whole world had accepted in the 7th and 8th century," Renan admits that "Arab philosophy, particularly in the 11th and 12th centuries, achieves true originality. Here, I am prepared to make certain concessions." Let us see what these concessions are:

> Arab philosophy provides us with a virtually unique example of a high culture almost instantly vanished, leaving not a trace, and virtually forgotten by the people who created it. Islamism revealed in those circumstances the irremediably narrow nature of its specific genius...Incapable of transforming itself, of admitting any elements of civil and non-religious life, Islamism tore from its breast all traditional culture. This fatal tendency was fought whilst the hegemony of Islamism lay in the hands of that fine, spiritual race, the

> Arabs, or the Persians, with their speculative proclivities; but
> it held unswerving domination ever since barbarians (Turks,
> Berbers, etc.) seized the direction of Islam.[45]

Despite the fineness of the Arabs, observes our man of science, the genius of Islam was stillborn, the product of an "incomplete race"[46] — a quality which authorized the erudite Westerner to single out the one instant (the 11th and 12th centuries) when this genius merited being sought out and removed from the drifting sands of barbarism.

Though this reductionist vision has been since rejected — by Henri Corbin in particular — it remains dominant to this day in so-called cultivated circles: Islam and Arab civilization were a great, but short-lived moment in history, a "concession" which made it possible to deny the present and the recent past in good conscience. Edward Saïd has eloquently demonstrated and abundantly illustrated all of this, quoting, in addition to Renan, figures as diverse as Sylvestre de Sacy, "father" of modern erudite Orientalism, Chateaubriand, Cromer, Balfour, with whom the serene negation of the Other found expression in the full authority of the man who wielded unchallenged dominion over the object of his contemplation: the authority of science (Sacy and Renan), the authority of prose (Chateaubriand), the authority — without qualification — of the rulers (Cromer, Balfour).

But this was only the tip of the iceberg. The image of the Orient which we associate with the 19th century (but was already available in the 17th century) was that available to the leisured, educated strata of the population. But in the 19th century, another Orient began to emerge: an Orient for the masses, exemplified by Eliot Warburton's *The Crescent and the Cross*, which went through 18 editions during its author's lifetime.[47] Warburton presented himself as a purveyor of cheap excursions for the working classes. Formerly the preserve of philosophers and travellers, knowledge could now be distributed to virtually all homes "like gas and water."[48] Warburton wrote accordingly. His Orient was a picturesque one, modeled after popular views of Cairo, "a source of unceasing amusement and curiosity."[49] But it also provided an excellent opportunity for flattering the self-esteem of the dominant race by allowing the casualties of industrial growth, those poor souls whose ill-fortune allowed them to travel only on the wings of imagination, to revel in the arrogance of the beys and pashas pushing passersby aside as they passed, to interject: "Unless they recognize you as an Englishman — one of that race whom they think the devil himself can't frighten or teach manners to."[50] The industrial worker of the Midlands could comfort himself in his misery; from afar, his authority was acknowledged by the potentates of the Orient through the respect inspired by the representatives of his race. This sense of haughtiness was in striking contrast with Richard Pococke's observation of a century before, that "the meanest Mahometan thinks himself above any Christian."[51] The difference tells little about the evolution of Muslim attitudes, but it demonstrates how the European mindset had changed. Between these two "snapshots" fell not only the Napoleonic expedition, but also the rise of English and French interventionism in the Levant.

It comes as no surprise to see Gérard de Nerval, the poet himself, swagger pompously about as he unveils the dominator-dominated nexus which, despite his best efforts (if we are to believe his account), had taken root in his Arab entourage:

> I may well have yielded slightly to the desire to impress these people, now insolent, now servile, always in the throes of intense, fleeting sentiments of the moment, and whom one must understand in order to comprehend to what extent despotism is the normal government of the Orient. The most modest of travellers finds himself rapidly led, if a sumptuous manner of living does not procure the necessary respect, to strike a theatrical pose and to apply, in a multitude of cases, energetic measures which, thenceforth, can be undertaken without danger. The Arab is a dog which will bite if one retreats, and which will lick the hand raised against it. When he is struck, he knows not whether, at bottom, you have the right to strike him.[52]

The European well knew that henceforth this right was his to claim: the theory of despotism now found expression as individual behaviour. Even had Thévenot, Chardin, or even Volney brandished a big stick, they would never have boasted of it. In the 17th and 18th centuries, violence was a function of class. In the 19th, it became the punctuation of international relations. Neither Warburton or Nerval drew their sense of superiority from their modest social station, but from the nation to which they belonged. Whatever its specific qualities, the Orient's general inferiority was henceforth taken for granted. The atmosphere was rife with the vanity of colonial self-admiration.

Paternalism, appreciation

Colonialism was a creature of many faces. But so ingrained had their conviction of superiority become that most Europeans could hardly observe, barely act without it. It had tainted their entire outlook, no matter how benevolent or enlightened they might be as individuals. "What might we not have expected from such men," noted de Chabrol for the Egyptians, "if we had been able to introduce among them the more just ideas and the enlightenment of European civilization."[53] The raw clay of the Orient needed only be shaped by the genius of the West to produce worthy offspring. Only Europe, by its existence, could breathe worth into "this unfortunate and heretofor uselessly fertile land" fated, under its governance, to "advance rapidly to a state of prosperity."[54] Appreciation of that which had been denigrated became a colonialist leitmotif, beginning with the French colonization which subjugated Egypt to nothing less than a cultural invasion bearing the hallmark of the Enlightenment.

The flowering was short-lived. European material power was increasing rapidly, and its penetration took other forms, though the gunboat was never far away (outright war was needed to seize Algeria). Egypt was no longer tempted by the siren song of the Enlightenment, but, as Warburton explains, "She is becoming gradually and unconsciously subsidized by the wealth that England lavishes, and hourly more entangled in those golden chains from which no nation ever strove to loose itself."[55] London, manifestly, was best outfitted to forge such chains. The means at its disposal were different — but so was the prevailing temperament across the Channel. The remote and phlegmatic Englishman knew he was inimitable, and saw the natives who sought to assimilate the customs of Albion as little more than poor copies of himself. The Frenchman, meanwhile, sought in every way possible to shape the Other in his image, with the indelible mark of his culture. In the Near East, France had lost the commercial primacy it had enjoyed up until the end of the 18th century. It now attempted to make up the ground which had been lost — by force of arms if necessary — with a more symbolic but no less significant retaking of possession. Witness this purple passage from a speech by the representative of the Marseille Royal Academy of Sciences, Belles-Lettres and Arts to the poet Lamartine on the eve of his departure for the Levant:

> Orient, land of powerful memories, cradle of the world, source of divine belief, the Occident wishes to possess you; we shall conquer you, shall bring freely to you our homage, like pious children who crave only to honor and glorify their mother. Long ago, you received our warlike peoples; then the great man who caused the world to tremble left his indelible seal upon your brow; you have known our most illustrious author [Chateaubriand]; now take the holiest, best-loved of our poets, for it is by allowing you to contemplate our great men that we wish to consummate our modern-day crusade.[56]

The effusion matched the man for whom it was intended; he, in turn, was to prove worthy of it. Lamartine would go on to develop colonialism's most purely distilled, ideal, thoroughgoing — and most smothering — sympathy for the Orient. Unlike his predecessors (notably Volney and Chateaubriand), Lamartine[57] accepted and embraced the Orient, whose alterity he minimized. But his acceptance was more like an invasion which transformed the Levant into a simple appendix of the West. The Orient, in Denise Brahimi's expression, became "to Europe as an empty receptacle is to one which is overflowing."[58] It was precisely this empty receptacle which Lamartine proposed to fill:

> If I had but one quarter of the riches of a Paris or London banker, I would have transformed the face of Syria within ten years…. A European adventurer with five or six hundred European soldiers could easily overthrow Ibrahim and conquer all Asia, from Smyrna to Basra, from Cairo to Baghdad, were he to procede one step at a time, using the Maronites of Lebanon as pivot, and in organizing the Christians of the Orient behind him, as he advanced, as his means of action, administration and recruitment.[59]

For:

> Time has come, I submit, to establish in the heart of Asia a colony of Europe, to bring modern civilization to those lands whence emerged ancient civilization, and to construct an immense empire from the huge fragments of the Turkish empire as it collapses from its own weight, and whose only heir is the desert, and the dust of the ruins into which it plunges.[60]

Lamartine gave short shrift to the critical distinction which, for the majority of his contemporaries, underlay the very concept of Orient: without the breath of Europe the Orient did not exist. Even the Christians, its only living fragment, had limited usefulness as a base of operations for Europe's colonial mission. The fraternal embrace of the poet carried negation beyond the abasement of ordinary colonialism. It had become a kiss of death.

Analyzed against the political background of early 19th century Lebanon, Lamartine's prose had a decidedly cynical air. He had written the above in 1833 when, at the instigation of their respective English and French "protectors," conflict had begun to flare between Druzes and Maronites. Here, high flown rhetoric about civilization found perfect harmony with the crudest *realpolitik*: the Maronites were a nothing but a "pivot" not only for foreign intervention but also for inter-imperialist rivalry. The Orient could be reified no further. Concentrated in this "beautiful soul" were all the components of the colonial spirit: invasive generosity, the messianism of the conqueror, the negation of the Other, the exploitation of physical and human resources, and the utilization of local particularities and enmities to secure foreign domination and fuel competition among European powers.

Imperialist rivalries long impeded direct military occupation. But when the powers broke into open hostilities over the spoils, they accelerated the dismemberment of the region. The political divisions which were the legacy of the protecting powers to the contemporary Arab world, particularly in the Mashrek, persist today: a mutilation from which that world has not yet recovered.

Self-criticism, re-appreciation

Thus was colonialism's progress, from depreciation to re-appreciation, so intense was the need to devalue the better to re-value that which it was ultimately to fragment. This is not the place to put colonialism on trial yet again, but to recall briefly how the justificative ideology which accompanied the rise of competing imperialisms and the growing intervention of the Western powers in the Near East was articulated. It was inevitable that the images most often employed to describe the Orient — the images which were everywhere to be found in Europe — increasingly became a function of imperial and colonial policy. The colonial spirit nurtured a seemingly inexhaustible reservoir of stock phrase and image, so vast that it survived the colonial period proper. Today, in the West, we find ourselves in a paradoxical situation: *ad nauseam* condemnation — a commonplace, almost obligatory reference wherever the Third World is to be mentioned — continues to coexist with the scarcely concealed persistence of the ideological output which accompanied colonialism. Behind the ostensible triviality of anticolonialism there remains the vital necessity to challenge our current outlook, and to appreciate its debt to the recent past. Conversely, we must remember that the critique of colonialism does not begin with decolonization, but with colonialism itself — not only amongst the anticolonialists of Europe, but up to and including several European "colonialists" themselves.

John Ninet, the Swiss entrepreneur and agronomist who took up residence in Egypt in 1839 was such a person. Given charge of Egyptian cotton production by Mehmet Ali before becoming an independent planter in 1843, he spent more than one-half century along the banks of the Nile before his arrest and expulsion by the British in 1882 for active participation in the Egyptian national movement. Ninet was a friend and confidant of Ahmed Urabi, leader of armed resistance against the invading British forces, and was probably a principal (if not the principal) drafter of the *Manifesto of the Egyptian National Party,* which was published on November 4, 1879.[61] In articles and letters to European newspapers and periodicals (*le Siècle, l'Intransigeant,* the *Times,* the *Journal de Genève,* the *Revue des Deux Mondes*), Ninet denounced the double plundering of the fellahs by the Khedive and by the Europeans: "The Egyptian peasantry is in an unbearable position. It will not be too long before the fellah will not even be able to enjoy the fruits of his own harvest."[62]

He writes, on the forced departure of the "ex-Khedive-vali, Ismail Pasha" and his followers, "banished from Egypt by the Porte,":

> All of them were odious to the people. The Europeans, like true pharisees, blamed them for their methods but joyfully accepted the profits of their abominable exactions in the attractive form of dividend coupons, etc....There is serious discontent among the educated classes of the population who suffer at beholding the Europeans administering, making and unmaking, behaving as masters in their house, when the devastation and the ruins which surround them are the work of these self-same foreign elements.[63]

How far we have come from the lyrical transports of the colonial spirit! Ninet shows us an Orient disfigured by the creeping colonialism[64] of which he himself was a part. Without calling his own presence into question, without pondering the meaning of European expertise or its long-term effects on the economic and social structures of the country, Ninet lashed out at the behaviour of his Western colleagues and at the abuses they had committed or concealed in their cowardice, stupidity, and thirst for short-term enrichment. But, he consoled himself, "Egyptians are intelligent, they are transforming themselves more rapidly than we may think."[65] There is no structural analysis, no broad overview of that which the Marxists were soon to analyze as imperialism, or, latterly, what would be described as dependence or unequal trade. But Ninet's lonely voice may well have been the ultimate personification of "benevolent" colonialism.

Confronted with exactions he condemned, limited by his own particular circumstances, Ninet faced a choice: either carry his Eurocentrism to its extreme limits by adopting the Egyptian cause — or leave. He was the concrete expression of a contradiction that had continued to smoulder deep in the consciousness of the West even during the most evil hours of the colonial enterprise. Competition between the powerful — and the powers — in the exploitation of lands overseas had not totally extinguished the ideals of the Enlightenment. But those who nurtured such ideals against all obstacles could not avoid being trapped in the massively unfavourable balance of forces which generated colonialism and imperialism. They found themselves in the position of the followers of Saint-Simon who, driven by a generous vision of East-West relations, went in Egypt to study and promote the opening of the Isthmus of Suez, only to turn against Ferdinand de Lessep's venture because it would "open Egypt to international capitalism." Having first believed that they would make ready the "nuptial bed of Orient and Occident,"[66] the Saint-Simonists discovered that they had prepared the bed of capitalism.

The West could never bring itself to relinquish what it viewed as its civilizing, regenerating mission in the Orient. The excesses of colonialism were mere historical accidents, lapses in the selfsame progress of which Europe and its bourgeoisie were unconscious agents: an intellectual alibi whose most complex and powerful version was to be created, from the early 19th century on, by the "universalizing history" of German philosophy. In this philosophical vision, the place assigned to the Orient was to reveal its integration by the West in stark clarity.

THE INTEGRATED ORIENT

> North, West and South disintegrate,
> Thrones burst, empires tremble.
> Fly away, and in the pure East
> Taste the Patriarchs' air.[67]

For Goethe, who had integrated it into his poetry sight unseen, the Orient was at once a return to the sources and flight forward toward the still-intact obverse of a shattered world. Nowhere more than in Germany was the Orient so vividly integrated into the imagined world, and into thought, into the *Weltanschauung* of poets and philosophers, as genesis and as complementarity.

But as a source of inspiration it raised problems; its complementarity was a troubled one. Like a repressed memory, the Orient kept re-emerging in a semi-conscious process of integration as the unavowed dark side of the Western psyche, as an empty canvas awaiting the expression of all phantasms.

The stanched source

While the Enlightenment, in France, used the Orient as a political fulcrum and foil (in the form of despotism), German romanticism sought in it an oneiric and ideological counterweight to the rationalism of the *Aufklärung*, then to the productivism of nascent industrial society. The

Orient was not simply a mirror, but the indispensable complement of a Western civilization which searched for totality and plenitude in fusion with it, sought coherence and continuity in a philosophy of history which saw pre-Hellenic antiquity conscripted into the service of European universalism.

From Herder to Schopenhauer, via Novalis, Frederick Schlegel, Wilhelm von Humboldt, Görres, Ritter and others, René Girard has traced the itinerary of this enigmatic quest.[68] The itinerary was a complex one, fraught with twists, turns, and missed directions, leading beyond the Mediterranean Orient all the way to India, often even to China. "Indiamania" spread rapidly in Germany thanks to Novalis, Fichte and Schlegel; sublimated India became the prism through which the critique of a West whose decline was already being stigmatized a full century before Spengler must pass. But the brilliance of the new crystal was short-lived: even among the most fervent Indophiles (such as Schlegel), disenchantment increased as "knowledge" of India deepened. "Dreams gave way to reality"; and with disillusionment "the attempt at oriental-occidental syncretism"[69] began to fray around the edges, or at least to retreat, toward Persia and the Mediterranean Orient. "Rather than break with Judeo-Christianity, the romantics preferred to break with India," concludes Gérard.[70] What better way to return to the "miracle of Greece" which romantic orientalism had set itself the task of overcoming, or better still, refuting.

This turnabout was symptomatic of the progression of Herder, spiritual father of German orientalomania; a progression at whose end point "the Orient was relegated to the childhood of humanity and its art considered as the dream of a pre-world, the veritable world being understood to begin only with the advent of Greece."[71] Having failed in his attempts to fuse contemporary, living India with his world, the German westerner reduces all Asia, and more specifically the Near East, to the speaking in tongues of infancy. The Orient thus became at once one of the ages of humanity, and a stanched source, a dried-up river bed in which nothing but rich silt remained to be stirred through and picked over. Its entire contribution consisted of this rich alluvium; henceforth it had nothing more to say. The Orient was of interest to the West only as a chapter, long since ended, of the universal history into which it had become integrated — a process of which Hegel was the outstanding theoretician.

Hegelian integration

With Hegel, the Orient as historical moment took on new dimensions and broader currency, in keeping with the immense intellectual corpus into which it was now integrated. Hegel's work was immense, above all, in its exceptional synthesis of the vision to which the West strove to subordinate the world.[72] He gave such magisterial voice to the Western *Weltanschauung* that he remains virtually unsurpassed. Despite the successive reversals suffered by Europe, then the United States on the international scene, the West's power and viewpoint still dominate the world; beyond shifts in style, beyond the *mea culpas* directed — more hypocritically than not — to the Third World, the core of this viewpoint has remained fundamentally Hegelian. The Orient of Hegel's *Weltgeschichte* has remained, down to our day, the Orient of Western consciousness: its place, role and historical meaning remain narrowly subordinated to the West's own conception of itself and of its universalizing function.

True, the Hegelian perspective has been subjected to simplifications and distortions. Our intention is not to restitute Hegel in all his truth — as if such a thing were possible — but to understand where, independent even of his own intentions, his thought leads. Call it popularization if you will, but such an approach has a solid basis in the philosopher's work. The Hegelian schema, for instance, took pains not to present the Orient as "blocked" in relation to a putative norm (the West), but depicted it instead as "instinctively refusing to evolve."[73] But the Orient was nevertheless represented as immobile, not to say stagnant. The value judgement is difficult to ignore: the West may well be the exception, but it and no other civilization has contrived to endow universal history with its full meaning.

Hegelian philosophy was not the first to present the West as fulfillment — still in the process of becoming though it might be. But Hegel was the first to invest the idea with all its latent power. His Universal History placed the West in the vanguard of the march of Reason, just as, two and one-half centuries before, Bodin had made Europe the head of the great body of the Universe. The general idea was the same, only the method was different: where Bodin's petrified anthropomorphism makes us smile, Hegel's powerful dynamic swept industrial society along before it. In the age of the steam engine, Hegel perfected the motor of History which was to propel the world toward a predetermined objective: consciousness of self, and the liberty which such consciousness implied. Universal history was the history of Reason becoming itself, knowing itself, through the tribulations of peoples and empires. "But the only thought which philosophy brings with it is the simple idea of reason — the idea that reason governs the world, and that world history is therefore a rational process."[74] Hegel denied formulating mere "general reflections" on history. He delivered to us "universal world history itself;" and "the philosophy of history is nothing more than the application of thought to history."[75] That such reflection took place in the West only confirmed its decisive place in the *Weltsgeschichte*. Though Hegel himself might not have approved, it was difficult for Westerners not to feel a mixture of pride and presumption at being the incarnation of the "Idea" (that Reason governs the world), and therefore, reason itself:

> That this Idea is true, eternal and omnipotent, that it reveals itself in the world, and that nothing is revealed except the Idea in all its honour and majesty — this, as I have said — is what philosophy has proved.[76]

"Philosophy" indeed. What praiseworthy simplicity! What generalization, which both proved and created its universality! It was the ultimate presumption: that all the threads of history, all of its meanings could be brought into convergence. But Europe alone was speaking; European thought alone which — before propagating its "verities" overseas — had come to know in all its plenitude "being in itself"; that is to say, "consciousness of self" as condition of liberty, which was to transform it into the active subject of history.

On the other hand:

> The Orientals do not know that the spirit or man as such are free in themselves. And because they do not know this, they are not themselves free. They only know that One is free, but for this very reason, such freedom is mere arbitrariness, savagery, and brutal passion, or a milder and tamer version of this which itself is only an accident of nature, and equally arbitrary. This One is therefore merely a despot, not a free man and a human being...Only the Germanic nations, with the rise of Christianity, were the first to realize that man is by nature free, and that freedom of the spirit is his very essence.[77]

Universal history, as "progress of the consciousness of freedom,"[78] proceeded from the oriental unconscious to German consciousness. What power of seduction the idea had: it gave the history of humanity a profound, simple, reassuring and redemptive meaning, of which every Westerner might knowingly partake. Like Christ's Calvary, the bloody progression of history could be understood, and made acceptable by its end. Hegel explains God in terms of dynamism, a dynamism whose end point was modern Europe. The European character of the Hegelian idea was seen as the objective fruit of the march of history and not as that which it was in reality (Hegel notwithstanding): a Eurocentrist beatification of Western world domination. Beatification is by no means too strong a word: history merely revealed the eternal immanence of Reason in the universe. So it came to pass that Europe regulated the world, and in the mouth of Hegel, revealed the meaning of history: Reason, in other words God, had spoken.

Its meaning thus given, history needed only reveal its inner logic, each civilization representing another step forward in the "great journey of the spirit" which symbolized its onward march.

> World history travels from East to West, for Europe is the absolute end of history, just as Asia is the beginning...for although the earth is a sphere, history does not move in a circle around it, but has a definite eastern extremity, i.e., Asia. It is there that the external and physical sun rises, and it sets in the West, but it is in the West that the inner sun of self-consciousness, which emits a higher radiance, makes it further ascent.[79]

Several intermediate stages marked its itinerary, each as essential as its predecessor: after infancy (the Orient) came Greece, youth, "like a lovely but ephemeral and quickly passing flower;" then Rome, "manhood of history;" finally, the "Germanic nations," "the fourth phase in history," an adulthood not of the body, nor of weakness, but "of the spirit" which had attained "complete maturity."[80] Not all civilizations could occupy a place of equivalent importance in the trajectory of the Spirit (setting aside those which were automatically excluded because of their remoteness from the Euro-Asiatic core). Though the Orient represented the infancy of history, "History is still predominantly unhistorical, for it is merely a repetition of the same majestic process of decline;" "no progress is made."[81] From the entire Orient, taken in the largest sense, only the ancient civilizations of central (or "anterior") Asia stood out as precursors to the "boyhood of history, which no longer displays the calm and thrusting qualities of the child, but behaves in a boisterous and turbulent manner."[82] Indeed, something must have happened, for "it is in Asia that the ethical world of political consciousness first arose." Nor did it happen in some distant and ill-defined region, but in ancient Asia, where geography (high plateaux and fluvial plains) had "drawn toward Europe."[83] Was it coincidence? Certainly not; the light, fleeing its temporary birthplace, was rapidly to come to rest on the continent where it would ultimately take root:

> It has not retained its own productions, but has passed them on to Europe. It has given birth to principles which were not developed in their country of origin, but were brought to fruition in Europe.[84]

Not only did the near or extreme contemporary Orient, mired as it was in infancy, have nothing further to add or contribute. Worse yet, entire sections of its past fell beyond the frontiers of universal history. Only those rare Oriental peoples to have contributed to the march of the Spirit — of which Europe was the only true arena — found favour in the philosopher's eyes. These peoples were three: the Persians, "the first historical people," the first bearers of the light (that of Zoroaster), which "belongs to the World of Consciousness — to a Spirit as a relation to something distinct from itself;"[85] the people of Israel, in its role of announcing and preparing the coming of Christ (whose universal message it could not understand), as unconscious complement to the Roman spirit; and, in a marginal sense, the Egyptians, enriched by an immense "subterranean knowledge," a "people-chrysalis, unintelligible to itself," to employ Michel Hulin's terms, which "carried out in silence the metamorphosis which was to produce Greece."[86]

These three peoples had one thing in common: the inability to realize that which they bore within themselves, to grasp fully their own genius; but at the same time each contributed to the engendering of Greek and Roman civilization. With these two civilizations, the Mediterranean occupied the centre of the world. But the occupation was to be a transitory one, which entered into decline after the conquest of Gaul by Caesar. With "the greatest vigour and practical skill" action (as compared to Alexander's "juvenile" action), "he originated a new (world) across the Alps."[87] From that day on, whatever occurred to the south and to the east of the Alpine barrier was without apparent consequence, as seen from the viewpoint of the progress of the Spirit.

Islam, born more than six centuries after the decisive crossing, provided a telling, and embarrassing example. While Islam could hardly be ignored, the philosopher was ill at ease in dealing with it. Michel Hulin may well explain that the Islamic religion represented the "Oriental counterpart of Christianity's *penetration* of the customs and institutions of the Germanic peoples," but Islam still amounted to little more than a brief — though brilliant — parenthesis which Hegelian discourse could accommodate only at the cost of radical reduction. *Philosophy of History* concedes Islam all of one three-page chapter incongruously inserted into a section dealing with the Germanic world (Chapter II, Part IV), and whose principal intention is to explain why "Mahomet's" extraordinary enterprise was destined to fail:

> Abstraction swayed the minds of the Mohametans. Their object was to establish an abstract worship, and they struggled for its accomplishment with great enthusiasm. This enthusiasm was Fanaticism, that is, an enthusiasm for something abstract — for an abstract thought which sustains a negative position towards the established order of things. It

is the essence of fanaticism to bear only a desolating, destructive relation to the concrete; but that of Mahometanism was, at the same time, capable of the greatest elevation — an elevation free from all petty interests, and united with the virtues that pertain to magnanimity and valor...But all this is only contingent and built on sand; it is today, and tomorrow it is not. With all the passionate interest he shows, the Mahometan is really indifferent to this social fabric, and rushes on in the ceaseless whirl of fortune. In its spread, Mahometanism founded many kingdoms and dynasties. On this boundless sea there is a continual upward movement, nothing abides firm; whatever whirls up into a form remains all the while transparent, and that very instant glides away. Those dynasties were destitute of the bond of organic firmness.[88]

Hegel did not deny the accomplishments, nor the splendours of the first caliphates: after first undertaking, in the name of the Qur'an, to "destroying everything concerned with art and science," the Arabs "became zealous in promoting the arts and spreading them everywhere."[89] Hegel even reintegrated Islam, albeit stealthily, into universal history, recognizing that "science and knowledge, especially that of philosophy, came from the Arabs to the West" and that "a noble poetry and free imagination were kindled among the Germans by the East."[90] No sign here of anti-Muslim obscurantism, no desire to minimize the Arab contribution (which was all too evident with Renan); these were traits of generosity which some observers wished to see as the hallmark of the Hegelian vision of Islam.[91] There is nothing mean-spirited about Hegel; nothing but a pure, unadulterated incapacity to incorporate Arab civilization into his linear scheme, as a stage of history. Not because "purification" had not taken place, but because the spirit envisioned by this purification was "abstract" (in opposition to the "concrete" spirit of the West), and because it emerged rapidly (while, in the West, it took the form of a gradual evolution). In short, Islam was nothing but an ephemeral flame, which Ottoman domination, though "establishing as firm dominion," was unable to fan back to life. "Fanaticism having cooled down, no moral principle remained in men's souls." The West had appropriated whatever Islam had to offer: this was the sum total of the Arabo-Muslim contribution. All the rest was decadence:

> But the East itself, when by degrees enthusiasm had vanished, sank into the grossest vice. The most hideous passions became dominant, and as sensual enjoyment was sanctioned in the first form which Mahometan doctrine assumed,

and was exhibited as a reward to the faithful in Paradise, it took the place of fanaticism. At present, driven back into its Asiatic and African quarters, and tolerated only in one corner of Europe through the jealousy of the Christian powers, Islam has long vanished from the stage of history at large, and has retreated into Oriental ease and repose.[92]

Considered from the vantage point of the march of the Spirit, the entire Orient, with the exception of Zoroastrianism and Judaism, was without significance. Even these two beacons in the Oriental night were without meaning and impact except as they impinged on the destiny of the West, whose path they helped light. The third and last light to flare brightly in Asia came too late, though Europe succeeded in capturing its brightest beams; too late for the Orient to join universal history, to emerge lastingly from its immemorial dormancy. Lighted out of time and prematurely extinguished, the glowing ember of Islam was reduced to little more than a lump on the slag heap of history.

Ultimately, Hegel was to include only a tiny fraction of the Orient in his *Weltanschauung*, but this fraction, drawn from Asia nearest Europe, was the object of an integration which was no less absolute for being philosophical. That which could be salvaged from the Orient existed only by the grace of the West. Beyond European philosophy's view of it, the Orient was nothing: nothing more and nothing less than what Hegel's philosophy had declared it to be.

"Hegel's children"

As Albert Hourani has noted, the majority of 19th (and 20th) century historians and philosophers are, in one way or another, "Hegel's children."[93] The convergence between spirits as disparate as Auguste Comte and Karl Marx is unequivocal.

Comte, in whom the Hegelian formula is reduced to its flimsiest expression, decrees the expulsion of all that its not the West, all that is not Catholicism from what he terms "the whole of the working of history" But this does not imply that other civilizations should be abandoned to their lethargy:

> Such a manner of proceeding must appear all the more indispensable if one is to consider it in its practical aspect, to recognize its necessary participation in all wise regularization of an important order of political relations, those which concern the general actions of the most advanced nations for hastening the natural development of inferior civilizations.[94]

Though Marx's register was different, his concerns were similar. In "materializing" the Hegelian schema, Marx took it to its radical, logical conclusion. All things considered, Hegel had left the Orient where he found it — or more precisely, where he could ignore it. His selective integration of several of its contributions was strictly spiritual. But Marxist integration focused on the socio-economic reality of the Orient as a whole. The idea that other civilizations would ultimately, in one way or another, become a part of the West is probably implicit in Hegel; but as far as we can tell, the idea was of little import to him. What was to obsess Marx, and especially the Marxism which followed him, was the seemingly inexhaustible question of the notorious "Asiatic Mode of Production (AMP)."[95]

For Marx himself,[96] the question was "secondary" and of minor interest. Its interest lies, for us, in how it exemplified historical materialism's scientific predicament in integrating the Orient into the succession of modes of production which it propounded. What place amongst the great historical stages — Antiquity, feudalism and bourgeois society — was to be assigned to Asia? How could an apparently "immobile" mode of production be correlated with the dynamics of the class struggle? The Orient could not simply be relegated to "Antiquity" because of its failure to evolve toward more "advanced" forms of society. The AMP had no other function than to express by magic formula — a "concept" which was more catch-all — the "immobility" of the Orient: Oriental societies did not pass through the phases which Marxism assigned, rightly or wrongly, to the extraordinary historical evolution of which Western Europe had provided the model. Such societies did not therefore evolve. The problem was one of impediment rather than inertia. But the Orient could not be abandoned to its indolence: to speak of "blocked" societies was to identify the log jams to be blasted apart. For Marxists, the Orient could not long remain outside history; it must return to the fold, by force if necessary. Societies must either discover a method of "transition" from "community" to socialism (as Marx suggested for a Russian rural commune in his celebrated letter to Vera Zassulich[97]), or — the greater probability — they would bear the brunt of transformations imposed on them from without, driven by the world-wide expansion of the "bourgeois mode of production."

> Just as it made the country dependant on the towns, so it has made barbarian and semi-barbarian countries dependent on the civilized ones, nations of peasants on nations of bourgeois, East on West.[98]

Here, Marx was merely explaining — in forceful terms — an unfolding reality, a dynamic process which was already, in his day, discernible to whoever wished to see. The question is not an abstract one; the theoretical importance Marx attached to what he termed the "unchangeableness"[99] of Asiatic society is unimportant for our purposes The author of *Capital* was often cautious about his own concepts, and was distrustful of the theories that certain "Marxists" hastened to derive from them. In fact, much of the interminable debate over the AMP seems to me completely sterile. Its only useful purpose can be to demonstrate to what extent, on the question of the Orient, Marx was subordinate to Hegel. For, not simply content to note the integration of the Orient into the dynamism of the West, Marx accepted the premise, and even accepted it as a lesser evil, a necessary stage for wresting the Orient from stagnation. Miklos Molnar has demonstrated that despite his "violent criticism of colonialist methods" Marx "approved the results."[100] No further demonstration was needed. In a practical sense, the autonomous evolution of the Orient, using its existing institutions as a point of departure, was doubly impossible: first, because Asia's incapacity to transform its economic and social structures on its own initiative had been well established; second, because the Western breakthrough seemed irresistible, and represented, realistically, the only path toward socialism. In this regard, Marx was a full-fledged participant in the most resolutely West-centred intellectual current of his day.

For both Marx and Hegel the Orient — past or future — possessed no historical destiny worth speaking of: it was fated either to merge with Western universality or sink into insignificance. Marxism, however, would attempt to rescue the Orient from insignificance by locating it squarely within Western modernity. How could this process of insertion be hastened, and improved? The entire question could be reduced to one of pure form; the ultimate negation of the Other. Eurocentrism was nothing else, in the end, than the intellectual expression of the West's all-encompassing material superiority over the world. Seen from this perspective, any unique or positive qualities which the Orient might have cloaked *hic et nunc*, were utterly without pertinence.

In many ways, this reductivist attitude still typifies the Western sociological view of the Orient. Traditional Oriental social structures are still seen as relics of the past, as doomed resistance to modernity rather than as source of a distinct destiny — no matter how curious the idea might strike Westerners.

Oneiric integration

The oneiric integration of the Orient is a direct descendent of "scientific" reduction. Because the 19th century Orient had no interest as a society, it conserved great attraction as myth; what it lost in historical reality it gained in the power of dreams. Just as the social Orient could be ignored, denatured and destroyed, the Orient of dreams must be preserved, as a precious bauble in the mental universe of the West. Corresponding to sociology's integrational negation is a poetic appreciation based on another form of obliteration: the Orient as flight, as fugitive apparition:

> Oh! qui fera surgir soudain, qui fera naître,
> Là-bas — tandis que seul je rêve à la fenêtre
> Et que l'ombre s'amasse au fond du corridor —
> Quelque ville mauresque, éclatante, inouïe,
> Qui, comme la fusée en gerbe épanouie,
> Déchire ce brouillard avec ses flèches d'or?[101]

First victimized by neglect of its concrete reality, the Orient now became Europe's imaginary world. It was not the first time. We now know that in the Middle Ages the mythical Orient embodied paradise. Later, in the 17th and 18th centuries, it stood in for historical distance (as in Racine's *Bajazet*) and provided a change of scene — what we would call exoticism.

Come the romantic era, the taste for the Orient grew into necessity. No longer a simple diversion or object of curiosity, the Orient had become an antidote, a homeopathic prescription for the anguish induced by industrial civilization in the hearts of poets and philosophers. Not without reason did Nietzsche express himself through the mouth of Zarathustra. The Orient as paradise or wisdom lost was to the West what the Middle Ages of the cathedrals were to industrial progress. The West secreted the Orient as progress did anti-progress (for, as Valéry notes, the two go together[102]).

Though it corresponded to a profound impulse, the newfound need for the Orient often assumed such superficial forms as fashion or fascination, familiar lyrical or esthetic pursuits. Saïd perfectly illustrates what had happened when he shows how Chateaubriand "attempts to consume the Orient," travelling there "to replenish his stock of images." But the images he brings back have clearly been retouched. As Saïd engagingly puts it: "the Orient was a decrepit canvas awaiting his restorative efforts."[103] Certain parcels of the dream had to be kept intact, the prestige which the journey to the Orient confers upon the traveller — who in turn must mark his passage — had to be preserved. Chateaubriand saw the pyramids only from a distance, but he took care to have his name etched upon them! With Chateaubriand, and even more with Lord Byron — romantic hero-in-spite-of-himself and pilgrim-warrior of Greece and the eastern Mediterranean — the Orient became the required itinerary of poets and artists. Lamartine, Nerval, Flaubert were among the many who observed the rite. The Orient supplied Lamaratine (his colonial functions aside) with both a reservoir and a foil, as the Parisian press of the day innocently explained:

The sight of such an ancient, poetic world must provide the poet with the most brilliant and true of harmonies and colours, and his universal voyage, undertaken at personal expense to complete an epic poem, holds out for France the promise of an as-yet-unattained glory.[104]

The utility of the poetic Orient and the universal voyage as a source of glory was well understood by Lamartine, who, in a letter intended for newspaper publication, adopted a Caesarian style ("I have seen everything, visited everything, understood everything"), describing his epic voyage to the "great scene of the Biblical drama," and demonstrating the superiority which Oriental distance conferred upon his views:

I have told you before: to properly see Europe, one must be in Asia. All the noise, all the systems of Paris have a pathetic air when seen from the heights of Lebanon, or from the middle of the desert.[105]

Expression of the Westerner's imagined view of the Orient was not limited strictly to displays of smugness, though. It also corresponded to the search for what we might call an "extra portion of soul." Putting vanity aside, why should Chateaubriand's pilgrimage back to his roots not fill his "empty world" in which he "lives with a full heart"? The pilgrimage need not even be a physical one, as Goethe (and Hugo after him) demonstrated in his *West-East Divan*. In it, the poet's intention was to "penetrate right to the first origin of the human races" through symbiosis with the celebrated Ha'afez.

Hafis, with thee, alone with thee
Will I contend! joy, misery,
The portion of us twain shall be...
Like thee to love, like thee to drink —
This be my pride — this life to me!
Haifs, straight to equal thee
One would strive in vain
Master, pardon me.[106]

The association with Ha'afez was a flattering one, indeed. But the poet of Weimar hardly needed such lofty sanction at the time (1814-1816). Goethe sought in the Orient of yore a variant of lost — or threatened — classicism; a quality of seeing that he feared would vanish from the West in the wake of science's reduction to technique in the apprehension of nature. The Orient, for Goethe, was not so much a place of escape as part of a search for authenticity and wholeness. Not the authenticity of the Orient, of course (for this would mean nothing), but of being itself. Only, paradoxically, because the poet of Weimar never set foot in the Orient might Goethe truly become one with Ha'afez. And even then, he realized, the search for oneness would be circumscribed by the hoariest of commonplaces on the societies of the Orient. "Persian poetry, and all that approaches it, will never be accepted by Westerners with pure and complete pleasure" Goethe observes. Not because of religious differences, but because "the Western spirit could never accept...the corporal and spiritual submission to one lord and master."[107] Though he only half-subscribed to such crudely identifiable theses, Goethe perceived Oriental despotism as an obstacle to total poetic communion between the two opposing poles of his Divan; at least at the reader's level. Only poets could understand one another beyond time and space: only through them could the "pure Orient" be attained.

But woe to the poet who might actually make the journey. The Orient corresponded not at all to the images which caused him to depart. Confronted with the sobriety of Mousky's café in Cairo, Nerval dreamed of the lushness of the Parisian Orient. "Only in Paris can one encounter such Oriental cafés." His *Voyage en Orient* was more an account of disillusion than of enchantment. The Oriental world might well have been "the perfect antithesis of our own," but it was not the world of the poet's dreams. He would have to wait until the homeward journey, course firmly set on Europe, to rediscover a whisper of the oneiric charm which he had left behind.

> I return to the cold, stormy lands, and already the Orient is, for me, nothing more than one of those early-morning dreams which are soon followed by the cares of day.[108]

But the dream itself suffered irremediably from contact with reality, as he complained to Théophile Gautier.

> Kingdom by kingdom, province by province, I have already lost the most beautiful half of the universe, and soon I shall no longer know where my dreams can seek refuge; but it is Egypt which I most regret having driven from my imagination and into the miserable lodgings of my memories! You still believe in the ibis, the purple lotus, the Yellow Nile, you believe in the emerald palm, in the nopal, perhaps in the camel. Alas, the ibis is a wild bird, the lotus, a vulgar onion; the water of the Nile is reddish with touches of slate, the palms look like frayed feathers, the nopal is nothing but a cactus...

Oh! How curious I am to visit Philastre and Cambon's Cairo in Paris; I am certain that it will be my Cairo of bygone day, the city I beheld in so many dreams, in which I felt, as did you, that I had lived I do not know how long ago, in the reign of the Sultan Babars or the Caliph Hakim!...

Let us think of it no more! That Cairo lies beneath the cinders and the ashes, the spirit and the needs of the modern day have triumphed, like death.[109]

Thus did the West become the executioner of its own dreams; thus was the Orient destroyed twice over: first, as a society condemned by history; a second time as "the stuff of dreams" devastated by progress.

With Flaubert the combination of escape, fascination and disillusion was even more promiscuous, even more cynical. He gazed coldly upon both his petit-bourgeois dream and the destruction of its concrete underpinning (the societies of the Orient themselves) by the inexorable penetration of capitalism. Escape, you say? Our poet could only vent his spleen by the banks of the Nile.

A gandja under sail passes before me; this is the true Orient, melancholy, soporific; already you feel something immense and pitiless pressing down upon you, in which you are lost.[110]

Re-establish contact with the past? Only the present remained:

I spent a night at the feet of the colossus of Memnon, devoured by mosquitoes. The old scoundrel has a good face, covered with graffiti; graffiti and bird droppings are the only two things in the ruins of Egypt that give any indication of life. The most worn stone doesn't grow a blade of grass, it falls into powder, like a mummy, and that is all![111]

To conclude, his peregrinations come to an end: "Yes, indeed I have seen the Orient, and I am no farther ahead, for I still wish to return." The reality of the journey had only strengthened the longing for escape and sensual release: "Of all possible debauches, travel is the greatest I know."[112] But Flaubert was never to return to the Orient, except in his imagination, in the writing of Salammbo, whose "Oriental" coloration had little connection with his real experience. The journey to the East was but a brittle reverie, continually threatened by swooning spells. No need for Victor Hugo to have been there to put it bluntly:

Devant le sombre hiver de Paris qui bourdonne
Ton soleil d'Orient s'eclipse et t'abandonne
Ton beau rêve d'Asie avorte...
Alors s'en vont en foule et sultans et sultanes,
Pyramides, palmiers, galères capitanes,
Et le tigre vorace et le chameau frugal
Djinns au vol furieux, danses des batadères...
Alors éléphants blancs chargés de femmes brunes,
Cités aux dômes d'or où les mois sont des lunes,
Imam de Mahomet, mages, prêtres de Bel,
Tout fuit, tout disparaît: plus de minaret mauve,
Plus de sérail fleuri, plus d'ardente Gomorrhe
Qui jette un reflect rouge au front noir de Babe.[113]

Thus the poet dismisses the imagery which, for a few moments of escape, he himself had called into being. Later, in speaking of the "Orient of the mind," Valery was to lay down this "essential provision":

If this name is to have its full and entire effect on the mind, one must, above all, never have been in the ill-defined region it designates...

It must be known only from pictures, from stories one has heard or read, and from a few objects; and then only in the least erudite, most inexact and even muddled fashion. This is the way we amass good material for reverie.[114]

THE DEATH OF SARDANAPALUS

The 19th century's "gallery" of the Mediterranean Orient is so inexhaustibly rich that we could spend long hours perusing it. The canvasses we have examined are, I believe, representative, fraught with meaning whose subtlest nuances I have been far from successful in capturing. Is there a common trait which unites all of them, from Volney to Renan, from Napoleon to Hegel? Victor Hugo, in his preface to the *Orientales*, describes the need to which his collection responds as a "general concern." But what lies at the innermost core? Oblivion or negation (disparagement), domination or return to the source, nostalgia or raw material to be transformed, promiscuously penetrated or dreamed about, vaporized vision — is there a common thread? The more I reflect on it, the more convinced I become that such a thread exists, and that we can trace it into its innermost lairs: sociology and philosophy, the colonial mind-set, even poetry. That thread, at once incomparably trivial and grimly unbreakable, is death. Beneath its multiple disguises, the Orient constructed by Western modernity is death. In the strongest sense of the word, the Other world: successively to be conquered (the idea of "conquering death" dates from the 19th century, does it not?), a vanished and now moribund past, and a precarious after-life as refuge against this world.

By way of illustration, I propose to examine a painting — the only work of visual art we shall have the opportunity to study in the course of our excursion, though 19th century painting is particularly rich in its expression of Orientalism.[115] I trust that I may be forgiven as I stand before Delacroix, for being unable to resist the temptation to emulate Foucault before Velasquez.[116]

The painting itself is better known than the violent event which its depicts. But our only concern is the image held up to our gaze.

The despot reclines, impassive, in the midst of fervid disorder underscored by the horse which bursts into the lower left-hand quadrant of the canvas, so terrified that his handler can barely keep it under control. The ambient penumbra is illuminated by the nudity of the women disposed around a monumental bed which is tilted on the diagonal toward the centre of the scene. An orgy may have taken place. Certainly this sanctuary of debauch has known orgies in the past. But now, butchery is taking place.

In the foreground, almost at the foot of the master bed, arched violently toward it by the hand that grasps her, the body of the most visible of the women, brutally pulled from her luxurious bedclothes, offers itself to the dagger. The breast, marking the precise spot where the killer's short blade will strike — and where his glance has already struck — leads the eye toward another gaze, this one imperturbable, remote, half obscured in the darkness of the canvas. The dissimilarity between the two could not be more glaring: the intoxication and covetousness of he who is about to strike with his dagger at the body whose possession is forbidden to him contrasts sharply with the indifference of the possessor who has delivered her over to the executioner. Is he simply a spectator to the senseless murder which he has commanded? We do not know, so remote does he appear from the furor and the passion he has set loose. The attitude is mirrored in the body of the other woman, prostrate on the bed at his feet: is she imploring, is she offering herself, is she dead? We do not know. But we do know that she, along with the others, is a sacrificial victim. The scene is played out as though the spirit of the master had already departed the theatre of its own accord. The fate of the despot matters little: despotism itself is all-pervasive, omnipresent in the fullness of its absurdity, in the excitation which it commands, in the flood tide of purple coursing through the tableau in all its majesty, in a vortex of sanguinary, tyrannous indifference, prefiguring the blood-letting and the carnage which are about to commence.

Riveting in its morbidity, extreme and cruel in the nervous excessiveness of its sensuality, numbly subjected to the caprice of a jaded despotism and all the more destructive for it, this is the capricious Orient: master and slave, grand and contemptible; but, above all, doomed by the double affliction of its own dementia and the painter's genius. The artist's palette transforms the carnage into festivity; suggests in fact that carnage is a festivity, because it takes place outside this world, in a hermetic and inaccessible place. The pleasure of the eyes and the exoticism conveyed by pleasure conspire to absolve the darker pleasure of the senses, a darkness drawn from the very barbarity which the painting at once displays and condemns.

The extraordinary vivacity which Delacroix breathes into his costume jewelry Orient does not alter its use, only its intensity. What he displays with such extraordinary power is the mirror of our repressed selves. The fabulous Orient is an executory for our innermost drives, languishing, erupting in orgiastic rage, killing on our behalf (was Sade not punished for daring have us do so without an intermediary?). The Orient is dream and nightmare: more than quenching our unspeakable desires, the Orient exorcises our terrors and dies in our stead.

I make no claim to have exhausted the meaning of *The Death of Sardanapalus,* and I cannot judge to what extent my reading is the product of my own phantasms. However, they tend to be trivial enough to jibe comfortably with the commonplaces of the Western psyche. Delacroix returns us precisely to these commonplaces. The Orient depicted in his painting unfolds only within the world of our collective imagination. Beyond clichés, it is as remote as the despot's gaze. This gaze, ours in reality, is sufficient to convey the message that, beyond the excess ordained by unrestrained power, the Orient is nothing: the Orient has expired, drowned in indifference, murdered by the blind servility to which we have condemned it. The Orient is the death agony of our modernist dream.

NOTES

1. Hugo, Victor, *Les Orientales*, XL, "Lui" (Sublime, he appeared before the dazzled tribes/Like a Mohammed of the West!)
2. *Mémoires de Baron de Tott sur les Turcs et les Tartares*, Amsterdam, MDCCLXXXIV (1784), Tome 1, p.xxxii.

3. Saïd, Edward, *Orientalism*, op. cit.

4. Saïd, op. cit., p.42.

5. Saïd, op. cit., p.39. "To say simply that Orientalism was a rationalization of colonial rule is to ignore the extent to which colonial rule was justified in advance by Orientalism."

6. Saïd, op. cit., p.40. "Knowledge of the Orient, because generated out of strength, in a sense *creates* the Orient, the Oriental, and his world."

7. Volney, Constantin-François Chassebeuf, *Voyage en Egypte et en Syrie*, Paris et La Haye, Mouton, 1959. Quoted by Jean Gaulmier in his introduction, p.16.

8. *Description de l'Egypte* ou Recueil des observations et des recherches qui ont étés faites en Egypte pendant l'expédition de l'armée français publié par les ordres de sa Majesté l'Empereur Napoléon le Grand, Paris, Commission d'Egypte, 1809-1828.

9. See Wortham, John David, *British Egyptology*, 1549-1906. Newton Abbot, David & Charles, 1971.

10. Article by Volney reprinted in *Le Courrier de d'Egypte*, No. 33, le 3 thermidor, an VII (1798).

11. The argument of authority was later refined by the British administration in Egypt (and by London itself) almost a century later. See Edward Saïd's analysis, op. cit., p.34-39. "England knows Egypt; Egypt is what England knows; England knows that Egypt cannot have self-government; England confirms that by occupying Egypt." (Ibid., p.34.)

12. Ibid., p.81-82. See also Brahimi, Denise, *Arabes des Lumières et Bédouins romantiques*. Paris, Le Sycomore, 1982, p.188. Volney is seen as "drawing up a comparative list of forces from which France could formulate policy."

13. Volney, *Considérations sur la guerre actuelle des Turcs*. Quoted in Gaulmier, op. cit., p.132.

14. Ibid., p.59-60.

15. Quoted by Gaulmier, op. cit., p.50.

16. Among the "voyages" which could be compared to Volney's are: Thomas Shaw, *Travels, or Observations Relating to Several Parts of Barbary and the Levant*, Oxford, 1738; Edward William Lane, *An Account of the Manners and Customs of the Modern Egyptians*, London, Dent, 1954; as well as Richard Burton, *Personal Narrative of a Pilgrimmage to al-Medinah and Meccah*, 1839.

17. Volney, *Voyage...* op. cit., p.149.

18. Ibid., p.156.

19. Ibid., p.156.

20. Ibid., p.405.

21. Ibid., p.28.

22. Ibid., p.399.

23. Ibid., p.412.

24. Ibid., p.410.

25. Ibid., p.371-373. Volney's version of the passage from the Qur'an (Surah II) is hopelessly skewed. See *The Meaning of the Glorious Qur'an*, Text and Explanatory Translation by Marmaduke Pickthall, Tehran, Salehi Publications. "This is the Scripture whereof there is no doubt, a guidance unto those who ward off evil/And who believe in that which is revealed unto thee and that which was revealed before thee, and are certain of the hereafter."

26. Ibid., p.114-115.

27. See Amin, Samir, *The Arab Nation*, London, Zed Press, 1978; Rodinson, Maxime, *Islam and Capitalism*, New York, Pantheon, 1974.

28. Montesquieu, *the Persian Letters*, op. cit., Letter XIX, p.72.

29. Melon, Jean-François, *Essai politique sur le commerce*, (1736) quoted by Marie-Louise Dufrenoy, *L'idée de progrès l'Orient*, Amsterdam, Rodopi, N.V., 1975, p.342.

30. Volney, op. cit., p.387.

31. Volney, *Considérations sur la guerre des Turcs,* Londres, 1788, p.94-95.
32. Ibid., p.89.
33. Ibid., p.17.
34. Ibid., p.93.
35. Ibid., p.99 and 106. Volney might well be suspected of choosing Russia precisely because the Tsar's empire was one of the least advanced in Europe.
36. Ibid., p.134-135.
37. Dufrenoy, op. cit., p.381.
38. Volney, *Considérations...* quoted by Denise Brahimi, op. cit., p.190.
39. See Note 18 above.
40. Volney, *Les Ruines,* présentation de Jean Tulard, Genève, Slatkine Reprints, 1979.
41. Ibid., p.84-85.
42. Ibid., p.93.
43. *Description de l'Egypte,*op. cit., p.LII.
44. Contrary to Edward Saïd's view. (See note 14 above), op. cit., p.81.
45. Renan, Ernest, *Oeuvres complètes,* Averroës et l'Averroisme. Paris, Calmann-Lévy, 1949, Vol. III, p.13-14.
46. Renan, Ernest, op. cit. Vol. VIII, p.156. (Quoted by Edward Saïd, op. cit., p.149: "One sees that in all things the Semitic race appears to us to be an incomplete race by virtue of its simplicity.")
47. Warburton, Eliot, *The Crescent and the Cross, or Romance and Realities of Eastern Travel.* London, Hurst and Blackett, n.d.
48. Ibid., p.iv.
49. Ibid., p.31.
50. Ibid., p.31.
51. Pococke, Richard, *A Description of the East, and Some other Countries.* Volume the First, Observations on Egypt. London, 1743, p.181.
52. Nerval, Gérard de, *Voyage en Orient,* Oeuvres II, Paris, Gallimard, Pléiade, 1956, p.281.
53. Description de l'Egypt, op. cit., Vol. II, p.424.
54. Ibid., p.lii.
55. Warburton, op. cit., p.185.
56. Bordeaux, Henry, *Voyageurs d'Orient,* Paris, Plon, 1926, p.17-18. Speech by M. Hippolyte de Villeneuve, reported in l'Echo du Vaucluse, le 4 juillet, 1832.
57. Brahimi, op. cit., p.201.
58. Ibid., p.209.
59. Lamartine, quoted by Denise Brahimi, op. cit., p.204.
60. Ibid., p.201.
61. Ninet, John, *Lettres d'Egypte 1879-1882,* présentées par Anouar Louca. Paris, éditions du C.N.R.S., 1979.
62. Ibid., p.52 (letter of June 15, 1879).
63. Ibid., p.60-61 (letter of July 1, 1879).
64. While formal power was still Ottoman, real power was in European hands.
65. Ibid., p.63 (letter of July 11, 1879).
66. Quoted by J.-P. Callot in "Suez (Canal de)" in *Encyclopedia Universalis,* Vol. 15, 1978, p.503.
67. Geothe, Johan Wolfgang von, quoted by Edward Saïd, in *Orientalism,* op. cit., p.167. See also *East-West Divan* in *The poems of Geothe.* Chicago, Belford, Clarke & Co. 1882. Vol. 3. In his preface to the Divan, Heinrich Heine writes: "This nosegay signifies that the West is tired of thin and icy-cold spirituality, and seeks warmth in the strong and healthy bosom of the East."
68. Gérard, René, *L'Orient et la pensée romantique allemande,* thèse présentée à la faculté des lettres et sciences humaines de l'Université de Paris, Paris, Marcel Didier, 1963.
69. Ibid., p.95.
70. Ibid., p.194.

71. Ibid., p.30.
72. The analysis which follows is based on my reading of Hegel's *Lectures on the Philosophy of World History*, London, Cambridge University Press, 1975. I have attempted to delimit the manner in which Hegel integrates the Orient, particularly the Mediterranean Orient, into his vision of universal history. My interpretation will undoubtedly strike philosophers acquainted with Hegel as superficial. I hasten to note that it is not my intention to deal with Hegel in his breadth, depth and complexity. My interest is in Hegel as he is commonly (and probably despite himself) perceived. The Hegelian philosophy of history (unlike other aspects of his philosophy) is accessible to the educated public. On the theme of the Orient in Hegel, I have also consulted Michel Hulin's *Hegel et l'Orient*, Paris, Vrin, 1979. I would, however, like to go beyond the "Hegelian" limitations of Hulin's book, particularly regarding Islam and the Arabs.
73. Hulin's interpretation, op. cit., p.141.
74. Hegel, *Lectures*... op. cit., p.27.
75. Ibid., p.11,25.
76. Ibid., p.28.
77. Ibid., p.54.
78. Ibid., p.54.
79. Ibid., p.197.
80. Ibid., p.202-203. To this diachronic argument are added the ancient climatic considerations dear to Aristotle, Bodin, Montesquieu, etc.: "It is therefore the temperate zone which must furnish the theatre of world history."
81. Ibid., p.199.
82. Ibid., p.199.
83. Ibid., p.190,192.
84. Ibid., p.194.
85. Hegel, *Philosophy of History*. Translation by J. Sibree. New York, Dover, 1956, p.173.
86. *Hulin*, op. cit., p.133-134.
87. Hegel, *Philosophy of History*, op. cit. p.312.
88. Ibid., p.358.
89. Ibid., p.358-359.
90. Ibid., p.360. "While, therefore, in the West, this long process in the world's history — necessary to that purification by which the Spirit in the concrete is realized — is commencing, the purification requite for developing Spirit in the Abstract which we observed carried on contemporaneously in the East, is more quickly accomplished. The latter does not need a long process, and we see it produced rapidly, even suddenly, in the first half of the seventh century, in Mahometanism." (p.355.)
91. Djait, Hichem, *Europe and Islam, op. cit., p.80-85.* For Djait, "the vision [of Islam] contained in these pages is striking — both profoundly true and remarkably poetic." (p.80.) Hegel saw Islam, explains Djait, as a "luminous force" which "transcended the negativity of the Oriental mind." (p.81.)
92. Ibid., p.360.
93. Hourani, Albert, *Europe and the Middle East*, Berkeley, University of California Press, 1980, p.57.
94. Comte, August, *Cours de philosophie positive*, tome cinquième contenant La partie historique de la philosophie sociale, 52e et 53e leçons. *Oeuvres*, tome V, Paris, Bachelier, 1841, p.3-5.
95. Literature on the subject is abundant. I have used Steard Schram's *Marxism and Asia*, London, Allen Lane, 1969, Miklos Molnar, *Marx, Engels et la politique internationale*, Paris, Gallimard, Idées, 1965, and Marian Sawyer, *Marxism and the question of the Asiatic Mode of Production*, La Haye, Nijhoff, 1977 (probably the most complete work on the subject).

96. Dhoquois, Guy, *Critique du politique*. Paris, Anthopos, 1983. "For Marx, the AMP is a secondary concern... He deals with the AMP in passing, and the term appears only once in his work. But in bringing together his scattered allusions to Oriental societies, a concept is arrived at." (p.14.)

97. Marx, Karl, *Collected Works*, New York, International Publishers, 1975.

98. Marx, Karl, *Manifesto of the Communist Party*, in Karl Marx, Frederick Engels, Collected Works, New York, International Publishers, 1975, Vol. 6, p.488.

99. Marx, Karl, *Capital*, Moscow, Progress Publishers, 1965, Vol. I, p.358. "...an unchangeableness of such striking contrast with the constant dissolution and refounding of Asiatic states."

100. Molnar, op. cit., p.224. See also Schram, *Marxism and Asia:* "England has to fulfill a double mission in India: one destructive, the other regenerating — the annihilation of old Asiatic society, and the laying of the material foundations of Western society in Asia." (op. cit., p.117.)

101. Hugo, Victor, *Les Orientales*, "Rêverie," XXXVI [Oh! Who will cause to rise, who to emerge/afar — whilst I dream at my window/And the shade grows dark at my door — /Some shining Moorish city/Which, like the rocket in a shower of sparks/Rends the mist with its golden arrows?]

102. Valéry, Paul, *Collected Works of Paul Valéry*, New York, Pantheon Books, Random House, 1962. Vol. 10, p.161. "...the idol of Progress was countered by the idol of damning Progress which made two commonplaces."

103. Saïd, op. cit., p.171,173.

104. *Journal des Débats*, October 6, 1832, quoted by Henry Bordeaux, *Voyageurs d'Orient*, op. cit., p.75-76.

105. Letter from Lamartine to Edouard Casalis, November 12, 1832, quoted by Henry Bordeaux, op. cit., p.75-76.

106. Goethe, op. cit., Vol. 3, p.392. Ha'afez (he who knows the Qur'an by heart) is the commonly used name of one of the great Persian poets of the Islamic era. He lived in Shiraz in the 14th century under his true name, Khadja Shams Eddim Mohammad.

107. Goethe, *Notes et dissertations pour aider à l'intelligence du Divan*.

108. Nerval, op. cit., p.142, 136 and 628.

109. Nerval, letter to Théophile Gautier, op. cit. p.120.

110. Flaubert, Gustave, *Voyage en Orient*, Paris, Société des Belles Lettres, 1948, Vol. 2, p.39.

111. Flaubert, Gustave, *The letters of Gustave Flaubert*, translated by Francis Steegmuller, Cambridge, Harvard University Press, 1980, Vol. I, p.119.

112. Ibid., p.309.

113. Hugo, *Les Orientales*, "Novembre" XLI.

114. Valéry, op. cit., Vol. 10, p.380.

115. Rosenthal, Donald A., *Orientalism, The Near East in French painting, 1800-1880*. Memorial Art Gallery of the University of Rochester, New York, p.19-31.

116. Foucault, op. cit., p.19-31.

VI

The Uneasy Orient

By the end of the 19th century, as industrial society, with the sanction of
Hegelian philosophy, completed its penetration into every corner of the
earth, secreting literary and artistic nostalgia for the Orient as antitoxin to
the ideology of productivism as it went, the expressions of the Orient
which to this day crowd our collective imagination had already taken
shape. Contradictory and confused, or well-ordered and rational, they live
on within us. From the heretically delimited "medieval" Mediterranean
world (whose symbiotic aspects we are still reluctant to accept) to the alien,
barbarous and voluptuous land laid prostrate before the jackboot, the
science and the delirium of the West, from exoticism to despotism, from the
magical to the sordid, the Orient — forgotten man and survivor of history
— has exhausted all possible forms, brought forth all possible phantasms,
held out all possible mirrors.

All mirrors but one, the product of the specific disquiet of our century,
and more particularly, of its second half. Through the disintegrating silver
glaze of its oriental psyche, the late-20th-century West has become uncom-
fortably aware that the Other has begun to gaze upon it. Accustomed, for
more than two centuries, to viewing the Orient as both subject matter and
object, the West, for the first time, must now confront it as a sentient,
bruised and exacting subject. Confrontation is the proper term: the reverse
shock of colonization has brought home to the West a new awareness of
the Other as actor on the world stage. Europe had long ago, of course,
considered the Other as subject. Collective memory knows that the words
Saracen and Turk in the Middle Ages stood for redoubtable adversaries
who were fought on equal terms. But it also knows that the Muslim threat
has since faded, that the Islamic world could no longer offer serious
resistance to the Western onslaught. Today, an awakened Islam is re-
emerging in the collective imagination of the West, no longer simply as an
army to be fought, but as a rebel, as an insidious enemy, as a challenge to
the established order, and even more recently, as immigrant pariah in the
heart of European society, ready at a moment's notice to disappear behind
the mask of the terrorist, or to sow disorder and fanaticism in the name of
the Qur'an.

Islam today, from within as well as from without, represents the only
ideology capable of articulating a radical challenge to Western hegemony

without simultaneously borrowing its intellectual weapons from the West. This, at least, is the often confused feeling of many Westerners, torn between pangs of conscience and apprehension — often ill-tempered — at the sight of a near-at-hand, and until recently "outdated," Islam suddenly become "overwrought" and "unpredictable." There is a sense of failure in the air: the failure of the West, ensnared in the trap of its own excess and confronted by the obstinate resistance of the Other. It may take the form of upheaval at the onrush of modernity, but it is resistance all the same. Occupied, studied, visited, exploited, fantasized, the Orient has remained unbent and incomprehensible in its outspoken or silent refusal; a barrier, a recurring closure which the West, despite its power, has been unable to overcome. Our anxiety, our desire to neutralize or to absorb the Other in our "universal" destiny remains so powerful that its resistance, even today, fuels our projections and our attitudes, from the most hostile to the most friendly. It has become the most recent addition to our imaginary construct; what we may term the Orient of disquiet.

This disquiet has kept our arsenal of prejudices well stocked. All that history has bequeathed to us is there, neatly stacked, ready to be used, to be brandished at the slightest sign of danger, to be oiled and sharpened to meet the needs of the day. Up to and including the idea of heresy: no longer religious, but economic or social. With each new crisis the same old stereotypes bubble to the surface. There is certainly no lack of crises in that part of the world where the West appears to have learned nothing from its painful colonial experience, where, since 1945, it has pursued reckless, short-sighted policies punctuated by moments of ineptitude or humiliation. Not every aspect of the endemic crisis which afflicts the Near East can be laid at the doorstep of the West. But it must be recognized that almost everything done by Europe, up to the invasion of Suez (1956) and the United States ever since, has exacerbated tensions.

Anti-Arab and anti-Muslim feelings (and until recently, anti-Sovietism) remain one of the modern West's strongest, most unreasoning negative urges. Anti-Arabism has grown even stronger since the end of World War II, and has now become the successor to anti-semitism. The Arab and the Muslim have in many ways replaced the Jew, both as undesirable elements in our societies (the immigrant) and as the malignant personification of wealth (petrodollars): while the Jews, under the banners of rampant Zionism have been handed the dubious mission of defending the West in the eastern Mediterranean and of cleansing Europe of its crime against Judaism. Our prejudices, both old and new, have been powerfully reinforced by this inversion. We know the constant replay of identical images kept alive by the Western media all too well.[1]

The 20th century view, like those of preceding centuries, is interesting only in its specificity. This specificity is the apprehension, or at least the anticipation of the decline of the West, and the angst that this feeling triggers in us, in our affluence, under the cold glare of the disinherited. The feeling is one of remorse, with an accompanying reflex of rejection, or more rarely, a desire for reconciliation. These desires are my main concern, particularly as they bode forth both our most generous and most deeply repressed collective fears, casting their shadow over the dialogue some of us wish to establish with the Other. The danger is two-fold: that of piteous condescension, and of guilty self-torment. But neither pity (over the fate of the Other) nor self-deprecation serve any purpose. Despite its inherent risks, the dialogue must be undertaken; our obligation is to reflect upon those conditions which would make it possible. Ethnocentric limitations aside, the thoughtful gaze of the West provides the Other — for whose heartbeat we listen, whom we seek out — with much to reflect upon. The "uneasy Orient" thus leads us straight to the question of cultural identity: a question as pertinent to us as it is to the Other.

THE DECLINE OF THE WEST

At approximately the same time — the late 19th century — as the West had completed its census of the emergent states and strengthened its material domination over other civilizations, Western thought gradually went over to the counterattack against its own triumphant nationalism and against the scientific underpinnings of universalism. The attack was marginal at first, but the massive shock of World War I, which was experienced as a titanic failure of Europe, opened the way for an outpouring of disenchantment.

While the European West's critical or disabused view of its own world vision gained prominence only after the most absurd of wars, its source can be traced much farther back, well before the conquering 19th century to the thought of the late 18th. To Herder, for instance, the repentant promoter of the "myth of the poetic Orient" whom Cassirer credits with the inception of a new, decisive stage in the "conquest of the historical world"[2] for having struck the first blows against the universalizing history of classicism and of the Enlightenment. Though Herder's quest for the "spirit of the peoples" was motivated chiefly by a nationalist desire to attend the birth of the German genius, his criticism of French universalism — beyond the quarrelling of philosophical schools — threatened to have an impact on the centripetal universality of the entire West. And Herder was not alone. In both France and England signs of anthropological relativism had begun to appear: in Hume's *Natural History of Religion* (1757) and in Diderot's *Supplément au voyage de Bougainville* (1772), and, of course, scattered throughout the works of Rousseau.[3] Some Enlightenment philosophers, or so it appeared, were already alert to the eventual havoc, and above all, to the universalist pretensions which were to spring from the very rationalism which they all cultivated.

The classical vision of universal man, who was to be measured against Greece, Rome and Europe, was to culminate in Hegel. But at the same time that the development of scientific rationality seemed to confirm the idea, new perspectives emerging from the natural sciences were already preparing the first challenges. In opening the door to anthropology in the early years of the 19th century, science indirectly called into question both the sovereignty and the universality of reason, which was to be further destabilized by the "discovery" of the unconscious. So it was that the self-same conceptual tools which contributed to the advent of European world supremacy also provoked an intellectual critique of the humanist underpinnings of this supremacy. It was a minority critique, to be sure. But that did not stop it from striking a first, though muffled blow against the untroubled conscience which had thus far accompanied Europe's conviction of superiority. It happened well before Europe was to enter into its own economic and political post-World War I decline. In fact, the challenge to the West by its own intellectual fringe came not as a result of decline, but emerged from the very structure of the thought processes which the decline provided ample reason to exercise.

The clear-cut leap from what I defined, in the previous chapter, as the spirit of the 19th century to that of the 20th came to light only after World War II (our secular *caesurae*, here as elsewhere, are more symbolic than chronological). It became particularly clear-cut in the way Europe used its knowledge of the Orient.

In his preface to the *Histoire des orientalistes de l'Europe du XII au XIV siècle*, published in 1868, Gustave Dugat clearly enunciated the functions of the Orientalists of the day:

> While continuing to delve into the sphere of pure science, they must mingle with the contemporary world as Europe invades the Oriental lands from every direction, and where agents of civilization must be trained, to initiate them to Asiatic studies in a political and commercial intent.[4]

The French occupation of Algeria was then twenty years old; England had been established in Aden for several years longer; both had intervened militarily in Lebanon to impose a political compromise; the Suez canal had been completed (to be followed 20 years later by the British protectorate in Egypt). Several years later, the European-controlled Ottoman Public Debt Administration was created; the Turkish Empire escaped dismemberment only because of the rivalries among the predators who coveted its remains. The final division of the spoils was to take place at the end of World War I, when the European colonial stranglehold on the Near East (and on the world in general) had reached its apogée, even as the war had weakened, and ultimately undermined the foundations of its hegemony.

Addressing a formally decolonized Orient one century later, Jacques Berque — another French orientalist — wondered aloud how it might now be possible to speak of Islam "from without," how the "inordinately underlined" disgraces committed by the foreign, and worse, Western, observer, be somehow redressed. "Our generation's self-doubt and its failures will have been necessary to refute the Eurocentrism which still dominates our vision of the world."[5]

Stretching between these two historical moments is a curve ascending from negation to a variant of guilty sensitivity itself not entirely free of fears and commonplaces (oil, fundamentalism, etc.). But behind it all remains a deepening dilemma: despite its position of relative weakness, beyond its threats — real or imagined — the Orient calls us to account, questions us. The questions it asks, and the questions we ask of ourselves through it, are of concern primarily to Europeans, less to Americans. The shadow of decline has crept over the former; the latter still believe themselves in the light. As the European-minded Jean Ballard remarked in 1947:

> At a certain point in the curve of their development, civiliza-
> tions come to doubt themselves; they become conscious of
> their possible end. Our civilization has been experiencing
> vertigo for the last 30 years, and continues to consult its
> physicians. God knows they have responded; first the
> visionaries, then the nay-sayers! The West's great neurosis
> led to the success of Spengler in 1920; created the success of
> all those soothsayers who, in our tower of Babel, drown out
> the aspirations of enlightened spirits towards affinity.[6]

Spengler, last of the monologues

Let the gentle spirits, those whose sympathies remain too disincarnate to be true, think what they will, but it is hardly possible to speak of the decline of the West without returning to Spengler, whose "Faustian" soul found itself in constant conflict with the "Apollonian" and "Magian" souls of the Mediterranean Orient. First of all, let us underscore the radical novelty of his proposition which, for the first time I am aware, located the West in a fundamentally different world — on the spiritual and intellectual levels — from that of ancient Greece: as foreign to the century of Pericles as to the century of Mohammed. His *Decline of the West* merits rereading for this iconoclastic enterprise alone: the opposition between Orient and Occident is suddenly bathed in fresh light.

No one showed better than Spengler the path that the European philosophy of history must tread in order to break free from the strictures of Hegelian thought. His "German philosophy" (as he himself described it) was probably the first Western vision of the world and of universal history which, despite the predominantly European focus of its concerns, brought full self-awareness to bear on the struggle to throw off its own guileless ethnocentrism. His efforts were badly served: a certain aristocratic nostalgia for the heroic days (visible in a different form in Nietzsche, whom Spengler admired), the convoluted impressionism of his thought, his Wagnerian mysticism, his exploitation by the Nazis — all conspire to make Spengler the kind of visionary one would rather avoid.

But the disfavour surrounding him also stems from the power and the obstinacy with which *The Decline of the West* poured salt on the wounds inflicted by the Great War on European consciousness, and on its belief in progress. We have, at last, reached a point — beyond spleen, beyond the lost paradise of the romantics — of confrontation with the certainty so succinctly summed up by Valéry: "We later civilizations...we now know that we are mortal."[7] We know, yet we do not wish to know. In laying bare our unavowed fears, Spengler shone an unpleasant light on the West's persistent denial of the idea, latent in its very being, that it too may be relative, finite. It is a harsh light, but one from which Spengler hoped a saving illumination would come:

> World-history is our world picture and not all mankind's. Indian and Classical Man formed no image of the world in progress, and perhaps, when in due course, the civilization of the West is extinguished, there will never again be a Culture and a human type in which 'world-history' is so potent a form of the waking consciousness.[8]

The extinction of Western civilization is not, then, inevitable, and Spengler himself wishes for nothing more than to repeal the fatal verdict. Our history may well not be universal, but it still possesses one unique particularity, one specific mission — fit for a Faustian culture — to be accomplished. It need only be aware of the mission. With an energy born of despair, *The Decline* strives to awaken this awareness.

> In this book is attempted for the first time the venture of predetermining history, of following the still untravelled stages in the destiny of a Culture, and specifically the Culture of our time and on our planet which is actually in the phase of fulfillment — the West-European-American.[9]

Only the West possesses the possibility, the unprecedented opportunity to bring about "the physiognomy of all becoming and the system of all things become."[10] What could be more Hegelian in its ambition! More

Nietzschean in its tormented striving to surpass itself! The West is the sole culture capable of realizing the universal for all humanity, on condition that it proceed properly, on condition that it first undertake the prodigious leap, the effort to establish the critical distance and thoughtful reflection to which Spengler summons it. In response to the serene ethnocentrism of the philosopher of Berlin, Hegel, who knew himself to be at the pinnacle of history (even though a call to conscience can be heard amidst the beatific serenity), comes the anguished ethnocentrism of the aristocrat who sees that the moment of truth is at hand:[11] universal history does not exist, but it can be realized — providing the West abandon its complacent vision of the world and set about reconstructing it in all its latent totality. Powerfully egocentric about the future (the preserve of the will), but lucidly pluricentric in his feverish meditation on the past, Spengler gave penetrating expression to the rending of the West in the face of the plurality of worlds, and of the eventual non-meaning of history. In all justice, we must grant Spengler at least this much: the desire to dominate the world (an entirely intellectual desire in his case) causes him to lash out at the hoariest, most persistent Eurocentric clichés, particularly those which locate ancient Greece within an exclusively modern Western perspective.

Spengler saw no need to establish continuity between classical antiquity and our age. The West came into being with the Gothic cathedrals, breaking with that which had come before. Furthermore, the break had come from within, not from without (as claimed by those who attempted to saddle Islam with the responsibility). "Thanks to the subdivision of history into 'Ancient', 'Medieval' and 'Modern' — an incredibly jejune and meaningless scheme which has, however, entirely dominated our historical thinking — we have failed to perceive the true position of the general history of higher mankind."[12] By destroying the "mystic number three" and with it, its seductive power, Spengler freed himself from a narrow linear vision of the past: he could now examine the cycles of history, and examine each culture in and for itself. "Here the Cultures, peoples, languages, truths, gods, landscapes bloom and age as the oaks and the stone-pines, the blossoms, twigs and leaves..."[13] His was a vision diametrically opposed to that of the historian in his ivory tower, who views universal history as the constant succession of epochs.

No more would there be any question, in this enlightened *Weltanschauung*, of tracing the conflict between the Orient and the West back to Marathon! Hellenic culture and its Apollonian soul are, in any event, foreign to our Faustian souls.[14] The Renaissance's reference to Antiquity is more theoretical than real. We are no closer to the Apollonian soul than to the "Magian" (or Arab) soul, of which original Christianity is one of the principal expressions. But, here as well, Western Christianity is related to early Christianity only in form. "What one people takes over from another — in 'conversion' or in admiring imitation — is a name, dress and mask for its own feeling, never the feeling of the other."[15] The religion of Saint Augustine (who lived from 354 to 430) is not our religion: it, like Augustine himself, who was born in North Africa, was Arab, in the broadest sense of the term — exaggeratedly so with Spengler, as Hichem Djait amicably admonishes.[16]

The projection of Arabicity in time and space is equally compelling in its transformation of the advent of Islam from a rift into a culmination. Indeed, the "Magian mentality of Arab culture" which was abroad in the eastern Mediterranean even before the coming of Christ, and was reinforced by it, rushed into the vacuum left in the Roman Empire as the Apollonian heritage grew old.[17] The process was not a formal borrowing, but a true substitution, a symbiosis made possible by the ossification of perverted Apollonian culture into a "civilization"[18] that had reached the end point of its decline as the Christian message had begun to triumph.

But how could Islam be viewed as a culmination if the Magian soul had already found vigorous expression in original Christianity? Spengler does not expressly resolve the contradiction, most probably because the Arab soul was unable to fully flourish under Christianity, and because Christianity was still ensconced in the "pseudomorphosis" where it had been so long confined. In Spengler, the concept of "historical pseudomorphosis" is used to describe the vegetative state in which the dead strictures of the ancient civilizations of Asia had long gripped Arab culture.[19] Those were the strictures which Islam shattered, setting the Magian soul free from its shackles. Whatever the significance and impact of ancient Christianity, only Islam brought about the flowering of Arab culture on every level, including the political, and thus brought the debilitating pseudomorphosis to an end.

> This alone is sufficient to explain the intense vehemence with which the Arabian Culture, when released at length from artistic as from other fetters, flung itself upon all the lands that had inwardly belonged to it for centuries past. It is the sign of a soul that feels itself in a hurry, that notes in fear the first symptoms of old age before it has had youth. This emancipation of Magian mankind is without parallel.[20]

This lateness of the flowering explained both its particular brilliance and the brevity of its political expression: the Arab Empire. As for the Muslim religion, it must be considered "as the Puritanism of a whole new group of Early Magian religions." Only in this deep meaning can "the key of its fabulous success" be found.[21] Islam's insertion into Magian culture — a vague, inadequate formula — its description as puritanism, as condemned by its pseudomorphosis to tardy maturity (or early ageing) which, after the decline of the caliphate, precludes any possibility of renewal...all this seems highly debatable. As Hichem Djait says:

> Islam would no longer be the dawn of a new world, but the twilight of a culture that has found in it the most beautiful and authentic winding sheet.[22]

One might well respond that Spengler never relegated Islam to any particular fate. In his universe, all cultures are fated to decline, even Faustian culture itself. But the two declines do not share the same contours: the decline of Arab culture belongs to the past and is irreversible, while that of the West, as we well know, remains hypothetical. Though it may be under threat, it still maintains real superiority, even though that superiority is one of material power alone: only the Faustian soul is capable of endowing history with universal meaning. But the hope is a paradoxical one, when we consider that the Spenglerian view of history has a propensity for cultural noncommunicability.[23]

We cannot assert that, in Spengler, the apprehension of decline leads to intercultural dialogue. But at least other cultures, in their historical development, are not subordinated to the Western imperative — to fulfill human destiny. For Spengler Islam, though implicitly obsolete, was neither negation, deviation, splendid anomaly, nor rift. It was, instead, a fruition and a deliverance; the liberation of the true Magian soul: a soul which felt at home not only in the Mashrek or the Maghreb, but also in Byzantium, Ravenna and Rome. Its spiritual presence was palpable in Christ and in the Gospels, before finding consummate expression in Mohammed, in an age when the Faustian soul had not even uttered its first stammerings. Spengler may well have turned a blind eye to the contemporary Orient, but he restored to Arab culture a broad and prestigious historical field which the West, to this day, has not ceased to claim as its own. This act of restitution had less connection with vague feelings of guilt than with a new, unexpectedly less inward-looking "morphology of world history." Spengler rehabilitated *cultures*. But his "generosity" was limited: the only cultures rehabilitated were dead ones, in what was to remain forever an internal monologue.

Toynbee: toward dialogue?

Are other cultures dead? The idea itself is challenged by a more level-headed, pragmatic but no less ambitious thinker, a specialist in world-history and the fate of civilizations for whom the Mediterranean Orient holds pride of place. For Toynbee, several non-Western cultures remain quite alive. The West has disseminated its mode of production, not its civilization.

> In its struggle for existence, the West has driven its contem-
> poraries to the wall and entangled them in the meshes of its
> economic and political ascendency, but it has not yet dis-
> armed them of their respective cultures. Hard-pressed
> though they are, they can still call their souls their own, and
> this means that the mental strife has not yet reached a
> decision.[24]

Among the twenty-one civilizations which figure in his history of
humanity, Toynbee distinguishes five cultures (or types of society) which
are still alive in the 20th century: the Western and the Orthodox (both
derived from Hellenic civilization), the Islamic (whose two branches, the
Arab and the Iranian, stem from Syriac civilization), the Indian and the
Far-Eastern. In its great cultural divisions, the world remains today what it
had already become in the 8th century of the Christian era, making Arab
and Western civilizations the last-born of history. Despite the ostensibly
homogenizing effects of the world economy, history itself remains open
and pluralist; the four non-Western civilizations have not had their last
word.[25]

In order to hear what these civilizations have to say, the West must
foreswear its unitarian conception of civilization and its linear vision of
history — mutually reinforcing concepts which stem in turn from three
"underlying misconceptions:" "the egocentric illusion, the catchword of
the 'unchanging East', and the misconception of growth as a movement in
a straight line."[26] In support of his deconstruction of dominant history,
Toynbee cites Volney's warning to his contemporaries:

> We have dealt only with the Greeks and the Romans, in
> servile fashion, following a rigid and exclusive method
> which attributes all to a minuscule Asian people, unknown
> in Antiquity, and to the system of Herodotus, whose limita-
> tions are infinitely restrictive: we have wished to see only
> Egypt, Greece and Italy, as though the universe existed
> within those small confines alone; and as if the history of
> those small peoples were anything but a fable, a late-bloom-
> ing branch of the history of the entire species.[27]

Toynbee underscores with scant ceremony the specific role played by
Protestantism (particularly Anglo-Saxon Protestantism) as a result of its
close relationship with Judaism. The Bible Christians (as he calls them)
identified consciously with Israel, casting themselves as the chosen people.
This myth which, for Toynbee, lies at the heart of all white racism, was
utilized and reinforced wherever Europeans established their colonies.
The Anglo-Saxons applied it in its most radical form.[28] In the Near East, the

concept of chosen people takes on a particular resonance, manifesting itself in two forms, whose contradictory nature Toynbee curiously neglects to mention: on the one hand Israel, and on the other, the Aryan race — which, Gobineau insisted, had maintained its "original purity" through its peregrinations from Asia to Europe.[29] This contradiction surely explains why the Jews, depending on the circumstances, could function as scapegoats for the West (as a people which had forfeited its chosen status for having refused to recognize the authenticity of the Christian message), or re-establish, under arms, a variant of their mission as chosen people now that the Arabs were to be neutralized.

But in spite of the innovative nature of his views Toynbee cannot rid himself of one of Western historiography's most persistent myths regarding Islam. Though he denounces the absurdity, in geographical terms, of the dividing line between Europe and Asia he cannot resist the temptation to attribute it historically to the famous rift caused by the advent of Islam.

> This massive Islamic road-block was a challenge which evoked proportionally energetic responses from pioneer communities in the two blockaded Christian societies.[30]

But, by the same token, he suggests that the East-West dichotomy may well antedate Islam, having apparently been thrust upon the leaders of the Roman Empire. According to Toynbee, it was no accident that the Ottoman Empire ultimately came to rule the dominions of Orthodox Christianity.[31] Following in Spengler's footsteps, but rather more cautiously, Toynbee views Islam (as he does Christianity) as an expression of the "Syriac" germ: a return to the Syriac origins of Christianity and a reaction against its Hellenization.[32]

It should come as no surprise to uncover ambiguities in a work written over the span of several decades. What is perhaps most fascinating about Toynbee is his attempt to grasp civilizations (rather than states) as intelligible historical entities, and to understand the reasons — fundamentally internal — for their decline. For this historian of breakdown, Western modernity does not necessarily bring about the obsolescence of other cultures; it does force them, however, to enter into contact with it. Thus, despite the political and military collapse of the Ottoman Empire, Islamic civilization remains alive and well. But it must now deal with the modernity which, at the crucial moment, the Turkish leadership was unable to adapt as its own, becoming first mired in parsimonious reform (the Tanzimat in the 1830s, the Committee of Union and Progress — "Young Turks" — in 1908), then throwing itself head first (Mustapha Kemal, in 1919) into a process of radical modernization whose success is far from certain.[33] But Toynbee is unclear about the scope and vitality of non-Western cultures. On the one hand, he affirms that no culture can permit the penetration of as much as one foreign element without immediately neutralizing it, something which Gandhi understood, in theory.[34] On the other, he sweeps aside the illusion that a culture can choose "pieces" of civilization (the technique of the West without its institutions, for instance, or its political ideas without its economic organization), "as though a culture were not an organic way of life which must be taken or left as a whole."[35] How, then, can technical borrowings be reconciled with the preservation of cultural identity (which Toynbee appears to advocate elsewhere[36])? How, technical borrowing policies notwithstanding, can the world-wide shock wave touched off by Western industrial expansion be absorbed?

Toynbee does not take up this crucial contemporary issue. He attempts to appraise, here and now, the reality of those cultures which border on the West, and to warn against the deceptive appearances of world economic integration. The world economy which came into being with the expansion of Western capitalism has given cultural dialogue a greater urgency, and made it, paradoxically, more difficult. The complex, high level economic network woven by the operations of the world market, along with the planet-wide effusion of products of mass consumption, interconnect only a small number of social groups. Far from making communication easier, the thin coat of highly-polished lacquer which masks the world's diversity of living cultures sends back deceptive reflections much more likely to reduce contacts to the superficial or the illusory. The West's technological and material supremacy is temporary. Nothing permits us to assume that it will last indefinitely. The Western mode of industrial production which is rapidly contaminating all human society holds out no promise of a happy outcome. "Every civilization makes the same error of vision with regard to itself."[37] But Toynbee cannot avoid conferring a kind of historical centrality upon the West.

> The encounter between the world and the West may well appear in retrospect as the most important fact of modern history.[38]

For other cultures, the encounter appears to have been reduced to a kind of technical mimicry: when foreign peoples "have attempted to imitate something other than our technique...," the imitation has been "badly adapted."[39] Ultimately, Toynbee's dialogue has shrunk dramatically: the Other is perceived as an imitator, gifted perhaps, prepared perhaps to preserve an identity, but not as a true interlocutor capable of reflecting our thought and experience, capable of transmitting back to us uncertainties and values. The shift away from dialogue back to monologue is further confirmed in Toynbee's treatment of the encounter between the West and the world: "political and social unity on a world scale is necessary for the salvation of humanity, much more so today, in the Atomic Age, than ever before."[40] Unity was also the principal invoked as the United States (and until recently, the USSR) pressed its claim to world hegemony.

KINDRED SOULS

Spengler and Toynbee, each within different limitations, give voice to the disintegration of the unitary vision of history and human fate. The centrality of the West is no longer self-evident, but a problem which must be addressed. Only by adopting a fresh view of history and of other cultures can this centrality hope to survive. Twentieth century disillusion-ment and uncertainty have awakened in heedful Western intellectuals the near-conscious desire for *rapprochement* with the Other, the need for recon-ciliation with the colonized peoples. For some orientalists with particular sensitivity to the cleavage which underlies their knowledge, the new necessity for understanding would take the form of what we could define as the search for a kindred soul, with all the ambiguity that both the reality and the expression convey.

The impossible reconciliation

Ideas and collective mentalities merge and respond to one another as recurring motifs on the loom of history: themes disappear and reappear, echoing themselves, after long periods of eclipse.

So it is that pro-Arab 20th century orientalists hark back to the "peace-ful coexistence" advocated by Erasmus toward the Turks, to Postel's plan for universal concord, and to the religious tolerance of Bodin. Tolerance, as we well know, was also the hallmark of an Enlightenment serene in its immunity from military threat (which was not the case in the 16th century). But great dissimilarities separate the three "even" centuries: the 18th admits and accepts difference, and waxes ironic about itself through the prism which these dissimilarities hold up to a self-confident Europe, as-sured of its place in the world; the 16th century is still fighting to conquer that place; while the 20th fears losing it.

In our era, the work and commitment of Louis Massignon are reminis-cent of Postel's effort to neutralize Islam and the Ottomans in a thorough-going neo-Christian reconciliation. Only time differentiates the two: with Postel, the drive to amalgamate the Other is more crudely visible, despite all the qualities which he attributes to the Turks. As he labours under no guilt complexes, he may speak on an equal footing. Four centuries later, Massignon must suffer for all the sins of colonization, which makes his thirst for reconciliation more painful and his failure more poignant. Mas-signon embodies that portion of Western conscience wounded by contact with its own limitations, suffering from the wounds of its century, and from a world laid waste by modernity and imperialism.

Louis Massignon was a man of immense erudition, a beacon light, and an uncontested champion of Islamo-Christian *rapprochement* — for the limited circle of those who knew him. He may also have been the most committed, both in political and spiritual terms, of all the Islamophile thinkers. Indeed, alongside his moderately articulated criticisms, Edward Saïd's admiration is palpable.[41] Massignon, he argues, is, along with H.A.R. Gibb, one of the last "greats" of traditional orientalism. "The two scholars took the essentially *ecumenical* authority of European Orientalism as far as it would go…"; after them, "the old Orientalism was broken into many parts."[42] Massignon is doubly ecumenical: more than Gibb, he seeks less to represent Islam than to invest it as all embracingly as he can with his own sympathies. He suffers, in the most literal sense, along with Islam; his suffering is all the more acute in that he feels at least partial responsibility for Europe's failure in the Muslim Orient.

> …the Oriental, *en soi*, was incapable of appreciating or un-
> derstanding himself. Partly because of what Europe had
> done to him, he had lost his religion and his *philosophie*;
> Muslims had 'un vide immense' within them; they were
> close to anarchy and suicide.[43]

But this is the concealed face of the Massignonian discourse: no matter how revelatory of the manner in which the Westerner looks upon the Other, it must not obscure its real, visible face. Massignon speaks not simply as a scholar but as a true believer bearing witness, as one who senses in the "confrontation between European and Muslim," the European's "terrible moral inferiority."[44] The "immense emptiness" which we find in the Other is also, and *above all*, our emptiness. Here I am drawn more by the witness than by the scholar.

The act of bearing witness is indissociable from the personal upheaval which Massignon experienced on his first journey to the Mashrek, an experience to which he would return shortly before his death:

> …In 1908, I found belief, making my first, tremulous prayer
> on the Tigris, imprisoned for suspected espionage aboard the
> *Burhaniye*, at the end of my archaeological tour of the Kar-
> bala desert.[45]

A fugitive from "productivist and Taylorized Europe,"[46] Massignon found in the Orient not only faith and authenticity; he also encountered — on the same occasion — the sacred character of Arab friendship and hospitality which was, by his own account, to save his life.[47] But the paradox persists:

the bonds of emotional intensity which he forged with Islam did not stop him from placing his convictions, his talents and his knowledge at the service of French colonial policy as an officer of the Armée d'Orient, and crucially, as adjutant to the French High Commissioner for Palestine and Syria.[48]

Massignon brings to mind T. E. Lawrence. Both were employed by their respective government as what Saïd calls "orientalist agents,"[49] with all the ambiguity attached to the function. But here the comparison ends. Lawrence could boast of having been a direct participant in an action around which a legend was created, and which *Seven Pillars of Wisdom*, despite its veiled disclaimers, could only reinforce. Lawrence shows enough of his personal aspirations that the alert reader will not be misled by his "Arab" sympathies. Not only are these sympathies constantly subordinated to the political imperatives of his homeland (however he comes to judge them), they evaporate on contact with his extraordinary egocentrism: no sooner does he feel he has exhausted its substance than the hero looses all interest in the cause for which he has fought. The book perfectly reflects the act: its historical interest is limited (the narrative thread is often difficult to follow), but it is fascinating as an account of human experience, and in the density with which this experience is expressed. Not that the reader should scan its pages in search of revelations about the Arabs. Virtually everything said about them can be found elsewhere, and corresponds to the image created by most European Arab specialists. The tale of the *Seven Pillars* is, first and foremost, that of the impossibility of entering into another culture, and of the threat to the identity of he who makes the attempt.

> I had dropped one form and not taken on the other, and was become like Mohammed's coffin in our legend, with a resultant feeling of intense loneliness in life, and a contempt, not for other men, but for all they do. Such detachment came at times to a man exhausted by prolonged physical effort and isolation.[50]

We encounter nothing of the kind in Massignon, who never sought to divest himself of his culture, and for whom contact with the Arabs made it possible for him to return to his own (Christian) values. The necessity and possibility of communion with the Other was what Massignon sought to evince in his life and work, both of which, despite his unquestionably greater erudition, caused much less of a stir than that of his English "rival."[51] But above all, Massignon, who was far more politically naive than Lawrence, could never choose between patriotism and friendship for the Arabs. Caught between two irreconcilable loyalties, he suffered their countervailing pressures for an entire lifetime. The contradiction was to further deepen in the wake of the failure of France's Oriental policy, which Massignon had come to recognize as not corresponding to the humanist hopes he had placed in it. But despite the succession of disappointments, he continued to believe in his country's mission in the Islamic world because, as he wrote in 1939, ever since the Revolution and Napoleon these lands have represented for France "a new school of energy" spurring it "to go beyond itself." While Lawrence had pursued his personal destiny, Massignon's dream was to witness the attainment of a nation's destiny.

> ...The call of the Desert, the lure of the rocks and the dunes, of the mental horizon, await our race, so that it may renew, beneath the blazing sun and in the arid air, its struggle to the death with destiny...But there is more, in Africa, than the desert; there are also travelling companions, Muslims, tough, hardy men who must be confronted, tested, penetrated, understood...Islam, against which our race fought, toe to toe, in the Middle Ages, during the Crusades, without ever having attempted, with few exceptions (like Raymond de Lulle) to understand its psychology, now stands once more before us, in Egypt and in Algeria, technically less well outfitted but morally impenetrable, barricaded behind the discipline of a shared religious existence. But our race, by a process of sympathetic uplift, through comprehension and adaptation, faithful to its historical vocation, may at last give of its full human measure; on condition that, whilst keeping intact its own heritage, it at least tastes of the exquisite qualities of the Muslims of which the West has virtually no conception, their delicate spontaneity in welcoming the stranger, to salute their guest as though he were sent by a dear friend; and their forbearance with life, their resigned contentment in the hands of God, their silent, serene and immaterial certitude of a divine, sovereign and veiled omnipresence. It is a substantial patrimony, the only one which Abraham could bequeath to his son Ismael as he abandoned him at the edge of the desert, and which one of his descendents, Mohammed, would one day reclaim.[52]

Is it possible to be so ethnocentric and at the same time so taken with the Other? Yes, in the heat of love-passion; in the all-consuming thirst to possess, to understand (to take away with oneself). Could Massignon be like the heros of *Gerusalemme liberata* by Torquato Tasso, the poet whom he adored for having imagined the "loving adversaries who are, in the end, reunited in the love of God?"

> Tasso avoids depicting a Muslim smitten by a Christian
> woman, so easily beheld, preferring instead to lift the veil —
> or the helmet's visor — from the Muslim girl, and in so doing
> represent the image of divine Love in the mirror of a hand-
> some enemy's face, and lead them thence to the baptism of
> desire.[53]

With good reason. As Massignon well knows, there is no obstacle for a
Muslim to marry a Christian woman; but it is much more difficult for a
Muslim woman to wed a non-believer. His favourable account of the
transgression clearly indicates the seducer's side: the masculine West must
guide his Arab beloved to answer the call of his desire — while respecting
her virtue. The imagery and the language may be beautiful, but the
representation of platonic wedlock is faintly ridiculous...

His admiring commentary is particularly troubling in its guilelessness.
Massignon, after all, is no cerebral recluse perched high atop an ivory
tower, but a man well versed in the material wellsprings of the Orient-Occident confrontation.

> In the Near East, expanding European colonialism was only
> able to take the offensive militarily after having prepared
> the ground with an economic and financial offensive.[54]

Lenin himself would not have disapproved. How then can Massignon not
realize that his passion for the Other, no matter how straightforward, is
disfigured by the interplay of forces (economic, military and political) of
which it is, inevitably, a part? Was it not precisely the divorce between ideal
and reality which led Sheik Ibrahim, leader of the reform *ulema* in Algeria,
to criticize him for having made of his mysticism "a kind of mask," beneath
which lurked the "most effective agent of the colonialist fifth column"?[55]

> 'I cannot forgive myself for having loved you,' one of my
> former Arab students wrote him, 'because you disarmed me.
> You were worse than those who burned our homes, who
> violated our daughters or expelled our old folk. For many
> years of my life you disarmed me by leading me to believe
> that there existed the possibility of reconciliation and con-
> cord between a Christian Frenchman and a Muslim Arab.[56]

Massignon, in quoting from this letter, gives proof of his honesty and his
clear conscience. Confident that the passage condemns itself by its excess,
he avoids delving deeper into its meaning.[57] The student of whom he
speaks could not have wished to suggest that Massignon was literally
"worse" than a brutalizing soldier, but that he had become an accomplice

in the crimes of the occupying forces by disarming the Arab intellectuals who might have fought against them. Hence his perfectly comprehensible outrage. Massignon avoids the painful question, regretting only that he is so poorly understood. But is this too political an approach? Youakim Moubarac, one of the master's most fervent disciples, may be right when he affirms that "this 'inward-looking' vision of history, originating in the dark reaches of his entry into pain" allowed Massignon to lay the groundwork for "a geopolitics of the spirit which illuminated each of his political decisions and his activity as a French friend of the Arabs and the Muslims."[58] Perhaps. But if such a friend intends to speak and act on the political level, the Other can hardly accept the impasse into which the spirituality of his geopolitics has led him. Instead, the process of reflection should begin at the impasse, in an effort to escape. But Massignon seemingly prefers to block all exits, as his passionately contradictory positions on Zionism and the Palestinian question indicate.

When he turned to the Arab-Israeli conflict, Massignon — like so many other European intellectuals attuned to all facets of this tragic predicament — had to understand and reconcile in himself two estranged souls: "kindred souls" perhaps, in terms of "spiritual geopolitics," but implacable opponents on the battlefield. In the state of Israel he rightly discerns a "lance" wielded by "Western colonialism" which "pierces the heart of the Orient."[59] But, entrapped by his culture and his faith, he cannot bring himself to reject what he had affirmed five years before: "A Christian must avow that the Holy Land belongs to the descendants of Isaac, and thus to the Jews. To those who return in the spirit of Abraham more than in the spirit of Moses or Joshua."[60] Abraham, founding figure and myth of the three great monotheistic religions, is the central figure in Massignon's work. Thus, ever the devout Christian, he commits the warring brothers to the great patriarch's shadow, and adds, on the subject of the Jews (toward whom, especially since 1945, Westerners feel a very particular responsibility): "The salvation and the spirituality of the world depends on Israel": but for this salvation, and "for its own" that country "must attempt to respect, not tactically but genuinely, the Abrahamic authenticity of Islam and of Christianity."[61]

The exhortation was wasted. Massignon's spiritual Israel bears no relation to the raw reality of Zionism. The "excellent sheik" (as Jacques Berque calls him) may well exclaim, on the eve of the first Arab-Israel war that "Israel cannot hope for more temporal independence, given today's geopolitical reality." But temporality won the day, in the test of strength through which the new state asserted itself. From that moment on, the confusion between myth and politics would only work to the advantage of the victor: Israel "must be free, for I expect that it will surmount itself," insists Massignon in an article written in 1949 on "The Refugee Problem and its Impact on the Near East."[62] Finally, he can do little more than exclaim in desperation:

The God of Abraham...is...today the most profoundly displaced of all displaced persons.[63]

Massignon's cry of resignation is a general expression — beyond the
failures of any specific conflict — of the depths of inner exile into which the
failed reconciliation between Jews, Christians and Muslims had plunged
him. Massignon remains alone at Abraham's side: alone in the spirituality
of his myth as a unifying symbol, while nationalist ideologies clamour to
recruit him to their particular causes. Abraham thenceforth opposes
Ibrahim, and Jesus, Issa. Some may see the openly religious expression of a
man's anguish as antiquated and ultimately unrepresentative. I believe
they are wrong.

Through the voice of Christian conscience, the voice of Western conscience cries out in torment: agnostic or believer, it can absolve itself
neither of the Nazi genocide nor the Palestinian exodus — or any other
form of dispossession or racism. This double guilt can be found in a perfect
atheist like Sartre, who was never able to draw a distinction between his
horror of anti-semitism, which led him to support Israel, and the fight
against colonialism and neocolonialism, whose logical implication is the
defense of the Palestinian cause. In every other region, the anti-colonialist
struggle unhesitatingly took priority. Only on the minefield of the Near
East, plunged through the fault of the West into the complexities of the
Jewish question (which was a European question), could a man like Sartre
have so hesitated, pondered, attempted to reconcile extremes. As he himself said:

I find myself torn between contradictory friendships and
fidelities...Today we find ourselves, as Israel and the Arab
world confront one another, divided within ourselves, and
we experience this confrontation as if it were our own personal tragedy.[64]

As Abdelkebir Khatibi explains it, Sartre "exemplifies, in his own way, the
terror of the guilty conscience," so typical of the West.[65] This is the shifting
ground where believer and agnostic converge — and the agnostic is more
lucid than the believer about his ambiguity.

But Massignon finally admitted the yawning chasm which separated
his mystical views from reality, when he discovered among more than a
few Zionists the same "disregard for the Other" which he had denounced
among the French in Algeria. He, the man who participated directly in the
tutelary enterprise which he had hoped would transform France into the
"uncontested educator of the Orient," knew that the educator had not
proved equal to the task. He was forced to confess that the French state had
used him as a "policy alternative" where force had failed, and used him "to

sanction words which, deep down, he never wished to speak."[66] For Massignon, nothing is more degrading than breach of trust. Speaking of the Arabs of Algeria, he uses this terrible phrase:

> They will never forgive us for having degraded them in the eyes of their own conscience...[67]

From this point on, all cultural intercourse between dominator and dominated is irremediably compromised. At the outset, in spite of everything, the colonized has expectations of the colonizer: "He is offered the pipe of peace...The newcomer — that foreign barbarian, that enemy — is regarded as sacred; he may bring something good, something precious, something unknown...*But the white man expects nothing of the colonized...*"[68] And when this realization sinks in:

> The clash of culture between the European colonizer and the Muslim colonized inflicts a psychic wound on the latter, and an even graver misunderstanding; for the European, to be able to enter into relations with him, has participated in a ceremony of welcome and hospitality.[69]

Louis Massignon's experience and testimony are of prime importance even today. Not only has decolonization — not to minimize its importance as the most recent phase in a process — healed no wounds, it has inflicted new ones. Relations between the West and the Orient in the Mediterranean (like North-South relations in general) remain outrageously unequal. Tormented conscience or clear conscience, the fact of inequality is there, massive, obvious, and brutal. The balance of power has lost nothing of its bitter edge, and may well have gained in cynicism; the white man now imagines having thrown off Kipling's famous "burden." Any attempted reconciliation which ignores this hard fact can only be doomed. Massignon stands as proof: his failure, and its profound significance, constitute the new starting point for reconsideration of our relations with the Other. Are relations even possible? If so, at what level, under what conditions? Above all, how authentic can they become?

In the footsteps of Massignon, minus the faith, another friend of the Arabs and advocate of cultural dialogue — Jacques Berque — has raised such questions, and sketched out answers.[70]

Acceptance by analogy, first case

Two sentences from Berque, deliberately quoted out of context, sum up what could be termed a method for relations between cultures:

> Respecting the Other in his difference is not enough. We
> must accept him analogically into ourselves; there is no other
> legitimate way for us to project ourselves into him.[71]

At first glance, the formula is seductive. Acceptation implies hospitality. And legitimacy of projection provides relief of a sort: no longer we are unalterably trapped within ourselves. Analogy (a recurring expression in Berque's work) remains, as the open door of imagination: all resemblances, associations and correspondences (esoteric or profane) are possible. We cannot but agree in principal. But a question persists: *which* analogies respect the differences in the Other, *which* analogies legitimize projection of ourselves onto it? Berque offers us a pure form, a framework, a vessel. Before examining how it can be filled, let us examine how others have used it, particularly in terms of religion.

Is not acceptance by analogy the same as Massignon's tragic desire, and that of Postel four centuries before him? With Postel, the matter was of little consequence: the Ottoman Empire was strong and the Roman Church was not prepared to listen (no analogy with heresy was possible). With Massignon, desire became spiritual tension, despair in the face of (our own) barbarity which made desire unattainable, and in the face of the spurned partner's vulnerability. As Abdelkebir Khatibi, a critic who wishes "to grant orientalism all its desire for nobility" argues:

> More than any other orientalist, Massignon felt the question
> of being glimmering in him. But it was to remain a glimmer,
> determined by a mystical bent: having transformed al-Hallaj
> into a Christ-like savior, he ended up by christianizing
> Islam.[72]

Even the best-intentioned, most passionate acceptance can become misinterpretation, as happened with another lover of the Orient, Henri Corbin, who "*shi'ified* the thought of Heidegger."[73] "Just as the God of the scholastics was departing the scene in the West, in the 19th century," Khatibi reminds us, "leaving man as the subject of history, orientalism revived him amongst the Arabs."[74]

This revival of God did not escape the notice of the Catholic Church which, since Vatican II (1962), has begun its own belated efforts at *rapprochement* with other religions — Islam in particular — as part of a general initiative to breathe new life into faith. Despite the death of God and the advent of man, so the reasoning goes, the West still nurtures in its heart of hearts a thirst for spirituality which, if the Church cannot rejuvenate its image, will be slaked elsewhere than from its tarnished chalices. From this perspective the Other, and the attraction which could ensue from the discovery in him of an unsullied spirituality, warranted consideration, if not annexation. After crying heresy for centuries, the Catholic hierarchy now drew superficial conclusions from the teachings of Massignon (who, as late as 1960, did not hesitate to describe the role of the Church as "worthy only of disdain"[75]) and set out in search of the very analogies which it had, only a short time earlier, rejected. All things considered, Islam was not far from accepting several of the Church's fundamental dogmas (such as the immaculate conception); in fact, it was almost Christian — not in the Spenglerian, but in the Catholic sense of the word. Some, such as father Michel Lelong, quickly launched into rather simplistic effusions of admiration. But the higher echelons of the hierarchy remained cautious: the tone would be adjusted, the message of the Gospels would be given a fine dusting of ecumenism, but care must be taken — analogies might cut both ways. The Church had no intention of renouncing its fundamental dogmas, nor its universal messianism. The most lucid and honest Catholics, those most faithful to the line of thought of the "excellent sheik" expressed the need to go toward the Other, rather than draw the Other toward them: "To understand the Other, Louis Massignon would say, one must not make him ours, but become his guest," note Louis Gardet and Rev. Joseph Cuoq in a training document prepared for the Church.[76] In their view, the most urgent task is not to "convince the Muslims to enter into a dialogue with us" but to "change the mentality of our Christian brethren...The task is immense. It will be a lengthy one."[77]

To suggest the extent of the task, I suggest we set aside for a moment the Western outlook in the strictest sense of the term, and turn our attention to that of the Christian Orient, or, more precisely, of a certain Christian Orient. The legitimate desire of certain Catholics in the Arab world to unite their faith with their Arabness leads straight to the annexation of Islam. In his *Pentalogie Islamo-chrétienne*, abbot Youakim Moubarac, a perhaps over-zealous disciple of Massignon, acknowledges (as did Massignon) that "the Arab Koran is the cry of protestation of all those excluded from the Promise, against the 'scripturists' of the day, the Jews of Medina and the Christians of Byzantium..."[78] and that "textual correspondences between Judeo-Christian scripture and the Qur'an are few, and where they do exist, signal different meanings."[79] But he also asserts, invoking the authority of Louis Gardet, that "the Qur'an does not reject the fundamental dogmas of the Church." If necessary, Muslim tradition itself could even be corrected.

> Yes, Islam, insofar as it endorses what could be considered a traditional interpretation, and rejects the Christian mysteries, exists in a tragic misreading of its own Scriptures. And we have not only the right, but the duty to correct this misreading, through a methodical return to these very Scriptures.[80]

We might excuse this Christian-centred approach its impudence if it expressed the desire of Christians who practice the Eastern rite to return to the historic roots they share with Islam (the foundations of the "Magian soul" so dear to Spengler). But such is not the case at all: Moubarac's stifling ecumenism (completely contrary to the spirit of Massignon) invokes strict Catholic verity as promulgated in the West. In fact:

> The native (Christian) communities of Syria, Iraq and Egypt
> have undertaken, with Islam, an enterprise which is doomed
> to fail, the result of their break with the doctrinal orthodoxy
> and with the catholicity of the Church.[81]

This is the voice of the West, its ingenuousness magnified by a spokesman who has no need to conceal his message. As an Arab he harbours no feelings of guilt toward Islam, and though divided by his double allegiance, he refuses to admit the dichotomy running right through him. Instead, in his eyes, Christianity and Islam *must* be necessary to one another, as Lebanon, "eldest son of the peaceful cohabitation of Islam and Christianity" demonstrates. If this sentence, written two or three years before the outbreak of the Lebanese civil war, rings tragically hollow today, it is precisely because Orient-West relations (without blaming them for every aspect of the war in Lebanon) have not, for a long time, been played out on strictly religious ground. Islam's specific role derives from the invocation by certain Muslim groups or parties of the *Sharia* in resistance to the westernization of their society. But this alone does not make religion the main issue in Orient-West relations, and even less a ground for significant relations or exchanges. Religious feelings may well bring believers from different faiths together on an individual basis. But religious affiliation as an element of collective identity tends to reinforce existing barriers. On the collective level, ecumenism is a modern form of proselytism, a trap placed in the void for those very persons who would set the trap.

Acceptance by analogy, second case

If religion cannot provide hospitable surroundings for acceptance by analogy, can the encounter of affinities find another venue? This is the hope of Jacques Berque, in his wish to establish "secular" communication with the Other, not "sacred" as Massignon once hoped.[82] Are the West, partially distanced — on the purely intellectual level — from the progress it continues to pursue, and Islam, confronted with the violence of unequal and destructive growth (raising the few to wealth and plunging the majority into misery), capable of joining together in reflection on modernity? Perhaps the appropriate starting point would be to ascertain who is speaking of what. What do we mean by Islam? What do we mean by the

West? What do we mean by modernity? Let us hold these questions for later: for, as a river flows down to the sea, the meanderings of our own reflection inexorably lead us there.

Let us, along with Jacques Berque, admit for a moment that Islam and the West exist, that both are confronted by the problem of modernity, but from a different point of view or "point of development." Could this be the problem? What of the hoary commonplace of plurality, the bridge to the very analogies Berque seeks, feeling his way forward, guided only by his sympathies? With the liquidation of the colonial regimes, common exploration becomes possible; now the Other must confront itself. Describing "in partly imaginary terms" the first day of Algerian independence, Berque remarks:

> The old demons have returned to the past. Or at least, so we hope. They will give way to new demons, which will be no less despotic, albeit more "national" than their predecessors. The devil, having amiably become my compatriot, whether in the guise of a capitalist or a bureaucrat, an agitator of egotisms or a provocateur of chimeric generosity, counsellor of inertia or of convulsion, will inflict upon me more bitter hurt that the colonial devil, for against him I could always invoke the guilt of the Other, whereas now I shall be less and less able to do so.[83]

Who said sympathy led inevitably to the complacent third-worldism of the day? For Berque, the reconquest by the decolonized peoples, and by the Arabs in particular,[84] of responsibility for their fate, no matter how difficult the general context, confronted the sociology of the Orient with a dilemma "proportionally analogous to what the proletarian uprising offered Marx in relation to Hegelian philosophy: at once a concrete content, and a logical renewal."

> It may well be that a planetary reality, in demanding of mankind, and specifically of us, a new sense of space to be discovered and to be revealed, may resolve in its unique fashion, certain of the questions which it poses. Such a possibility, were it ever to materialize, would allow us to understand one of the movements of our age, and would provide this movement with perspectives for ideas and action corresponding to its meaning. It would relieve us from the anguish which overcomes us when that which has brought us thus far, and that which we have thus far achieved, is called into question. We would then see, thanks to the enormous progress which the emancipation of the

World would impose upon us, the onward march of history
as it moves to conquer, with its full anthropological
plenitude, a decisive rationality.[85]

Invoking at once a hypothetical planetary reality — and a liberation — as
demanding as the Hegelian advent of Reason, Berque, with the sanction of
Marxism, proposes to transform the emancipation of the colonized peoples
into a tool for world integration. History may well judge decolonization to
be a step in this direction; the hypothesis is seemingly reconfirmed every
day. But here (with Berque), we are dealing with more than a simple
statement of fact. We find ourselves enveloped by a will whose objective is
to reassure itself about the scope of its own history, and about the premises
of its own universality. What the "emancipated" peoples themselves might
want is of little moment. Are we Westerners not merely relieving our
anguish as we reinvest our onward march with meaning?

This is the essence of the challenge which, via Berque, the West has
thrown at the feet of Islam.[86] Islam is called upon to respond to our
expectations, and even more, to repair the damage which we have
wrought, and to remedy our own failings. But what then of respect for the
Other? The requirement is to remake itself. In the manner of strict yet
tender-hearted parents watching their child grow up, we expect a double
achievement: Islam must both negotiate modernity (with all that it entails)
while remaining or re-becoming itself. The modern Orient is not only
expected to confirm that the world (our world, naturally) is rolling down
the right track, it must also safeguard its oasis-like coolness from the heat
of its own harsh sunlight, it must protect the evanescence of being against
the "de-signification" which looms over us. It is nothing less than an
"instrument enjoining us to carry on, atop the ruins of the first Orients,
with the resurgence of a second Orient."[87]

We have little alternative but to accept Berque's argument that "the
second Orient," "much more than an exotic inspiration," is the locus of a
"deeply buried truth" which it is incumbent on the West to discover.[88]
But Berque does not see Orientals themselves as cut off from this truth.[89]
Bruno Étienne, on the other hand, is quite candid in expressing this need
for Orient, comparing it, not without a tinge of provocation, to a "secondary residence." Like the city-dweller who structures the "countryside"
in a way that has little to do with the way of life of country people, the
Western intellectual imputes to the Orient the words he wishes to hear,
with scant concern whether his wishes correspond with the feelings and
interests of the peoples who populate it. In short, the Orient is reduced
to a *topos*,[90] a bundle of imaginary significations only tenuously linked to
reality: an intellectual investment ("intellectual necessity," Renan termed
it early on) whose creative profitability, and emotional fecundity must be
constantly stimulated.

Within this framework, Berque continues to exhibit a beguiling *savoir-faire*, or more properly, *savoir-écrire*. With consummate mastery of ellipsis and half tone, he carries on with Islam a dialogue enveloped in perpetual pedantic imprecision. At the midpoint between poetic essay and erudite anthropological observation, Berque (particularly in *L'Islam au défi*) seems intent on displaying Islam to advantage. Unless, all things considered, it is Islam which is expected to display Berquian philosophy to advantage. But on closer inspection, what we really have is a dialogue between Berque and himself, with Islam as little more than the scaffolding of his own thought process. The Other is simply a catch-all, a receptacle of convenience for the thoughts of a given moment. With Berque, the entire process is so wrapped in sinuous connivance that we feel as though we are penetrating into the inner sanctum of the Muslim faith through an unguarded door. Berque knows very well that he "speaks from without"[91] and designates himself a "travelling companion." But is it not he who has chosen the path? Is it not he who points, however vaguely, to the utility of an Islam which could become "a new idea in the world"?[92] But not so fast; the Iranian experience, still fresh and relatively novel at the writing of *L'Islam au défi*, was already evidencing "expressions" which were sufficient "to cause fear, accrediting as they do an unwelcome synonymy between preoccupation with the past and authenticity."[93] Could it be that these "expressions" have disturbed and clouded the Western-centred vision of the world, that they do not jibe with the comforting schema of history as progress? Why must Islam, as a matter of obligation, present a face which Western intellectuals can unreservedly love and embrace? Why must it have only one face?

A kind of unity fixation is all but inevitable when contemplation of Islam becomes part of a search for meaning by a non-believer titillated more by the divine in the Other's culture than by his own. On contact with a modest Muslim scholar Berque discovers plenitude, and the universal.[94] And with it, method:

> For the man who does not consider the Book of Islam as an archaeological relief, but as a presence which has been experienced, providing this presence is experienced, the question is simply not asked: one can only study Islam from the starting point of belief in Islam, even though one is not of this belief oneself.[95]

More rigorous respect for the Other would be difficult to imagine. But here, too, certain limits must be recognized: belief as reference point can no longer be defined from without (except in the most formal manner). Instead of retreat in the face of potential accusations of break and entry, Berque uses his sympathy to justify an incursion into the very heartland of a belief which is not his own:

> How simple it would be to deplore that, between textual analysis, stylistic commentary, philosophical excursus, and even the deduction of principles of action adjusted to the present day (the Manar school), Koranic exegesis has not yet made use of the resources which progress in the humanities and social sciences could have placed at the disposal of those of the faithful who seek to cast the greatest possible illumination on the word of God.[96]

Here we encounter a radical antinomy. The word of God, its origins beyond doubt, can only be illuminated by itself or by those who profess it, surely not by our social sciences, whose efforts the believer considers — justifiably, from his point of view — as derisory. Berque hastens to add that "these methods are far from being uniformly pertinent, let us admit as much."[97] But the nuance changes nothing. Though it is true that history and sociology "begin…with the admission of the Other's absolutes,"[98] that is also their end point, at least where this particular absolute is concerned. Only the outward contours, the forms can be "sociologized." But Berque's empathy rejects this kind of limitation, attempting instead to circumvent it by dialectical definition of his object:

> The object which I wished to grasp is more and more clearly defined by its encircling dangers: to take Islam either as an ideality under the purview of the philosophy of religion, or as a factual whole under that of the social sciences, whereas Islam sees itself as *din wa dunya*, the mediation between the one and the other. Thus it must be apprehended in the very act of mediation, precisely at that moment when the transformation of the world raises new problems before it.[99]

The approach is as seductive as it is impracticable for the non-believer, who can only purport to grasp one of the two poles of the mediation which he has observed. The knowledge that this mediation forms part of Islamic writ (though it remains a principle whose historical application is yet unconfirmed) is not enough to carry us into the heart of Berque's dialectic. We cannot automatically discount attempted observation and analysis, but the view "from without," fraternal or not, remains outside its object: sensitive to the Other perhaps, intelligent (the intelligence of the heart included) perhaps, but still outside. One might even affirm that recognition of this insurmountable limitation (we shall be returning to the issue) is the first condition of intelligence about the Other. Berque would be the first to agree…only to wriggle away, so powerful is his need to infiltrate. As Massignon understood so well, the desire for spiritual osmosis with the Other can only be expressed through faith, each through his own; but one must believe, one must accept without restriction — as an obvious manifestation of divinity — that many paths lead to God. Moreover, spiritual communion at this level has little to do with sociology; there it runs, as we have seen, a high risk of being transformed into political impotence and division. Once he ventures onto religious ground, Berque's undeniable political sympathy for the Arab world is transmuted into false communion. Perhaps this is why Khatibi asserts that "by insulting the nobility of radical orientalism, Jacques Berque reduced the Orient to a misleading rumor."[100]

I suggest that Berque employs his "baroque" constructions the better to avoid stating exactly the conditions and the limitations of "acceptance by analogy," a concept which, for him, remains a vague yet immense desire for integration and escape. Berque, like so many intellectuals before him, needs the Orient, needs an Islam to invent as he ponders the world. His invention is well informed, but it is still an invention, one whose prime purpose is to respond to the disquiet generated by modernity. Arching across the world from west to east, this critical issue develops even sharper contours when it reaches the land of Islam.

> All this, which poses severe problems of adjustment to in-
> dustrial society, poses the same problems to Muslim society
> with a vehemence heightened by newness, by contrast, by
> the excitement of the newly enlightened...[101]

And heightened above all, we must add, by "external impingements," as Berque himself half admits. His reticence springs from the legitimate fear of sanctioning a "colonialization of the problematic."[102] The danger is real, recognition of the effects of imperialism is not the same as imperializing science (though this may not be enough to assure its decolonization). But Berque, I believe, has another fear: brute force having been accounted for, precious little of the fragile edifice of complicity may remain. The loss could well be irreparable: where can the lover of the Orient find a home for his philosophy? Where is the magnifying mirror of his anguished fears? Berque is by no means deceived by his own aspirations. Meditating on the future of Islam in a preface to a collection of articles by von Grunebaum, in 1973, he writes:

> Yes, what will it, *like I myself*, become in the onrush of history,
> and what, too, will it become under my gaze?...
>   Such is the fate of the orientalist: to postulate, despite the
> fact that, for better and for worse, his own experience of the
> Orient, that is to say, of *his own personal Orient* and of the
> *Orient within him*, may be all too human.[103]

Acceptance by analogy is little more than a relatively brief process of returning to oneself; the Other is but the landscape of our own reflection. It is a majestic landscape, and is well worth the detour, providing we have not concealed from ourselves the meaning of the journey. But the journey toward the Other brings us no closer, and may even lead us astray, into a false sense of complicity. Precisely because of his ambiguity, Berque leads us less far afield than does Massignon. Not only does he not overcome the failure of his master but, with his purposely muddled effusiveness, camouflages or at least smooths over the breach left by the zealot of al-Hallaj. Far from being better articulated, the relationship with the Other is subtly submerged in a vague universalism meaning, quite simply, our own. The nostalgia for authenticity has changed nothing.

The return of the repressed

My survey of acceptance by analogy has focused neither on the effort it requires nor on the desire which drives it, but on the partially illusory nature of its results: they have not met our expectations — hence the risk of self-deception, of deepening, in the best of good faith, the very gulf we thought we were bridging. We shall soon be attempting to ascertain if the trap is avoidable. But first, I believe I should set out, with maximum clarity, the limits of my critique.

Undifferentiated rejection of any approach to the Other — for whatever reason — must not be allowed to lead to what we might term the return of the repressed: that is, the rejection of the Other through subtle appeals to the irreducibility of its otherness, the irrationality of its attitudes, or simply to the behaviour of certain groups with which an entire society has become implicitly or abusively linked. These groups, according to our Western criteria, behave in such a "retrograde" manner, are so unjustifiably violent and intolerant, that the society which produces and tolerates them merits neither our attention nor our respect — to say nothing of those societies where extremists themselves hold power. The reader will by now have recognized Muslim "fundamentalism," and behind it, Islam itself as source of fanaticism. This is the image held up for the reprobation of a Western public prepared to fall back on the old negative clichés about the eternal enemy rather than attempt to make sense of the "Near East's" climate of crisis and endemic disorder. It also offers a convenient way of sidestepping questions about the role of the Western powers.

A favourite method of fomenting mistrust of Islam is to vilify or mock those who, in the West, clearly identify themselves as friends of the Muslim religion, those whom Jean-Pierre Péroncel-Hugoz contempt-uously describes as "professional Turks."[104] Insults of this kind would hardly be worth countering if they were completely without pertinence, if they did not have some basis in the clumsiness and the complacency of

Islam's rare unconditional zealots in the West; if they did not coincide with a much wider movement, among many Western intellectuals, of turning away from the peoples of the third world. In the case of Pascal Bruckner, the movement is both welcome and ambiguous.[105] It is hard to take issue with his claim that Western leftists, for all their fine intentions, were quick to transform the "Third World" to suit their own needs, to invest it with the revolutionary aspirations which they had seen melt away in their own countries — not to mention their consuming desire to distance themselves from a world system of exploitation which they condemned while being incapable of not benefiting from, however remotely. Insofar as it focuses on the ethnocentric underpinnings of "third-worldism," Bruckner's exercise is a salutary one. But the difficulties must be carefully evaluated: the thin line of defense separating lucidity from disenchantment, from disillusioned and even cynical withdrawal, can collapse at any moment. The major danger facing Western intellectuals today vis à vis the peoples of the non-Western world — particularly in the light of the long-term economic crisis — is still loss of interest, and turning inward. Whether the result of hypersensitivity, insouciance or arrogance, this inward turning is first and foremost a danger to us. While we need feel no obligation to envelop the Other in our verbal solicitude, we must attempt to establish an intelligent liaison, if not with it directly, at least in relation to it — if for no other reason than to understand ourselves in the world. The stakes are high.

This is precisely what the Péroncel-Hugozes of this world would prefer to ignore. Is it necessary to taunt Western supporters of Islam as, for instance, he does Roger Garaudy?[106] Garaudy's profession of faith may be faintly amusing, and I admit — speaking as a non-believer — to preferring Massignon's Christian option, which seems to me more solid, more consistent. If, as Garaudy himself admits, there is no difference between the message of the Qur'an and that of Christ, why disguise oneself as a Muslim? His gesture might be easily mocked, but it should be closely examined. Beyond the man's personal motives (which are quite adequate in themselves), the political dimension of Garaudy's conversion transforms it into a symbolic act. In adopting Islam he affirms in the most concrete, most manifest way, the equivalence of religions, as well as the necessity for mutual respect. This does not make him a "Muslim" in the cultural sense of the term, as he himself hastens to point out, unambiguously defining himself as a Westerner. In fact, his affirmation of Western values enables him to criticize the intellectual strabismus of many Orientals who covet the material advantages of the West with one eye while contemplating the past splendours of the Orient with the other, all the while marching backwards into the future.[107] In truth, if one were to reproach Garaudy for anything, it would be for concealing a comforting universalism, the sign of a rather superficial and highly Eurocentric approach to the Arabo-Islamic world, beneath his profession of faith. This hardly makes him, politically speaking, an unconditional Muslim or a "professional Turk" as Péroncel-Hugoz would have us believe — far from it.

Is our world so afflicted by Islamomania and by Arabophilia that Islam and its admirers should be pilloried for their troubles? For my own part, I see racism, contempt for and ignorance of the Other at work everywhere in the West, to such a degree that I have come to despair of the mental progress of our civilization. Péroncel-Hugoz has chosen his target well: by singling out the most obvious aspects of Muslim fervour, he was sure to curry public favour (as the commercial success of his book demonstrated). He believed that by carefully focusing his attack on his adversary's weaknesses, he could put himself beyond criticism; he knows the Arabo-Islamic world well enough to avoid the grossest errors. Indeed, all is not well in the lands of Islam, any more than anywhere else. No need to lie to inflict hurt. Most of Péroncel-Hugoz's criticisms, in and of themselves, pose no problem. The problem is the tone and the intent which underlie them; and even more, their author's obvious in-sensitivity to the place in which he expresses himself and to the state of mind of this readers: both are Western. In the name of what, and for whose benefit does he imagine he is administering such a lashing? How well-intentioned can it be to feed public prejudice and repugnance toward Muslim practices, particularly in a country where the integration of North African workers has already given rise to a climate of dangerous animosity? Why not make the effort, as Claire Brière has done, to explain how and why, in the face of their own rejection, im-migrants — or certain of them, at least — find in their religion an indis-pensable tool for consolation and resistance?

Most distressing of all, relatively well-informed observers of Islam and its problems pretend that nothing can be learned from history, that no new perspectives could be gained and no lessons learned from the compen-dium of images over which we have poured in our voyage down through the centuries. Worse: they act as if these images had never been produced, as if we ourselves were faultless before the Other.

What does this mean? That if Westerners cannot approve of what goes on beyond their borders they have only to keep their mouths closed? Is the Other capable of using our guilty conscience to silence us (as Edward Saïd sometimes appears to be doing)? Perhaps reactions like the *Radeau de Mahomet* can be justified by underlying guilt, by the complacent recitation of a certain Western culpability. But this is the wrong response, and no better than the *mea culpa* which it ridicules. Worse, in fact: it encourages the intolerance which it condemns in the Other, and locks us into our cen-turies-old clichés. But could not the bitterness or the hostility of the Other be transformed into the stuff of reflection? No, we should not throw ourselves at its feet, nor should we smother it in an embrace which it has every reason not to want (or at least find suspect). But the effort of cognition which its presence encourages in us, or, if you prefer, the knowledge of it we wish to obtain, can only gain from integrating the Other's critical reaction to the way in which it has been scrutinized. Only on this condition — with no guarantee of success — can an exchange of views or a cultural dialogue begin with the Orient. This condition is particularly vital in that mutual perception and the encounter between the participating partners (or adversaries) must take place against a backdrop of material inequality.

True dialogue is unlikely as long as the dominated party feels incapable of modifying the balance of power — intellectual power included — which underlies the exchange. The balance of power is not simply military, economic or technological; it is also "scientific." Modern science, and the social sciences in particular, were, after all, developed in the West. Now, thanks to them, the West purports to be able to examine the Other more objectively, more completely.

Is this pretension well-founded? Can we move beyond the limitations of Orientalism and envision a new way of relating to the Other, a knowledge which is truer because it is better informed on the snares which waylaid our predecessors? Do the social sciences of today enable us to formulate, in a rational manner, the double question of identity and of otherness?

THE DIALECTIC OF IDENTITY

As the dialectic of identity (or identity/alterity) runs like a thread through the history of the West's view of the Orient, so our scrutiny of it constitutes the natural end point of that thread. But to raise the question of identity is to conjure up, at the same time, a broader problematic which, in its epistemological implications, goes well beyond the object of this book. I have decided to take up these matters, in closing, as quick sketches of a more thoroughgoing reflection I intend to pursue in future. It is a task I, as a simple knowledge practitioner, undertake without theoretical pretension and in all epistemological candour. I undertake it, furthermore, within the same limits all but explicitly laid down by the epistemological postulates of the "specialists," making no attempt to exhaust their full meaning. I am aware that this dialectic is drawing me beyond a dividing line which, until now, I have been reluctant to cross; it impels me to breach, however haltingly, the Other's "reality." Short of simply paying lip service, this end-of-course deviation was unavoidable. One cannot live outside one's own time.

The scientific approach to the Other

The "science" of the Orient begins well before the 20th century. The modern concept of science is based on the idea of objective knowledge, systematically organized and methodically elaborated. By this definition, orientalism (here taken in the limited sense of erudition about the Orient, and primarily, about Oriental languages) has considered itself a science from at least the end of the 18th century. And, as we have seen, certain elements of the scientific discourse on the Orient (considerations of method in particular) were already in place two centuries earlier, in the work of Postel. So conclusively has Edward Saïd demonstrated how orientalism abusively constituted its object, isolated that object, and even created "its own" Orient, that we need not go over the same ground here. Today, I believe there is nothing to be added to the critique of the ethnocentrism which characterized traditional 19th and 20th century orientalism — which by no means invalidates the sum total of the work of the orientalists, and leaves the question of scientific knowledge of the Other still unsolved.

It is widely admitted today that orientalism, from an essentially philological starting point, defined its field of study too narrowly; that it reduced the Orient to an archaeological excavation zone, a dead thing having little relation — aside from the colonial relationship — with the modern world.[108] The rise of nationalism, the struggle for political, then economic independence (however defined) and, more recently, the apparent reinvigoration of Islam have brought Western observers to view the Orient as a subject of history. It was understandable that this "new" subject should draw the attention of the social sciences (or humanities, the two expressions are used interchangeably), but to consider this development as a pure product of our times would still be an exaggeration. The late 18th century produced, in Volney, a man whose on-the-scene investigation had much more in common with modern-day sociology than with the dominant, learned orientalism of the day. Today, with orientalism in retreat, hardly conceivable without the protection of the social sciences, the social sciences themselves must be held up to scrutiny, whether practised by orientalists or not.

Science, the scientific approach, the scientific viewpoint: in everyday language, these expressions all connote, to one degree or another, the idea of objectivity, seriousness, or exactitude. This idea of scientific objectivity is not a creation of this century. In fact, Western social science harks back, in many ways, to a certain positivist optimism more characteristic of the 19th century than of our own. The problem of objectivity has always impinged on the social sciences in a more direct and troublesome way. Their development has stimulated examination of their limits, and made it possible to expose their underlying ethnocentrism — if only in terms of their concerns.

Today, we know that ethnocentrism is not simply a flaw which, given a bit of mental gymnastics, can be set aside at the threshold of scientific activity. It is the very prism of our perception, it is *our* view of the world, a lens whose necessity we would be better off to admit, instead of imagining it can be discarded. Seen in this perspective, self-knowledge becomes a precondition for approaching the Other, a fragile and uncertain precondition. The Other is, as we have seen, the medium by which we all but consciously define ourselves. Such is the identity/otherness dialectic which must be brought into full consciousness. Knowledge of the Other means full self-knowledge, an accomplishment that once claimed implies instant reversal of decision.

But notwithstanding the difficulties, notwithstanding the limitations of Western epistemological consciousness, the idea of objective, value-free science, of science as a universal *lingua franca*, remains deeply rooted in our minds as, if nothing else, an objective to be pursued.[109] Today the social sciences enjoy, often for good reason but oftimes abusively, a favourable bias, particularly as far as orientalism is concerned. Conscious, too, of its greater vulnerability, the West's contemporary knowledge of the Orient has learned to outwit its critics. Though it is no more objective than before, it shows a new craftiness, displays greater dexterity in manipulating the object of its intentions. Emboldened by its newfound flexibility, it can now conceal itself behind a screen of rigor, all the better to shut itself off from the Other more radically, or, conversely, create the timid, lucid beginnings of a still-unequal dialogue, given the objective conditions in which dialogue must take place.

The use of science as a protective shield or as a device for deflecting subjective criticism hardly warrants discussion. Bernard Lewis provides the classic example in his long article on Saïd's *Orientalism*, whose weaknesses he pitilessly enumerates.[110] Weaknesses there are, of course, and most of Lewis' criticisms are accurate. Lewis strikes the pose of the school-master who sends the chastened pupil back to his desk to correct his work: what is being administered is a lesson in erudition. I use the term "erudition" — and not method — advisedly. Lewis confines himself to a catalogue of Saïd's "errors and omissions" (fair game, after all), but he painstakingly refuses to address the heart of Saïd's discourse. He is critical of Saïd's failure to do justice to orientalism (particularly to his own erudite research). But Saïd's primary objective is to reveal the frequently *a priori* negative judgements underlying this specialized knowledge, to protest a certain reification or fabrication of the "Orient." Here, Lewis has nothing to say. But his disdainful silence indicates that he considers Saïd's approach as impertinent. He would disqualify Saïd by demonstrating the unscientific quality of his discourse: that which is unscientific cannot be used to impugn science; science need not deign to pay heed.

Saïd's charges against Orientalism may indeed be partial and repetitious, an indication that their author has had difficulty in extracting himself from the skin of the victim. But his criticism is also an act of witness: the "object" of Orientalism reacting — subjectively — to the "scientific" treatment inflicted upon it. Lewis, however, from the lofty heights of knowledge, cannot or will not see the Other as subject. Science and its objectivity serve, in fact, as a safeguard against the reactions of the subject. Within this artificially determined framework, one may discuss the methods and the technicalities of knowledge, but there is no place for a full debate on *the* method, meaning the epistemological foundations of the study of the Other. Within this narrow perspective, the advent of the social sciences has changed nothing, fundamentally, in the West's scientific approach to the Orient.

Whether as process of objectivization or closed system ostensibly immunized against the intrusion of value judgements, "science" has little to contribute to the deepening of communication between cultures. The idea of scientific objectivity itself postulates the general existence of references and criteria common to all humanity. All attempts at dialogue must, by default, be couched in a particular language which excludes all other forms of verbalization, all outside criticism. Communication which has not first accepted its premises is forbidden. The "scientific approach" may not necessarily invalidate *ipso facto* everything produced under its aegis, but it seriously restricts and distorts its range.

In his study of the Assassins,[111] this self same Bernard Lewis methodically assembles factual information on the history of several 10th to 13th century Muslim minority sects: reason enough for Maxime Rodinson to urge us to read this monograph, while "disregarding Bernard Lewis's opinions on contemporary politics" (opinions which Rodinson himself does not share). All well and good. Particularly since the specialist's verdict confirms my own layman's impression: that of "serious historical work, written with competence and clarity." Rodinson goes on to add: "Nothing else should be taken into consideration." Nothing else, really? Not the choice of subject, nor the title itself? Why the sub-title (worse still in the French version: "Terrorism and politics in Medieval Islam") which so poorly translates the author's efforts at rehabilitation? If Lewis has indeed taken such pains to go straight to the Ismaelian sources to correct a negative image based primarily on Sunnite sources hostile to the movement, why "A radical sect in Islam," which suggests some relationship between Islam and one of the running sores of our times? The reason, explains Rodinson, is that:

> The history of the Assassins fascinates us because the echoes which it touches off within us, the reminders of contemporary events which it offers at every step, are by no means

anecdotal coincidences. This story is an archetype, a *first* (my emphasis) and fascinating representation of the multiplicity of tragic occurrences which recur later, again and again, even to this day, in a new context.[112]

Rodinson may very well have faithfully interpreted the spirit of Lewis's inquiry. But whether the author likes it or not, the book's subject matter closely reflects a certain outlook which it is difficult to ask those who might feel affected to overlook. Perhaps another title would have been as easy to find, one less commercial, perhaps, less in keeping with the Western public stereotype of Islam.

Granted, no subject is taboo. But if this is so we must realize that the ingrained capacity to respect nothing *a priori* is typical of the modern West; we must also accept that science — our ultimate refuge of the sacred — is no exception. The revocation of taboos implies a higher awareness of our choices, including on the scientific level, and particularly when the Other is called into question. No matter how rigorous our science may be in terms of the internal standards which govern it, that science which takes the Other as its object enters onto the ground of the Other's sensibilities — which become keener as differences and disparities deepen. We may well decide to ignore these sensibilities. But it is a choice which condemns us to speak only to ourselves. In such conditions, scientific objectivity is more than the striving for the honesty and rigor which govern the relations between the method and its object; it becomes prophylaxis against anything which might eventually attack the method from without: it is, succinctly stated, the "scientific" justification for turning inward upon one's self.

Ideally, however, objectivity and its inherent distancing should lead to the establishment of relations between method and object, so that the latter can then function as subject. Only by exhibiting its openness, and thus accepting its vulnerability, can science lead to true intellectual exchange. The aim of science, after all, is not to silence passions but to arm them with more effective weapons, to make them as comprehensible as possible.

True objectivity knows that objective knowledge of the Other does not exist, and redefines its objective as the critical appreciation of the conditions of our knowledge: "This is how I view you; these are my sources, my tools. Now, it's your move." The game is not an easy one, and may have its brutal moments. But a sharply worded exchange is often better than equivocal complicity. Still, nothing can obligate the Other to take part in an exercise which is not desired — whose rules are rejected in the name of an absolute or of a fundamental claim which supersedes any exchange. Should we decry this intolerance without trying to understand, only strengthening this rejection? Or should we challenge the Other to respond to our science? Neither, I would hope. We know well enough the distance which separates science and the experience of transcendence not to throw down such a meaningless challenge. Here again, science can only acquiesce in its limitations, and accept being impugned without allowing itself to show contempt. Three conclusions seem apparent: first, the experience of transcendence is neither incompatible with science nor with openness toward the Other (it could be fairly argued that the living experience of faith has never been a source of intolerance); second, the Other is no more monolithic than we are, even when conformity with dogma seems at its most opaque; third, faced with the signs of intransigence we believe we detect in the Other, we must ask ourselves how much of this radical attitude is due to our own view, and in more general terms, to the context in which these views intersect with ours'.

It is a lot to ask. Openness to the Other can never be more than intermittent or partial. Necessarily, for it lies under constant threat of being swallowed up in a never-ending dialectic, in the mutual reflection of opposing mirrors. But we have not yet reached this point. Our social sciences are not yet at the point of being seriously shaken in the ethnocentrism of their approach to cultural otherness. In fact, ethnocentrism is stimulated by the dynamics and the apparently integrating impact of the world economy: the selfsame forces which propound the idea that cultural diversity is fated to disappear before the onrush of modernity and its avatars, to survive only as folklore.

More than ever before, the issue of cultural identity is being raised in a world which has been blithely presented (at this cultural level) as polarized between "modernity" and "tradition," — the general form of the Occident-Orient dichotomy. Several western sociologist/orientalists have focused on this quandary, pregnant as it is with potential misunderstandings, in contemplating at once the Orient and their own approach. Could the act of contemplation become the point of departure for eventual dialogue with the Other? Or could it be an ultimate turning inward? Or could it be merely a transitory phase...

Cultural identity and modernity

What is cultural identity? My intention is not to explore this "self representation" in all its extraordinary complexity. It is enough to say that cultural identity is formed in relation to the Other, that is to say, in opposition to it. If we are prepared to grant this assertion as true, then we may accept that cultural identity today (without, for the moment, specifying its locus) be provisionally defined as *that which the shock of modernity has called into question*. This is not a rigorous definition, but it has the merit of illustrating how the issue of identity has been shaped by the encounter with the Orient; in the force field of tension between "modernity" and "tradition." Islam, in our Western eyes, is both grounded in, and envelops,

this tradition; Islam also expresses the collective identity of the Mediterranean Orient. It is hardly surprising that Islam is so frequently challenged.

Here lies the gist of the challenge Jacques Berque has laid at the feet of
Islam, and the one to which he seeks to respond. We have seen that, for
Berque, modernity and the web of planetary interdependence which it
spins, are at once an inescapable constituent of the contemporary world
and an opportunity which Islam must grasp, while simultaneously remaining itself. The scope of the problem is clear: Islam must reconcile within
itself modernity and authenticity, the West and the Orient, while surpas-
sing itself at the same time. But how? Berque — thankfully — has no recipe.
He seems happy enough to hold out for us the state of human universality
which looms at the far edge of history. René Guénon performs an
analogous operation from a clearly more philosophical viewpoint, but
takes the opposite tack, inviting the modern West, or at least that part of it
which has disfigured its own tradition, to repudiate itself. It would be a
return to self in which the Orient (where tradition is still alive) could be of
powerful assistance, a return which "the crisis of the modern world" has
made inevitable. But whether Islam is to make modernity its own (Berque)
or the West is to reconquer tradition (Guénon), both leave unresolved and
unelaborated the problems they purport to address. Perhaps this is because
we are dealing with thinkers who are too receptive to the inexpressible, or
too close to the Other to be able to confront the question in all its latent
violence. Berque, in particular, wavers between (often highly lucid)
analysis and a nebulous empathy in which he expects contradictions to
dissolve. Little more can be said. "Acceptance by analogy" ultimately serves
more to obscure the question of identity than to illuminate it.

How then are we to illuminate identity? We may have to admit that, as
we attempt to delve more deeply into the issue, we are likely to stumble
over the old stereotypes and the old habits. In the duel between "tradition
and modernity" we have been too hasty to analyze the former as deficient
in comparison with the latter (implicit as a standard or accepted as ineluctable historical necessity). Hence the virtual impossibility of formulating a
diagnosis: of Islam, of the "Arab mentality" or of any other generalization
which purports to portray the Other in its collective essence, and of
identifying that which has thus far refused it full access to modernity.

Reminiscent of Renan, though less spiteful, H. A. R. Gibb cannot resist
sliding back into the traditional orientalist position. He attempts to locate
the historical moment when the "Arab mentality" would have been formed
(in the first centuries of Islam), thence to continue unchanged down to our
day. Tracing "the aversion of the Muslims from the thought processes of
rationalism" back to its sources, Gibb explains:

> The rejection of rationalist modes of thought and of the
> utilitarian ethic which is inseparable from them has its roots,

therefore, not in the so-called 'obscurantism' of the Muslim theologians, but in the atomism and the discreteness of the Arab imagination.[113]

Even though they developed the "experimental method in science to a degree[114] far beyond their predecessors of Greece and Alexandria," he writes, the Arabs never adopted their spirit of synthesis. The failed encounter with the Greek spirit (a spirit whose remoteness from our "utilitarian morality" Gibb seems not to perceive) has had the gravest consequences down to the present day: it has all but barred the Arabo-Islamic world from transforming its religion into humanism and from acceding to modernism. At the least, it makes the transition (for which Christianity provides the model) an extremely difficult one. The reason for the obstruction is historical in appearance only: in reality, its origins lie in the atavism of the Arab spirit. Ultimately, Gibb corrects one prejudice (Muslim "obscurantism") the better to fall victim to another (the "atomism...of Arab imagination") equally arbitrary one which drives its object into an impasse even more profound than the first.

But, come time to venture a prognosis, Gibb appears to forget his own diagnosis; paradoxically he places his hopes in Islamic continuity. "The essential relation between social behaviour and religious belief" appears destined to survive. As for the contradictions between tradition and social requirements, "they will find their own appropriate solutions:" they will be "realistic and far removed from the intellectual confusion and the paralysing romanticism which cloud the minds of the modernists today."[115] In dismissing modernism and conservatism, Gibb turns back to the "historical rationalism" which flourished in the third and fourth centuries of the Islamic era, but which was stifled by the hostility of the theologians[116] — a proposition which is jarringly out of tune with his insistence on the "horror of rationalism" inherent in the Arab spirit... In fact, Gibb finds himself trapped between the desire to see the Arabs emancipate themselves, and his determinist analysis of their mentality.

No other ground is as treacherous as that of collective mentalities. The spirit of a people cannot be described outside of time and space, on this much we can all agree. Still, Arab and Muslim societies are often depicted by Western science, even today, as timeless, particularly when it pretends to describe what we call, in relation to our modernity of course, their "blockage," their "backwardness" — concepts which are perfectly in tune with the traditional Western view of the Orient and of Islam as petrified societies. The "tradition/modernity" nexus stems directly from the process of simplification. As Marshall Hodgson so eloquently explains in his *Introduction to the study of Islamic Civilization,* the "dead hand of tradition" has been all too frequently "(Hodgson) invoked to explain the failure of other societies, such as the Islamicate, which are then compared, to their disadvantage, with the pre-modern Occident."[117] The dichotomy itself presupposes a clear explanation of the impact of the "modernity matrix" upon the West. Not only are we missing such an explanation; even were it to exist, it could never be boiled down to the "inherent traits in the Occident:" only investigation on a world scale — imagining for a moment that such a thing were possible — might enable us to understand why modernity appeared in Europe rather than elsewhere[118] (providing we could agree on the meaning of the term, and on the moment of its appearance). But, above all, there is no such thing as a petrified society.

> Historical change is continuous and all traditions are open
> and in motion, by the very necessity of the fact that they are
> always in internal imbalance.[119]

Thus the West's science of the Orient, in its most lucid moments, is able to begin the preliminary task of deconstructing the very general concepts and stereotypes about the Orient which it has helped create. In *Islam and Capitalism*, Maxime Rodinson devotes much effort to dismantling, through practical study of Islamic society and analysis of the Qur'an, the myth of the incompatibility of Islam and capitalism.[120] One of the most celebrated, though *a contrario*, perpetuators of the myth was — unsurprisingly — Max Weber, who attributed the emergence of capitalist "rationality" to the Protestant ethic.[121] Hence the idea that Europe has, in its (even post-modern) history, somehow embodied a "higher degree of rationality," and its corollary, which considers certain ideologies, including Islam, "un-amenable to a rational orientation of thought." However, nothing in the Qur'an can justify such a leap: Rodinson demonstrates, on the contrary, that "the Koran is a holy book in which rationality plays a big part," that "Allah never stops arguing, reasoning." In fact, the reasoning of the Qur'an is "identical with Pascal's famous wager." Logic likewise plays a key role in the Islamic polemic against the inextricable contradictions of Christian Trinity dogma.[122] In fact, the Qur'an lends itself to a "mercantile" inter-pretation of intercourse with God, on which point Rodinson quotes (without comment) this appreciation by a late-19th century British author.

> The mutual relations between God and man are of a strictly
> commercial nature. Allah is the ideal merchant. He includes
> all the universe in his reckoning. All is counted, everything
> measured. The book and the balances are his institution, and
> he has made for himself the pattern of an honest living.
> ...The Muslim makes a loan to Allah: pays in advance for
> paradise, sells his own soul to him, a bargain that prospers.
> The unbeliever has sold the divine truth for a paltry price;
> and is bankrupt. Every soul is held in security for the debt it

has contracted. At the Resurrection, Allah holds a final reck-
oning with all men.[123]

We can immediately appreciate how reductionist such a "strictly commercial" reading of the Qur'an can be. But is not the tone an ironic one?
Rodinson's apparently serious reference also serves to remind us of the
limitations of outside interpretation.

The reminder is a timely one indeed: it is not because Western science
"corrects" its own simplifications or *comes to grips with itself*, that it comes
any closer to the truth of the Other. As Rodinson himself notes (referring to
a socialist reading of Islam), it is "absurd to transpose" our ideal back to the
era of Mohammed, "trying artificially to discover in it that setting. Similarly, to try to reduce the demands of today's consciousness to the demands of
an age that is gone, is an operation that is, in the strictest sense, reactionary."[124] But the same caution should be directed toward his own method.
There is little to assure us that Rodinson's interpretation of Islam corresponds in the slightest with the ways Muslims today interpret their
religion. These ways are pluralistic, and open to tradition as a response to
the specific problems of the Muslims of a particular country or doctrine
(whether the return to the sources be revolutionary or reactionary, in the
figurative sense). Dissipating our own myths (such as those which posit
Islam and capitalism as irreconcilable — as Rodinson does) will always be
a significant achievement. But we cannot, in the same breath, create new
myths by drawing on our own newfound lucidity (which is little more, at
best, than lucidity about our past blindness).

So it is that Rodinson contradicts, ever so slightly, the spirit of his own
method when, at the end of his book, he scrutinizes "the claim put forward
by some to make a religion, Islam, the banner of socialist economic construction in the Muslim countries," a pretence which he rejects, affirming
that "the Muslim religion seems poorly fitted to play this role."[125] Rodinson
certainly has the right to express his views (which I tend to share). But this
is pure opinion. Islam has no other limits, in the future, than those which
Muslims themselves will impose upon it. Rodinson may well have excellent reasons for pessimism, but it is a pessimism which certainly does not
proceed from any known truth about the nature of Islam. No one knows
what "Muslim socialism" might become (or "socialist Islam," for that
matter), but nothing can prevent Muslims from attempting to build a new
society (whatever its name or its sources of inspiration may be). Only
Muslims themselves are capable of expressing — in word or in deed — an
eventual unity, or liaison between Islam (that is, their own *religious* practice) and the political (that is, their conception of social organization). We
can judge nothing of the future from our observation of what we judge to
be negative experiences (as defined by our criteria). As Hodgson says,
"every generation makes its own decisions." Even though this affirmation

cannot be verified, it has the signal advantage of prejudging nothing. Contact with the Other requires nothing but great self-restraint.

In reality, defining the identity of the Other is a contradiction in terms. Everything which we have seen through this book indicates that the definition of otherness can never be anything more than a method of self-representation — or self-refusal. Awareness of this limit, and of its insurmountable nature, is justification enough for the restraint I advocate. Seen from this perspective, a Westerner may no longer deal authoritatively with questions like Islamic cultural identity, as Gustav von Grunebaum strove so masterfully to do.[126] Grunebaum, in spite of himself, proves conclusively how vain is the attempt to externally encompass a totality called "Islam" or "Orient." These generalities express nothing more than one of the terms of a mental antinomy. Who would attempt to define the Orient, or Islam, if not to near-consciously place it in opposition to the West (or, in the past, to Christianity)? Likewise, who would dare speak of "tradition" in its generic sense if not in counterpoint to modernity, if this tradition is not simply to designate the negative of modern industrial society? Not that these concepts are devoid of meaning — instead, the larger and more malleable they become, the more they are charged with a multiplicity of meanings — but because they have meaning only in relation to the subject which employs them, not in relation to the object which they purport to define.

By way of the Other...

Grunebaum has a thoroughly remarkable way of illuminating relativity. To my knowledge, despite his ultimate failure to draw all the possible conclusions for his own approach, no other orientalist carried the question of identity quite so far in terms of method. With Grunebaum the contradiction expresses, deep down, the Westerner's difficulty in understanding the meaning of his own perception, and in accepting its limitations. Our purpose here is not to dwell at length on the negative aspects of this perception. Grunebaum cannot avoid the propensity for denigration which we have come to recognize among orientalists, indulging it with a unique combination of harshness, elegance and "loftiness" — but this is not what interests us. Grunebaum's interest, at this stage of our survey, lies in the way he expresses the imperious desire to arrive at the essence of Islam, *despite the clear indication, drawn from his own methodological reflections, that the enterprise is radically impossible.*

Abdullah Laroui[127] gives a convincing analysis of the reductionist consequences of Grunebaum's attempt at universal characterization, showing how it reduced to naught the temporal and spatial differentiations which the author of *The Search for Cultural Identity* attempted to inject into his arguments. But was Grunebaum truly seeking to introduce a spirit of differentiation into his proposed vision of Islam? Permit me to doubt it. Grunebaum is perpetually sliding from the religious to the cultural in expressing the recurrence, in Islam, of religious determination on society as a whole, irrespective of its geographical and historical situation. This use of *Muslim* history is all the more — or all the less — surprising in that it totally contradicts his proposed vision of Western history.

For Grunebaum, historicity — the capacity for experiencing historical time "as meaningful," belongs only to the modern West. This historicity, which "pervades every sphere of man's activity,"[128] is missing from the Orient, which lacks realism (*Sachlichkeit*) and openness to reality. Do we hear the distant, discordant echoes of a Hegelian *Weltanschauung*? Not entirely. Grunebaum, far from being indifferent to the destiny of Islam, attempts to posit a mechanism by which Arabo-Muslim society could join the mainstream of history, a kind of access road to historicity inspired — this much seems clear — by the Western experience. We have seen the paternalism before: Grunebaum is neither the first, nor the last, to attempt such a rescue operation — about whose success he continues to express certain doubts. But his effort has one innovative aspect: an intelligent explanation of the way in which the West itself has constructed its identity and built the central discipline which has today become anthropology.

Grunebaum is adamant: the one process springs, by definition, from the other. Its demonstration begins with a basic epistemological reflection on the social sciences, taking the concept of historicity as a starting point. History, for Grunebaum, is the bearer of meaning, not because it embodies an immanent Hegelian principle, but because *we* endow it with meaning through the ends which we set for ourselves:

> The purpose-directedness of human existence — in subjective terms, the primacy of the will — pervades every sphere of man's activity, the technological or the economic as well as the political or the interpretive...The *why* is secondary to the *what for*... Objectivity means object-orientedness. Thoughts, observations, interpretations receive their objectivity from the ends toward which they are oriented.[129]

This form of objectivity (which is a way of objectivizing subjectivity, or of relativizing what we normally call objectivity) brings culture (for Grunebaum, a hierarchical value system) into relation with "the persistence of the Muslim community and the growth of the Muslim civilizational area."[130] In this encounter of the self with reality, there also exists the Other: the capacity to "exploit..." is an element in the "readiness to open" characteristic of Western culture.[131] Thus we arrive at "a self understanding of man as a culturally conditioned being...based on analyzing and assessing one's own civilization against, ideally, all other civilizations...an end confined to the most modern West."[132] Hence the strategic position (formerly that of philosophy) held today by anthropology.

> Our need to review and construct ourselves against the background of the totality of the cultural achievement of mankind has made cultural anthropology a central concern of our time.[133]

In other words, the advent of anthropology is a result of the very process by which the West has constructed its self image, and "our self-understanding (which) must be based on an understanding of other cultures."[134] Here we find the germ of the expression which we could term the relativity of the historical and anthropological view.

But no sooner than it has been spelled out, this relativity is in danger of losing a substantial part of its epistemological scope: the centrality of anthropology expresses at the same time the centrality of the West which has produced it. This is the process by which the West has continued to reconstruct its self-image vis-à-vis the Other, to employ the formula Grunebaum borrows from Husserl. For Husserl:

> That idea is no other than the idea of philosophy itself; the idea of a universal knowledge concerning the totality of being, a knowledge which contains within itself whatever special sciences may grow out of its ramifications, which rests upon ultimate foundations and proceeds throughout in a completely evident and self-justifying fashion and in full awareness of itself.[135]

The "justificatory" tone of Husserl's conclusion aside, one would think that awareness of the element of self-justification in the Western anthropological approach should logically lead us to reflect on its limitations: its objective can no longer pretend to be the knowledge of the world (other people), but the knowledge of oneself in the world (among other people). But the logic of this proposition is more ambiguous than meets the eye. To know the relativity of our view, and to transform what we know into a particularity of the West may well be an ultimate form of self-reassurance, a way of elevating our lucidity above cultures: no sooner than it has impinged upon our consciousness, the relativity of our knowledge is dissipated in the pretension which it nourishes. So it is that Grunebaum can assert, with the best of good faith:

> In this sense one may speak of the superior attitude of the modern West for the analysis of civilizations. One may go further and describe the only civilization that has, in its

concept of man, fully utilized its *Kulturenfähigkeit*, that is, its potential (and largely actualized) cultural pluralism.[136]

As Islam (like any other non-Western culture or civilization) lacks this "higher aptitude," it is therefore incumbent on the West to provide it with the necessary investigational tools, to draw attention to the true problems, to tell Islam what it is — even though the responsibility for finding their way in the contemporary world falls to Muslims, and to them alone.

Grunebaum thus arrives at the following paradox: on the one hand, he demonstrates more thoroughly than any other orientalist before him to what extent the knowledge — or more precisely, the scrutiny — of the Other has helped the West to understand itself, and to understand the movement of self-analysis which leads by way of the Other; on the other hand, he speaks of the Other as a reality independent of his view, which science can envision at once as totality and in its component parts, which it can dissect and recompose at will. The paradox is a powerful one, and expresses a fragment of deep truth which it would be foolish to disregard: scientific assurance (not to say arrogance) reveals not only the author's naivety, but also reflects the position of strength which the West still momentarily enjoys in the economic and political sphere.

Grunebaum's reflections on cultural identity are rich in interest: no culture today, least of all Western culture, can sidestep the questions posed, directly or indirectly, by the expansion of the industrial mode of production. Despite our incapacity to define the Other, it remains entirely legitimate and necessary to reflect on the problems caused by the dynamics of material accumulation and technical change, both for others and for ourselves. Whether we regret it or draw profit from it, the West is present in varying degrees everywhere in the world. The weight and the ugliness of this presence so manifest in so many places and in so many ways (including in our midst) compels us to keep our eyes wide open. Our purpose is not to exonerate the Other *a priori*, nor to perform penance for the sins of the past, no matter how highly-charged that past may be, but to understand our relation to today's humanity. It is to establish with utmost clarity the conditions under which we can reflect on our collective destiny and identity, in an age when, more than ever before, no one is an island unto himself.

Seen in this light, Grunebaum is right to emphasize that the questions asked of the Orient by a "Westernization" at once endured and desired "become more burning as it is less possible to brush them aside by pointing to colonialism as the root of evil. And, even if colonialism is impugned, the problem is pushed back only one step, for it would be difficult not to ask further: What is it that weakened the Muslim world to such an extent that it no longer could or would resist the intruder."[137] This interpretation is not far removed from provocation. But I believe it essential to avoid eventual intellectual exchanges between the Orient and the West becoming entangled in a vicious circle of blame and recrimination. Every people must accept its situation in the world, if for no other reason than to escape it.

Taking this truism as a point of departure, I am in agreement with Grunebaum that a second truism should be formulated: *self-knowledge must lead by way of the Other*. As we are already perhaps too well aware, such a "passage" is in many ways typical of the Western search for identity. But it is also the reason why it represents one of the ultimate constraints imposed by Western expansion on the rest of the world. Added onto all those that have gone before, one last intellectual constraint may well drive the non-Westerner beyond the limit: to hell with the West, its economism, its values, its thought structures! But, as Mojtaba Sadria has shown, such rejection stems — *a contrario* though it may be — from the presence of the West, from interference which can be rejected and condemned. We cannot behave as though none of this ever occurred, as though history never happened.

Though possibly a consequence of imperialism, it is not necessarily imperialist — or, conversely, defeatist — to affirm, as does Grunebaum, that the road to awareness of self in Islam leads through the West. But on condition that there is no contempt for the meaning of the detour, that it imputes no intrinsic superiority to the Western approach over other modes of apprehending the real, that it does not imply that the Islamic peoples share our way of life, our aspirations, or our values. In truth, these peoples have all the less reason to share uncritically our fundamental aspirations (presuming that we ourselves know what they are) since these were the aspirations which helped to bring us down upon them and to shatter their way of life — not to mention the problems which they pose for us. Once more, as modernity works its way across the planet (at different levels depending on continent or region, but in one way or in another omnipresent) it constrains the peoples of the Orient, the West, the North or the South, to define themselves in relation to it, if only to resist those of its aspects they may judge as alienating and destructive.

No culture, no collectivity can escape the need to redefine itself, to rethink itself — mythologically or otherwise. Today, more than ever before, the awakening awareness of identity must take into account the alterity, the viewpoint and the presence (near or far) of the Other. This principal is equally applicable to both the West and to the Orient, even though, for historical reasons, the dialectic takes a different shape at each of its two poles.

For the Orient, dialectical necessity has a heartbreaking inevitability. Is it possible to think about the Other without thinking *like* the Other? As long as the balance of power, which is slowly changing beneath our eyes — even though we may not take the trouble to open them — remains unequal, the risk of intellectual colonization will persist.

The danger for the West is hardly less critical: as long as we have not decolonialized our view (our science), we will continue to be completely mistaken about the meaning of our so-called knowledge of the Other, whom we will continue to examine as a pure object. If it is true that the path to self-understanding leads through the Other, the aphorism, today more than ever, applies equally to the West. The Other may well shift the angle of the mirror in which we seek our own image, reflecting unexpected, perhaps even unpleasant images of ourselves.

If this book has demonstrated anything, it is that for a long time the West took interest in the Other without realizing that it's real interest was in itself; that it represented it in order to create its own identity, that it denigrated it in order to reassure (or frighten) itself, that it dreamed of it to escape itself. But why speak in the past tense? None of these diversions of identity has truly come to an end.

Still, something has changed; a hope more than a certainty. Among some Western intellectuals, the idea that the road to self-understanding goes by way of the Other has finally gained grudging acceptance. This does not necessarily mean that those intellectuals are in a situation of dialogue with the Other — if for no other reason than that the Other has rejected the dialogue. But this need not stop us from acknowledging a new and obvious fact: taking this path does not mean that we can or should define it, nor does it mean we can understand it in its fullness and in its essence. This, for me, is a decisive stroke of good fortune compared with the attitude of those who not long ago took for granted — and of those who today still believe — that Western science gives a truer image of the Other than the Other itself could ever provide.

Our view of the Other cannot — in all lucidity — set itself the objective of knowing it "in and of itself..." We must, henceforth, know that through it we seek ourselves. No longer will we find a passive reflection of our sense of the imaginary. We will discover that, longer ago than we suspected, it has begun to reflect back at us his own image of ourselves. Since the image is not a particularly flattering one, many Western intellectuals will persist in their refusal to awaken to the implications of our inevitable ethnocentrism — so unbearable do they find the notion that there may be truth in what the Other says about us.

NOTES

1. See Edward Saïd, *Covering Islam*, New York, Pantheon, 1981.
2. Cassier, *The Philosophy of the Enlightenment*, op. cit.
3. This anthropological relativism was itself quite relative; it could not escape the constrictions of ethnocentrism. No anthropology, and no discipline of the social sciences, can. But ethnocentrism's influence is mitigated by consciousness of it. In Hume, it expresses itself unconsciously in the idea — which for him is as obvious as

it is natural — that monotheism constituted undeniable progress over polytheism. See Hume, David, *The Natural History of Religion*. Stanford, Stanford University Press, 1956.

4. Dugat, Gustave, *Histoire des Orientalistes de l'Europe du XIIe au XIXe siècle*, Paris, Maisonneuve et cie., 1868, p.li.

5. Berque, Jacques, *L'Islam au défi*, Paris, Gallimard, p.30,46.

6. In *Cahiers du Sud*, Marseille, Rivages, 1947, p.7.

7. Valéry, Paul, *An Anthology*, Princeton, Princeton University Press, 1956. Bollingen Series XVL-A, p.94.

8. Spengler, Oswald, *The Decline of the West*. Authorized translation with notes by Charles Francis Atkinson, London, George Allen & Unwin Ltd., 1926, p.15.

9. Spengler, op. cit., Vol. I, p.3.

10. Spengler, op. cit. Vol. I, p.119.

11. Spengler was not the first — no one ever is — to express these feelings of anguish and pessimism (which can be found in Schopenhauer and Nietzsche, and even in the younger Hegel), but he gave them an original form by making them the motor of history. Spengler's concerns are ethnocentric in the extreme; I cannot countenance Hichem Djait's judgement that "Spengler rejects all forms of ethnocentrism." (op. cit., p.85.) He does, I suggest, relocate it.

12. Ibid., Vol.I, p.16.

13. Ibid., Vol. I, p.19,21.

14. Ibid., Vol. I, p.183. "The Apollonian existence is that of the Greek who describes his ego as *soma* and who lacks all idea of an inner development and therefore all real history, inward and outward; the Faustian is an existence which *is led* with a deep consciousness and introspection of the ego..."

15. Ibid., Vol. I, p.401.

16. Djait, op. cit., p.86.

17. Spengler, op. cit., Vol. I, p.213.

18. For Spengler, civilization, in opposition to culture, is synonymous with sclerosis and decadence; while culture is the expression of ascending life.

19. Ibid., Vol. II, p.189.

20. Ibid., Vol. I, p.213.

21. Ibid., Vol.II, p.260. Spengler goes on to add: "Dogma was complete, finished — just as it was...with the confession of Augsburg (1540)." (Vol.II, p.261)

22. Djait, op. cit., p.93. See also p.84-96 for Djait's critique of Spengler.

23. Not that communication between cultures does not occur, but that the innermost essence of any culture cannot be transferred to another. Forms alone can be transmitted — even thought the invasion of the Roman Empire by Magian culture would seem to contradict the rule. Here, as with many other aspects of his thought, Spengler is not without his contradictions.

24. Toynbee, Arnold, *A Study of History*, London, Oxford University Press, 1935, p.31.

25. Ibid., p.51. Further on, Toynbee notes what he detects as affinities between Western civilization and the Iranian branch of Islamic civilization, and Orthodox civilization and the Arab branch of the same Islamic civilization, as a way of introducing the debatable notion of "Indo-Europeanicity." Toynbee also seemingly accepts the culturally integrating effects of Western civilization on other cultures.

26. Ibid., Vol. I, p.157.

27. Volney, quoted in the original French by Toynbee, Ibid., p.154. (From "Leçons d'Histoire, Sixième séance. *Oeuvres complètes de Volney*, Paris, Firmin-Didot, 1876, p.588.)

28. Ibid., Vol. I, p.223. "In the 17th and 18th century of our era, in North America, when the English settlers were expelling or exterminating the Red Indians, the French settlers were intermarrying with them and assimilating them."

29. Ibid., Vol. I, p.216. See also Arthur de Gobineau, *Essai sur l'inégalité des races humaines (1853-1855)*, Paris, Pierre Belfond, 1967. Gobineau (who is said to have inspired

certain Nazi theses) is particularly praiseful of the Jews, whom he describes as a "free," "strong," and "intelligent" people.

30. Ibid., Vol. VIII, p.217. The two societies are the Western and Russian (Orthodox).
31. Ibid., Vol. VIII, p.723.
32. Ibid., Vol. I, p.83-91.
33. Ibid., Vol. VIII, p.237.
34. Ibid., Vol. VIII, p.542-547.
35. Ibid., Vol. VIII, p.237.
36. Toynbee, *The World and the West*, op. cit. p.33. From Jacques Madaule's introduction to the French edition.
37. Ibid., p.40.
38. Ibid., p.69. See also Toynbee's dialogue with Ragharan Iyer, *The Glass Curtain between Asia and Europe*. A symposium on the historical encounters and the changing attitudes of the peoples of the East and the West, Oxford University Press, 1965, p.329-349.
39. Ibid., p.34. Madaule's introduction.
40. Ibid., p.106.
41. See Saïd, *Orientalism*, p.265-274. Massignon's stature leads Saïd to qualify his own critique of orientalism, which he continues to condemn as a discipline explicitly grounded in the a priori concept of the Orient as global, unalterable alterity, the discipline's learned works only serving to further confirm and legitimize the stereotype.
42. Ibid., p.284.
43. Ibid., p.271. Saïd here paraphrases Massignon, quoted in Waardenburg, op. cit., p.219.
44. Massignon, Louis, "Le mouvement intellectuel contemporain en Proche Orient," in *Opéra minora*, Beirut, Dar Al-Maaret, 1963, Vol. I, p.230.
45. Massignon, "honneur des camarades de travail et la parole de vérité," 1961, in *Opéra Minora*, op. cit., Vol.III, p.840.
46. Ibid., p.840.
47. Massignon, "La situation sociale en Algérie," in *Opéra Minora*, op. cit., p.578.
48. The High commissioner in question was none other than François Georges-Picot, co-author of the celebrated Sykes-Picot agreement, under which, in 1915, France and England secretly undertook to divide the Near East with Russia following the defeat of Turkey. The planned partition negated Britain's promises to the Arab national movement, which had agreed to fight with the Allies against Turkey on condition that a unified Arab State be created after the war.
49. Saïd, op. cit., p.238-243.
50. Lawrence, T.E. (Lawrence of Arabia), *Seven Pillars of Wisdom*, London, Penguin, 1964, p.30.
51. The word may be too strong. But Lawrence and Massignon supported diametrically opposed views regarding the future of Greater Syria, reflecting the policies of their respective countries. Massignon wrote that Lawrence was jealous of his exclusive contact with Faisal, and feared the Frenchman's influence over him. "You prefer the Arabs to me," Lawrence allegedly told Massignon. See Massignon, "Mes rapports avec Lawrence en 1917," 1960, in *Opéra Minora*, op. cit., Vol. III, p.423.
52. Massignon, "Situation de l'Islam," 1939, *Opéra Minora*, op. cit., p.11-12.
53. Massignon, "L'amour courtois de l'Islam dans la *Gerusalemme liberata* tu Tasse," 1947, *Opéra Minora*, op. cit., Vol.I, p.106. Tasso completed *Gerusalemme* in 1580. As Massignon explains, the work became "for the great century of French classicism, the Epic, the Iliad of Christianity (Ibid.), the literary embodiment of the survival of the Crusade myth.
54. Massignon, "Le mouvement intellectuel contemporain en Proche-Orient," loc.cit., p.225. Written six years after the article on Tasso but illustrative of the same concern for the West-East relation.

55. The words, with the exception of 'mask' are Massignon's. See "L'Occident devant l'Orient, primauté d'une solution culturelle." *Politique étrangère,* Paris, juin, 1952 in *Opéra Minora,* op. cit., Vol. I, p.208.

56. Letter quoted by Massignon in "L'Occident devant l'Orient," loc. cit. p.209.

57. In this rambling exposition, Massignon details the comprehensions and ugly stereotypes of the Arabs held by Europeans, who are unable to imagine what the Arabs might be able to give them. It is enough for him to chastise the psychological errors of the colonizer toward the colonized. In the face of criticism, Massignon appears pained that his efforts have not been understood.

58. Moubarac, Youakim, article on Massignon in *Encyclopaedia Universalis,* Vol. 10, 1978, p.606. It should be recalled that Massignon's major work dealt with the life and thought of the Iraqui Muslim martyr al-Hallaj *(La Passion d'al-Hallaj, martyr mystique de l'Islam,* Paris, 1922), a choice often criticized for giving undue prominence to a marginal figure in Islamic history, whose 'Christ-like' character he had exaggerated.

59. Massignon, "Le mouvement intellectuel en Proche Orient," loc.cit., p.224.

60. Massignon, "Ce qu'est la Terre sainte pour les communautés humaines que demandent justice," 1948, Opéra Minora, op. cit., Vol. III, p.475.

61. Ibid., p.475-477. Massignon notes, higher, that "Marxist Zionism truly wishes to emancipate the Palestinian workers; all well and good, but it is not for this reason that the United States finances the Zionist enterprise, but because the 'colossal' exploitation of the Near East must be organized. Is this what Israel, in returning to the Holy Land, wishes? Its spiritual loyalty, however, forbids it." (Ibid., p.510.)

62. Massignon, Politique étrangère, 1949, in *Opéra Minora,* op. cit., Vol. III, p.514.

63. Ibid., p.510.

64. Sartre, Jean-Paul, *New Look,* mai, 1966. Quoted by Abdelkebir Khatibi, *Vomito blanco,* le sionisme et la conscience malheureuse. Paris, 10-18, 1974, p.67. It should be noted that Sartre was first to admit the ambiguity of his position, as attested in "Pour la vérité," preface to a special issue of *Temps modernes* (No. 253, 1967) on the Arab-Israeli conflict.

65. Khatibi, op. cit., p.47.

66. Massignon, "Colloque universitaire du 2 juin 1957 sur le problème algérien" in *Opéra Minora,* op. cit., Vol. III, p.608.

67. Massignon, "La situation sociale en Algérie," *Esprit,* août 1951 in *Opéra Minora,* op. cit., Vol. III, p.581.

68. Massignon, "Le respect de la personne humaine en Islam et la priorité du droit d'asile sur le devoir de juste guerre," Revue internationale de la Croix-Rouge,) No. 402, juin, 1952. *Opéra Minora,* op. cit., Vol. III, p.548.

69. Ibid.

70. On Massignon's and Berque's convergences and divergences, see their "Dialogue sur 'les Arabes'" *Esprit,* octobre, 1960, p.1506-1519. Berque: "I seek community with the Arabs, not so much in the semitic spirit of which you speak, but in the Greco-Oriental message" where Abraham is replaced by Heraclitus. (Ibid., p.1516.)

71. Berque, Jacques, *L'Islam au défi,* Paris, Gallimard, 1980, p.246.

72. Khatibi, Abdelkebir, "Jacques Berque ou la saveur orientale," in *Les temps modernes,* juin, 1976, No. 359, p.2163.

73. Ibid., p.2163.

74. Ibid., p.2164.

75. Massignon, *Dialogue sur 'les Arabes',* loc. cit., p.1515. Massignon does not distinguish between Catholics and Protestants.

76. *Orientations pour un dialogue entre Chrétiens et Musulmans,* Secretarius pro non-Christianis, Rome, Ancora, 1970, p.16. (this 144-page booklet was prepared by father Joseph Cuoq and Louis Gardet.)

77. Ibid., p.17.

78. Moubarac, Youakim, *Pentalogie islamo-chrétienne,* Beirut, Éditions du Cénacle libanais, 5 vols., 1972-1973, vol. II, p.284.

79. Ibid., p.60.
80. Ibid., Vol. III, p.19-20.
81. Ibid., p.283.
82. Berque, Jacques, *Dépossession du monde*, Paris, Seuil, 1964. p.21.
83. Ibid., p.11-12.
84. Ibid., p.42. In discussing the problems of identity created by industrial civilization among the decolonized peoples, Berque adds: "When they speak of these matters, the Arabs cry out and gesticulate with immense poignancy. Their violence, their solemn language, their old-school dignity, their Greco-Latin affinities, make them the most picturesque heroes of decolonization."
85. Ibid., p.66.
86. Berque, Jacques, *L'Islam au défi*.
87. Berque, Jacques, *L'Orient second*, Paris, Gallimard, 1970, p.295.
88. Ibid., p.111.
89. Ibid.
90. Saïd, op. cit., p.177. "In the system of knowledge about the Orient, the Orient is less a place than a *topos*, a set of references."
91. Berque, *L'Islam au défi*, op. cit., Chapter II.
92. Ibid., p.103.
93. Ibid., p.63.
94. Ibid., p.18.
95. Ibid., p.115.
96. Ibid., p.115.
97. Ibid., p.115. No explication of the Qur'an, he writes, "has shaken the conviction that it proceeds directly from direct, integral dictation from God. I would consider the contrary hypothesis needlessly provocative."
98. Ibid., p.43.
99. Ibid., p.39.
100. Khatibi, loc. cit. p.2160.
101. Berque, *L'Islam au défi*, op. cit., p.290.
102. Ibid., p.298.
103. Preface to Gustav von Grunebaum's *L'identité culturelle d'Islam*, Paris, Gallimard, 1973, p.vii-viii.
104. Péroncel-Hugoz, Jean-Peirre, *Le radeau de Mahomet*, Paris, Lieu commun, 1983.
105. Bruckner, Pascal, *The Tears of the White Man*. Translated by William R. Beer, New York, The Free Press. 1983.
106. Péroncel-Hugoz, op. cit., p.17-18.
107. Garaudy, Roger, *Promesses de l'Islam*, Paris, Seuil, 1981.
108. For a critique of the philosophical approach, see Marshall G.S. Hodgson, *The Venture of Islam*, Vol. I, The Classical Age of Islam, Chicago, Chicago University Press, 1974, p.39. On the "marriage" of Orientalism and the social sciences, see H.A.R. Gibb, *Area Studies reconsidered*, London, School of Oriental and African Studies, 1963.
109. This prompts Djait to remark (op. cit., p.51): "Seeking to head off these dangers, the Orientalist ensconces himself in the superiority of things European. Whereas the critically minded intellectual harbors doubts about his own society, the Orientalist assigns an exemplary status of the destiny of Europe."
110. Lewis, Bernard, "The Question of Orientalism," in *The New York Review of Books*, June 24, 1982, p.49-56.
111. Lewis, Bernard, *The Assassins, A Radical Sect in Islam*. The preface to the French edition (*Les Assassins, Terrorism et politique dans l'Islam médiéval*, Paris, Berger-Levrault, 1983) is by Maxime Rodinson.
112. Ibid. (Rodinson's preface to the French edition), p.8. The English title confirms the (false) definition of 'Assassins' (in the plural) found in The Oxford Universal Dictionary: "Certain Moslem fanatics in the time of the Crusades, sent forth...to murder Christians."

113. Gibb, H.A.R., *Modern Trends in Islam*, Chicago, University of Chicago Press, 1947, p.1.
114. Ibid., p.11.
115. Ibid., p.104. The "modernists" Gibb alludes to are those reformist Muslim thinkers (and believers) partially won over to Western liberal ideas. "So far from guiding Muslim thought…they have bound it still more firmly with the shackles of the romantic imagination." (p.127.)
116. Ibid., p.105.
117. Hodgson, Marshall, *The Venture of Islam*, op. cit., p.148. The extensive methodological introduction itself constitutes, in my opinion, one of the best cautionary notes on the study of Muslim societies.
118. Ibid., p.34.
119. Ibid., p.37.
120. Rodinson, Maxime, *Islam and Capitalism*. Translated by Brian Pearce. New York, Pantheon, c1973.
121. Weber, Max, *The Protestant Ethic and the Spirit of Capitalism*. Translated by Talcott Pearson, New York, Charles Scribner's Sons, 1958.
122. Ibid., p.78-79.
123. Ibid., p.81: Torrye, Charles C., *The Commercial-Theological Terms in the Koran*, 1892.
124. Ibid., p.27.
125. Ibid., p.224. Rodinson goes on (p.228) to enumerate the conditions under which Islam could be employed in other than reactionary ways. But here too, the enterprise can only be undertaken on the basis of a value structure — Western values in Rodinson's case.
126. Von Grunebaum, Gustav, *Modern Islam: the Search for Cultural Identity*. Berkeley, University of California Press, 1962.
127. Laroui, Abdallah, *La crise des intellectuels arabes*, traditionalisme ou historicisme? Paris, Maspero, 1974, p.56.
128. Von Grunebaum, op. cit., p.30. "An element of Schalichkeit — the readiness to open and surrender oneself to an encounter with reality, rather than to surrender to reality." (p.34) and, further along: "The scrutiny of modern Muslim self-interpretation, as much of the acquaintance with medieval Islamic theology, suggest some doubt concerning to which Islam is prepared to accept history as a binding experience." (p.47.)
129. Ibid., p.30-31.
130. Ibid., p.1.
131. Ibid., p.34.
132. Ibid., p.32.
133. Ibid., p.35.
134. Ibid., p.107.
135. Ibid., p.104. (Husserl quoted by Grunebaum.)
136. Ibid., p.108.
137. Ibid., p.25.

VII

The Deadly Frontier

The crushing of Iraq at the hands of the Western powers in 1991 provided a dramatic demonstration of the deadly nature of the frontier which has been the central concern of this book. The Gulf War, a punitive action of a magnitude unequalled since World War II, particularly in its combination of brevity and intensity, gave violent, destructive expression to the power of myth. Bubbling up blindly, in its dark potency, from a deep well of latent act, myth *acts* upon us collectively in the same way that a repressed urge acts upon an individual: *in our unawareness of it.*

If unawareness had been awareness, if understanding of how our vision of the Other functioned had been mutual, what we euphemistically describe as the Gulf War would never have taken place, would never have taken on the guise, nor won the support that it did. Only depreciation of the Other, only ignorance of the secular bases of the entire process of devaluation made it possible for Western leaders and media to wield so effectively the ideological weapons which assured consent and stifled dissent. But it is not enough to simply attach a label to the process of devaluation. Time spent re-examining the litany of anti-Arab insults which erupted during the conflict would be time wasted, a diversion from the central issue of frontiers, and from the spirit which has animated this book from its inception.

If certain reactions to the first French edition are any indication, this spirit has not yet been entirely understood — particularly by orientalists still smarting from Edward Saïd's *Orientalism*, a book from which I took considerable pains to distance myself. Saïd rightly censures the ethnocentrism and the colonialism of the learned (and less learned) view which has wounded his subjectivity, but he does not touch upon what, for me, is the crucial question: that of the frontier. This is why I return to the subject here. To liken my approach to Saïd's *j'accuse* is to make a highly superficial reading of the power of imagination whose sharp breaks and founding moments I have attempted to articulate. But while the reading may be superficial, it is not the result of laziness or negligence; instead, it suggests resistance to virtually any attempt to question the unconscious, to seek out those things which we prefer not to see. It cannot be said often enough: this book is not simply a catalogue of charges against Western ethnocentrism, nor is it an indictment of the erudite study of the Arabo-Muslim world known as orientalism. The book's first line must be taken literally: *it is about us*. It scrutinizes our knowledge of ourselves as seen through the prism of our knowledge of the Other. In attempting to sketch out the most striking phases of a certain relationship with the Other, I drew on our knowledge and collective perceptions of this Other's world as my guidelines. But my fundamental interest throughout has been the deeper meaning *for ourselves* of the emotional and intellectual evolution which permeates each successive function of this imagining vision.

Seen from this vantage point, the consensus surrounding the destruction of Iraq warrants serious consideration, not as the unclouded reflection of an amply demonstrated racism, but as the culminating point of a way of thinking which, all manipulation aside, today enjoys both coherence and respectability: a way of thinking which may be subscribed to in good faith. What manner of civilization is this whose discourse about itself is capable of legitimizing a destructive undertaking wholly out of proportion with its announced objectives, and contrary to its own universally proclaimed standards? What order of thought is this that sanctions action to safeguard the principals it violates? This is the root question, the one posed by the collective punishment inflicted on Iraq. It is all the more acute in that punishment was visited upon an age-old opposition, one in whose mirror the West has constructed a significant portion of its identity.

As we scrutinize the thought system which set the tone for the conflict, our central question — the question of the frontier — surges once again to the fore. It is, naturally, a geopolitical and cultural frontier, complete with a component of the imaginary which made the rift so effective. But it is, above all, a frontier of science, a frontier between knowledge and consciousness, mooted but not named in the discussion of the "dialectic of identity" which concludes the French edition. The timidity was mine: I had not fully grasped the epistemological implications of the road thus far travelled, had not taken my thoughts on the production of science to their logical conclusion. The criticism which greeted the book and the critical distance from it which I have since gained, taken in conjunction with the systematic obliteration of Iraq, now impel me to return to the problematic sketched out in the preceding chapter in greater depth and contour.

Iraq is an extreme example, granted. But it is also an ideal starting point. What does it tell us? The images of military operations provided by the enforcers are as good a place as any to begin. Cutting-edge techniques of destruction were applied to a new surgical method which isolated the object of its ministrations. The congruence of means to ends lent considerable legitimacy to the operation: precision bombing, like a scalpel wielded by a skilled surgeon, would make it possible to remove the malignant tumour with the least possible effect on the patient's body. But with all its nerve centres (water, electricity, communications, factories, etc.) under assault, the whole organism collapsed. The recovery period is likely to be a long one, what with post-operative treatment consisting of a strangle-hold. The same surgical skill flaunted its prowess with the media: a country was crushed, bombed back into the pre-industrial age without the appearance of massive destruction. The image has since suffered some deterioration, with revelation of the operation's devastating long-term effects. But this comes at a time when public attention has been diverted from a theatre emptied of spectacle. Only the scar remains, the frontier: on one side, the army returning home virtually untouched, well pleased with the efficiency of its arms; on the other, the unburied corpses. For us there is science, technique, logic, measure, law. For them ignorance, folly, destruction, and death.

This image — slightly overdrawn, I grant — does not address the issue of responsibilities: nor is it meant to do so. That responsibilities must be shared, that the "victim," and more specifically, its leadership, collaborated closely in its own chastisement does not alter the nature of the frontier. On the contrary, it confirms both its immutable presence and its depth. Only the irreducible nature of such a dividing line can explain why the protagonists, despite the increasingly disparate military and political balance, never hesitated, never faltered. Combat, in the strict sense, never took place; never was there a true test of strength, only the gradual preparation — active on one side, passive on the other — for execution of sentence, for consummation of the sacrifice. The balance of forces was a curious one indeed; it did not pit one military machine against another, one strategy against another (as in Vietnam, or Afghanistan, for example, where the defeat of the stronger adversary was, if not a certainty, at least a possibility) but logistics against a symbol.

There is more to the contrast than meets the eye. The confrontation was more than a clash on a battlefield (ultimately revealed as a fiction) involving modern weapons. Obscured by the immense inequality of material forces, a confrontation of imagined forces was also unfolding. Nor was the clash between a "realistic" strategy and an "unrealistic" one, but between two mutually-enhancing imaginary strategies, between two contrasting yet interpenetrating symbolic logistics: one gearing for victory, the other seemingly resigned to defeat. Though these two structures of imagination are complementary, they neither understand one another nor share equivalent strength. Victory for one side and defeat for the other did not flow from a confrontation where, though their respective means were unequal, the resources of imagination each could draw upon were equivalent. No; the inequality was double. The West's victory was more than material, it was moral: a victory of imagining power. This moral aspect of victory found its everyday expression in the clear conscience of public opinion: chastisement, no matter how stern, was justified.

The idea of the frontier reaches to the very depths of this juggernaut of justification.

Not only are the weapons themselves lethal, not only is the death they inflict more horrible. Far more deadly still is the principle of exclusion, which always contrives to find the weapons which best serve its needs. The principal is not peculiar to the West: every civilization, every community constructs its identity, to a greater or lesser degree, on the same foundations. The West's distinguishing feature is not exclusion, not ignoring the exclusion it practices, though its material successes over the last two centuries have tended, paradoxically, to obscure its vision of the world. The distinguishing feature of Western civilization, at its best, is the desire *in all honesty* to accomplish exactly the opposite; to be firmly convinced that, rather than exclusive, it is *inclusive;* and that it acts *out of respect for differences.*

As the preceding chapter indicates, the conviction is not entirely illusory. It is grounded, in fact, in incontrovertible reality: no civilization was ever so systematically curious about other cultures as Western civilization. But its vast storehouse of anthropological knowledge should have given it a sense of relativity, should have sharpened its self-lucidity. Given the scientific achievements of the West, such lucidity might well be possible. The exercise of it could lead straight into generalized relativism, could slide into the crudest kind of cynicism where only raw power relationships still matter. This discourse of disillusion, which sweeps aside all scruples, invoking as it does a narrow and irrevocable egotism, is neither lucid nor human; but it has enabled the mighty to avoid the opprobrium of the oppression they exercised — not a strictly Western trait by any means.

No, lucid awareness of the eventuality of which I speak can be found in Montaigne, in the philosophers of the Enlightenment; it opens onto the *possibility* of greater self-knowledge. Here, as in every facet of human wisdom, Western thought can make no greater claim to accomplishment than any other. But it has succeeded, slightly ahead of the others, in acquiring a critical mass of knowledge, an anthropology, from which it may derive conscious awareness of itself and of its place in the world. But the act of conscious awareness demands of us an effort of a purely philosophical order: it does not spring from knowledge like clear water bubbling from an artesian well. Knowledge, obsessed by absolute thirst, or threatened by self-satisfaction, has laid a trap for us, a trap which is difficult to avoid. This trap is the sentiment of the universal.

Strictly speaking, neither is this sentiment unique to the Western spirit: any human being may feel, in his own way, a participant in the universe, in this world, and in the human condition. "In his own way" is the operative phrase: for there exists a typically Western way (in terms of its origins, at least) of grounding this sentiment, of constructing a kind of intellectual insurance comprising the breadth and diversity of knowledge, its ordering and its methods. Today, knowledge and its scientific foundations — rather than human experience — underlie the Westerner's conviction that it holds the reins of the universal. This foundation itself must be closely scrutinized: what is this *certainty of knowledge* which so vigorously resists Cartesian methodological doubt? When did it arise? My intent here is neither to present a detailed analysis, nor to set out a chronology, which alone would demand an entire book (now in progress). For the moment, it is enough to note that this problematic can be traced back to approximately the same point in time as the emergence of the modern West and the appearance, in its bosom, of its antinomian concept: the Orient. The coincidence, we know, is far from fortuitous. By definition, the frontier which divides the modern era from all that precedes it comes into being with Western affirmation and negation — or imagined inversion. The frontier, in turn, is consolidated coevally with the scientific assurance which forms the foundations of the sentiment of the universal in the West.

The frontier is double. It is a construct of historical imagination, dividing before from after, whose genesis can be traced back to the concept of Renaissance, the first period to name itself and to organize time in accordance with its own self-description. It also traces a spatial and mental horizon which divides identity from alterity, with their respective traits arrayed behind them in perfect symmetrical opposition: universal rationality, an attribute of self; and narrow-minded irrationality, a residue of backward, pre-historic alterity. The former is destined to thrive and prosper, the latter to disappear.

Hatred or fear have nothing to do with the sentence of disappearance; it is not a product of the defensive reflex which nurtures everyday racism and exclusion. It proceeds, instead, from world-knowledge whose self-assurance grows stronger as it develops ever more powerful tools, which in turn bring mastery of nature seemingly within reach — within reach of technology, to be more precise. Modern technique is spreading inexorably, though unequally and in varying ways, across the entire planet, and for this reason alone stands as a challenge to all cultures. Given such efficiency and power of diffusion, it is hardly surprising that technique — the manipulation of things — would strengthen, in the civilization which initiated the process, the conviction that it understands the world of humans! Scientific, technical, economic, social and political progress, through an evolution unique to Western societies, have become indissolubly linked in our collective imagination, where they are subsumed under the general idea of progress. Despite the heavy blows inflicted on it by the history of the 20th century, despite being assailed by doubts from all sides, despite being drained of a portion of its substance, the idea remains, *like an empty shell crying out to be filled*, at the centre of the Western credo. The credo is modernity.

For us, as Westerners, this credo is all of a piece. The diverse components (scientific, economic, social, etc.) of modernity draw their sustenance from the same sources, from the same historical moment, at a point between the Renaissance and the Enlightenment: a debatable coincidence, to say the least, once we penetrate the innermost fibre of event, thought and interpretation. But it functions, *a posteriori*, as myth, as intellectual necessity, obeying the irresistible desire of reason which, as in Hegel, resumes, accumulates and surpasses all contradictions in one single project. Reason's project is nothing more than its own accomplishment, a powerful blending of ideal, desire and certitude.

But the hope of reason, in all its compelling power, cannot stand in the way of reality. It is almost impossible to resist seduction by the slippage which has taken place along the way from the modernist *project* to its *credo*: where once there stood an ideal, a sense of hope (the project), a construct of imagination has arisen, a moral code — the credo which trumpets: "we are modernity." As the threat of refutation at the hands of social reality grows stronger, the affirmation becomes all the more peremptory. We have difficulty accepting the obvious: social (not to mention intellectual) progress has not kept pace with technical progress and economic accumulation; the ideals of modernity have been diminished in the upheavals of modernization. The rule of law, citizenship, universal suffrage, equality before the law, distribution of wealth, basic freedoms — to sum up what remains of the modernist project — are by no means futile achievements. But great disparities persist: many of our achievements are fragile, often more formal than real, and, above all, counterbalanced by the negative impact of an overpowering system of production and exploitation in which the values of European humanism can barely survive.

Western thought has reflected these dissonances — while entrusting their resolution to the inexhaustible resources of the future. But curiously, our great self-lucidity suddenly clouds over the moment we confront the Other, and verges on the opaque when we face the outcry of protest aroused by the way we impose ourselves, and our knowledge. True, some well-meaning Western leftists experienced nearly two decades of "guilt" toward the Third World, at a time when the drive toward emancipation seemed to offer a stimulating diversion from the lassitude of material prosperity. Now, with economic crisis and fading prosperity, uneasiness has pushed lassitude into the background, and along with it, concern for the Third World, where rejection, inconsistency and treachery have conveniently betrayed our fondest hopes. The brief crisis of conscience has ended happily. Its remnants have been cleverly incorporated into the great ecological issues of the day, where the Other now joins us as co-accused — standing beside us in terms of responsibility, but under our vigilant supervision in terms of the measures to be taken, for "planetary management" represents today's leading-edge ideology, where the imperatives of the world market are joined with the necessities of the ecosystem in holy matrimony. The technical progress which, for the last two centuries, we have inflicted on the planet today obliges us to use the techniques which would, to the best of our knowledge, contribute to its regeneration. The frontier henceforth extends to the entire ecosystem, kept under close surveillance by our sophisticated sentinels in space. Today more than ever, world order is shaped by Western knowledge — as Japan looks on with polite curiosity.

This rather cavalier overview of the trials and tribulations of progress is not meant to justify devaluation of modernity itself, whose guiding utopia has lost none of its validity. Instead, it reveals the gulf which still separates us from modernity; reveals how flawed appreciation of the distance distorts our view of ourselves and of the world. Despite our occasional self-lucidity we, as Westerners, do not understand the world; what we understand is the world in us. We are the world — such is our desire. But knowing that we are not the world, we enjoin it to be what we are. These two dynamics, one imagined, the other material — the modernist credo and the relentless onrush of modernization filling the world — have imperceptibly broadened the scope of our ambitions to match the dimensions of the planet itself, and mistaken them for the scope of our knowledge.

It would be reassuring to extrapolate the future of humanity from the omniscient, seemingly inevitable progression of technique and modernization. But though the process is everywhere at work, its effects vary from one culture to another, and remains totally unforeseeable, proliferating independently of our will and our best laid plans. This is precisely what we find most disturbing: that the civilization whose knowledge has produced the universal concreteness of modern technique has not been universally accepted in its values. Meanwhile, these same values are far from being fully realized in our own societies, and we allow our leaders to make a mockery of them beyond our borders. But even if we disregard this last contradiction, the disenchantment we feel at the resistance of alterity is rooted in three false premises. First, the belief that our knowledge is purely, or essentially Western, a belief which only reinforces the chronological schema created by the Renaissance, relegating the Middle Ages, and with them the contribution of Arabo-Muslim science, to voluntary oblivion while annexing as "Western" the achievements of Greco-Roman antiquity. Second, paradoxically, the belief that Western knowledge enjoys the same universality as the technique which it has helped engender. Third, the belief that universality of knowledge necessarily carries with it a universality of values; that our values, in other words, body forth the universality of the Reason in which they are grounded.

The consequences of this triple conviction, in our relations with the Other, are so radical that they escape us altogether in their obviousness. Our anthropological knowledge of the Other, because it is real, precise, and ordered, because it proceeds from a universal rationality, is true. Because we know so much about the Other (more than it often know about itself), we know it. Because we know more about the world than any other culture we are best suited to decide where it is going, or at minimum, where it should be going. But the assurance that we derive from this knowledge ultimately reflects our own flawed knowledge of ourselves, undermining the doubt of which we are sometimes capable when the Other is not at issue.

No sooner is our relationship with alterity called into question than this deceptive certainty about ourselves and the world transforms the frontier into something quite different from a static line of demarcation. Like the American myth, the frontier keeps moving forward, until it has engulfed the entire world. The famous "end of history" is the myth restated, in the double sense of the term: spatially and temporally. Differences may subsist as marginal phenomena, or as folklore, providing they are compatible with the onward thrust. Any alterity which tries to resist this advance, even by force of arms, will be crushed. The necessity to crush resistance becomes all the greater when it touches the most sensitive section of the frontier. The Eastern Mediterranean is one such pressure point, both in terms of material interests and mythical significance. The difference which it begets is not politely expressed, as simple variance, but as dangerous irreducibility, little matter whether the danger be cast as radical Islam or militant nationalism.

There is no need to demonstrate the material significance of the region we have named the "Middle East." So powerful is our inclination to see nothing else, that we lose sight of the workings of our own myths. Throughout this book, as we have traced the construction of the imagining vision which sets us apart from the Other, we have seen how incomprehensible to us has remained the identary function of the selfsame frontier to whose erection we have so strongly contributed. We have seen how, today, we experience the frontier as a rift for which the Other, in its refusal, must bear ultimate responsibility. We have no such feelings toward East Asia (east of Iran), nor toward black Africa, nor toward so-called Latin America, even though our relations with these regions partake of the North/South cleavage. The symbolic resistance of Arabo-Muslim culture to the progression of our universal values in the Eastern Mediterranean is particularly irritating to us in that the region is firmly anchored in our collective imagination as belonging to us since the depths of antiquity. Not merely because of the transitory inclusion of the Eastern Mediterranean in the Greco-Roman sphere, but also because of the resonance of the Bible story within us. Here, myth unleashes its full — and negative —power: far from contemplating it in its inexhaustible human richness, we reduce it, semi-consciously, to a title deed, the legitimizing instrument of *one* civilization.

In spite of our knowledge, because of the power it has conferred upon us, and by our inconsiderate use of it, we have bypassed and ignored the very origins which we invoke. In the end, our failure is a failure to understand ourselves.

* * *

BEYOND HYPOCRISY

Decoding the News in an Age of Propaganda
Including a Doublespeak Dictionary for the 1990s

Edward S. Herman
Illustrations by Matt Wuerker

In a highly original volume that includes an extended essay on the Orwellian use of language that characterizes U.S. political culture, cartoons, and a cross-reference lexicon of *doublespeak* terms with examples of their all too frequent usage, Herman and Wuerker highlight the deception and hypocrisy contained in the U.S. government's favourite buzzwords.

240 pages, illustrations, index
Paperback ISBN: 1-895431-48-4 $19.95
Hardcover ISBN: 1-895431-49-2 $38.95
International Politics/Sociology/Communications

SHOCK WAVES

Eastern Europe After the Revolutions

John Feffer

John Feffer paints a vivid picture of the political and economic conflicts that are dramatically reshaping daily life in today's Eastern Europe. Covering Poland, Hungary, Czechoslovakia, Romania, Bulgaria, Yugoslavia, and the former East Germany, Feffer provides an incisive historical background to the current crisis and offers critical and guardedly hopeful speculation about the future of the region.

300 pages, index
Paperback ISBN: 1-895431-46-8 $19.95
Hardcover ISBN: 1-895431-47-6 $38.95
International Politics/History

DISSIDENCE

Essays Against the Mainstream
Dimitrios Roussopoulos

Dissidence reflects a range of essays, bold and acute that are fundamentally related to the most urgent and least understood problems and solutions that confront our society. This collection, written over twenty years, drives towards the building of the community way of life, and a participatory democracy.

250 pages, index
Paperback ISBN: 1-895431-40-9 $19.95
Hardcover ISBN: 1-895431-41-7 $38.95
Social and Political Theory

FROM CAMP DAVID TO THE GULF
Negotiations, Language and Propaganda, and War
Adel Safty

This book is about the Camp David negotiations between Egypt, Israel and the United States and their effect on the Middle East. It is about the injustices inherent in the destruction of the Palestine society; about the opposition of Israel and the United States to its free and unhampered reconstitution; and about the illegality of the continued Israeli occupation of Arab territories.

232 pages, index
Paperback ISBN: 1-895431-10-7 $19.95
Hardcover ISBN: 1-895431-11-5 $38.95
International Politics/History

TOWARD A HUMANIST POLITICAL ECONOMY
Harold Chorney and Phillip Hansen

Guided by a critical theory perspective, Harold Chorney and Phillip Hansen focus their attention on the neglected cultural side of society in order to chart the progress of political change. They feel that the simple economic explanations and the old radical conventions can no longer be relied on in explaining and pointing the way towards a fundamentally reformed society. Instead they use as background some of the insights of writers as diverse as Hannah Arendt and John Maynard Keynes.

230 pages, index
Paperback ISBN: 1-895431-22-0 $19.95
Hardcover ISBN: 1-895431-23-9 $38.95
L.C. 92-70623
Economics/Sociology/Politics

CULTURE AND SOCIAL CHANGE
Social Movements in Québec and Ontario
Colin Leys and Marguerite Mendell, editors

The renovation of society is emerging in the activities and ideas of both the new and the old social movements. In contrast with the current tendency to see 'culture' only as an increasingly commodified instrument of social control in the hands of a power elite, the work collected in this volume reveals cultural transformations occurring in the older social movements, such as the labour movement and the churches, and creative new energies being released in the culture of the new social movements such as the women's movement, the ecology movement and community organizations.

230 pages
Paperback ISBN: 1-895431-28-X $19.95
Hardcover ISBN: 1-895431-29-8 $38.95
L.C. 92-70625

BOOKS BY NOAM CHOMSKY

Judged in terms of the power, range, novelty and influence of his thought, Noam Chomsky is arguable the most important intellectual alive.
New York Times Book Review

A leading US dissident, he is the author of numerous books and one of the best known critics of US foreign policy.

RADICAL PRIORITIES
Carlos P. Otero, editor

2nd revised edition, 4th printing
...[a] critique of American foreign policy and the irresponsibility of intellectuals...another valuable collection of Chomsky's political and social criticism...
The Village Voice
307 pages
Paperback ISBN: 0-920057-17-9 $19.95
Hardcover ISBN: 0-920057-16-0 $38.95

THE POLITICAL ECONOMY OF HUMAN RIGHTS
Noam Chomsky and Edward S. Herman

Vol. 1: The Washington Connection and Third World Fascism

A brilliant and devastating book. Backed up by massive documentation from newspapers, government, church and relief agency sources. Chomsky and Herman draw attention to little published horrors committed by regimes.
Maclean's
441 pages, index
Paperback ISBN: 0-919618-88-X $9.95
Hardcover ISBN: 0-919618-89-8 $29.95

Vol. 2: After the Cataclysm: Postwar Indochina and the Reconstruction of Imperial Ideology

Volume II is devoted to postwar Indochina, with a preface explaining some of the factors contributing to the ongoing Vietnamese-Cambodian conflict.
392 pages, index
Paperback ISBN: 0-919618-90-1 $9.95
Hardcover ISBN: 0-919618-91-X $29.95

LANGUAGE AND POLITICS
Carlos P. Otero, editor

The interviews in this book merge Chomsky's linguistic theory and his politics, revealing the relationship between the two.
779 pages
Paperback ISBN: 0-921689-34-9 $24.95
Hardcover ISBN: 0-921689-35-7 $44.95

THE FATEFUL TRIANGLE
Israel, the United States, and the Palestinians

...a strongly-stated plea for all sides to cease arguing and to find a way to provide the Palestinians with a homeland.
Los Angeles Herald Examiner
481 pages, index
Paperback ISBN: 0-920057-21-7 $19.95
Hardcover ISBN: 0-920057-20-9 $37.95

BLACK ROSE BOOKS

has also published the following books of related interests:

Year 501: World Power in the "Post-Colombian" Era, *by Noam Chomsky*

The Culture of Terrorism, *by Noam Chomsky*

The Fateful Triangle, *by Noam Chomsky*

On Power and Ideology, *by Noam Chomsky*

Turning the Tide: The US and Latin America, *by Noam Chomsky*

Pirates and Emperors: International Terrorism and the Real World, *by Noam Chomsky*

Mask of Democracy: Labour Rights in Mexico Today, *by Dan LaBotz*

Common Cents: Media Portrayal of the Gulf War and Other Events, *by James Winter*

Germany East: Dissent and Opposition, *by Bruce Allen*

The Iran-Contra Connection, *by Jonathon Marshall, Peter Dale Scott, and Jane Hunter*

The New World Order and the Third World, *edited by David Broad and Lori Foster*

Voices From Tiananmen Square: Beijing Spring and the Democracy Movement, *edited by Mok Chiu Yu and J. Frank Harrison*

Friendly Fascism: The New Face of Power in America, *by Bertram Gross*

To Win a Nuclear War: The Pentagon's Secret War Plans, *by Michio Kaku and Daniel Axelrod*

The Radical Papers , *edited by Dimitrios Roussopoulos*

The Radical Papers 2 , *edited by Dimitrios Roussopoulos*

The Anarchist Papers, *edited by Dimitrios Roussopoulos*

The Anarchist Papers 2, *edited by Dimitrios Roussopoulos*

The Anarchist Papers 3, *edited by Dimitrios Roussopoulos*

Send for our free catalogue of books
BLACK ROSE BOOKS
C.P. 1258, Succ. Place du Parc
Montréal, Québec
H2W 2R3 Canada

Printed by
the workers of
Editions Marquis, Montmagny, Québec
for
Black Rose Books Ltd.